SUPER HOROSCOPE
GEMINI

2010

MAY 21 – JUNE 20

BERKLEY BOOKS, NEW YORK

THE BERKLEY PUBLISHING GROUP
Published by the Penguin Group
Penguin Group (USA) Inc.
375 Hudson Street, New York, New York 10014, USA
Penguin Group (Canada), 90 Eglinton Avenue East, Suite 700, Toronto, Ontario M4P 2Y3, Canada
(a division of Pearson Penguin Canada Inc.)
Penguin Books Ltd., 80 Strand, London WC2R 0RL, England
Penguin Group Ireland, 25 St. Stephen's Green, Dublin 2, Ireland (a division of Penguin Books Ltd.)
Penguin Group (Australia), 250 Camberwell Road, Camberwell, Victoria 3124, Australia
(a division of Pearson Australia Group Pty. Ltd.)
Penguin Books India Pvt. Ltd., 11 Community Centre, Panchsheel Park, New Delhi—110 017, India
Penguin Group (NZ), 67 Apollo Drive, Rosedale, North Shore 0632, New Zealand
(a division of Pearson New Zealand Ltd.)
Penguin Books (South Africa) (Pty.) Ltd., 24 Sturdee Avenue, Rosebank, Johannesburg 2196,
South Africa

Penguin Books Ltd., Registered Offices: 80 Strand, London WC2R 0RL, England

2010 SUPER HOROSCOPE GEMINI

The publishers regret that they cannot answer individual letters requesting personal horoscope
information.

A Berkley Book / published by arrangement with the author

PRINTING HISTORY
Berkley trade paperback edition / July 2009

ISBN: 978-0-425-22653-7

Library of Congress Cataloging-in-Publication Data

ISSN: 1535-895X

PRINTED IN THE UNITED STATES OF AMERICA

10   9   8   7   6   5   4   3   2   1

CONTENTS

THE CUSP-BORN GEMINI

Are you *really* a Gemini? If your birthday falls during the third week of May, at the beginning of Gemini, will you still retain the traits of Taurus, the sign of the Zodiac before Gemini? And what if you were born late in June—are you more Cancer than Gemini? Many people born at the edge, or cusp, of a sign have difficulty determining exactly what sign they are. If you are one of these people, here's how you can figure it out, once and for all.

Consult the cusp table on the facing page, then locate the year of your birth. The table will tell you the precise days on which the Sun entered and left your sign for the year of your birth. In that way you can determine if you are a true Gemini—or whether you are a Taurus or Cancer—according to the variations in cusp dates from year to year (see also page 17).

If you were born at the beginning or end of Gemini, yours is a lifetime reflecting a process of subtle transformation. Your life on Earth will symbolize a significant change in consciousness, for you are either about to enter a whole new way of living or are leaving one behind.

If you were born during the third week of May, you may want to read the horoscope book for Taurus as well as for Gemini, for Taurus holds the key to a hidden and often perplexing side of your personality—yet one that is the seed of your cosmic uplift and unfolding.

Mobility is your aim and variety your purpose. Yet you are drawn again and again to fixed, immobile Taurus. Your compulsion to settle down, find stability, wealth, and constancy attracts you to Taurus, and this attraction is a dilemma. For where is your true commitment? To variety—that old spice of life—or to the solid, substantial promise of Taurus?

At best, you symbolize the birth of perception, the capacity of the mind to know and communicate information.

If you were born during the fourth week of June, you may want to read the horoscope book for Cancer, as well as Gemini, for in Cancer you find not only financial security but a way of making all your assets grow.

You are about to settle down, about to dock your ship in a port and stay awhile; but there is a restlessness in you that is irrepressible. You are preparing to make yourself secure. You can be shrewd, money-minded, and practical despite your moodiness, naivete, and sometimes irksome adolescent approach to life.

Above all, you are a skilled manipulator of language and design and your powers of reason lie behind everything you think and do.

THE CUSPS OF GEMINI

DATES SUN ENTERS GEMINI (LEAVES TAURUS)

May 21 every year from 1900 to 2010, except for the following:

	May 20			May 22
1948	1972	1988	2000	1903
52	76	89	2001	07
56	80	92	2004	11
60	81	93	2005	19
64	84	96	2008	
68	85	97	2009	

DATES SUN ENTERS GEMINI (LEAVES CANCER)

June 21 every year from 1900 to 2010, except for the following:

June 20		June 22	
1988	1902	1915	1931
1992	03	18	35
1996	06	19	39
2000	07	22	43
2004	10	23	47
2008	11	26	51
	14	27	55

THE ASCENDANT: GEMINI RISING

Could you be a "double" Gemini? That is, could you have Gemini as your Rising sign as well as your Sun sign? The tables on pages 8–9 will tell you Geminis what your Rising sign happens to be. Just find the hour of your birth, then find the day of your birth, and you will see which sign of the Zodiac is your Ascendant, as the Rising sign is called. The Ascendant is called that because it is the sign rising on the eastern horizon at the time of your birth. For a more detailed discussion of the Rising sign and the twelve houses of the Zodiac, see pages 17–20.

The Ascendant, or Rising sign, is placed on the 1st house in a horoscope, of which there are twelve houses. The 1st house represents your response to the environment—your unique response. Call it identity, personality, ego, self-image, facade, come-on, body-mind-spirit—whatever term best conveys to you the meaning of the you that acts and reacts in the world. It is a you that is always changing, discovering a new you. Your identity started with birth and early environment, over which you had little conscious control, and continues to experience, to adjust, to express itself. The 1st house also represents how others see you. Has anyone ever guessed your sign to be your Rising sign? People may respond to that personality, that facade, that body type governed by your Rising sign.

Your Ascendant, or Rising sign, modifies your basic Sun sign personality, and it affects the way you act out the daily predictions for your Sun sign. If your Rising sign indeed is Gemini, what follows is a description of its effect on your horoscope. If your Rising sign is not Gemini, but some other sign of the Zodiac, you may wish to read the horoscope book for that sign as well.

With Gemini on the Ascendant, that is, in the 1st house, your ruling planet Mercury is therefore in the 1st house. Mercury in this position gives you a restless spirit, pushing you on a constant search for knowledge. You are always alert for new information, and your quest may take you far afield to explore unfamiliar subjects and even foreign lands. Mercury confers a subtle wariness that could be your best defense when people try to fool you or cheat you. On the other hand, that trait could be aggressively used as a weapon against people, giving rise to unworthy actions, tricks, or disputes.

The desire to express yourself will be very strong in your personality. You tend to rely on logic rather than intuition, and you could go to great lengths to prove to yourself and to others the validity of your ideas. This need for expression combined with an equal need for variety gives your life a lot of surface drama: you are endlessly changing your focus of experience. In your lifetime you may hold a series of seemingly unrelated jobs; move frequently to new residences in unusual surroundings; make friends, drop them, pick them up again; change your world view often. Although other people may judge you to lack seriousness, that is not really so. You seek ideas and experience to help you understand and order your environment because you want from it maximal comfort and constant ego satisfaction.

Human contact is another large need for Gemini Rising individuals. It gives your desire to express yourself an audience. Yours is the sign of brothers and sisters, relatives, family. If you do not have a closely knit blood family, you will create a familylike network among friends, workmates, neighbors, and community contacts. You like to keep up with distant acquaintances, even ex-lovers, just so you can invite them to participate in one of your shindigs. And of course your home will be the center of attraction. For you are more than just tidy and fashionable; you know how to arrange a setting and accommodate people in order to stimulate the greatest communication between them.

Your youthful appearance and pleasing speaking voice attract people to you, and you know it. You are not above heightening the effect of these natural assets. You have been known to adapt your costuming to suit the occasion, and you sometimes manipulate your speech patterns to display emotions you don't feel or to invoke emotions in other people. As a result, you can be accused of self-centeredness.

Charm is your great natural talent; you do it with words, words, words. Gemini teachers can fascinate bored students into enjoying, let alone learning, a boring subject. Gemini adults can sweet-talk unruly youngsters into rational behavior. Gemini people in general lighten the lives of their friends with endless small talk about clothes, things, events, places, other people. You also enlighten your friends when you talk on that deeper, more sophisticated level of patterns of experience and cause and effect.

Writing and public speaking are arts that you with Gemini Rising can rely on consistently. Scholarly work is a possibility in your lifetime. Intellect is the key word that will allow you to understand any environment. Although your financial fortunes may change, your mercurial talents will deepen and survive.

RISING SIGNS FOR GEMINI

Hour of Birth*	Day of Birth		
	May 21–25	**Mary 26–30**	**May 31–June 4**
Midnight	Aquarius	Aquarius	Aquarius; Pisces 6/3
1 AM	Pisces	Pisces	Pisces
2 AM	Pisces; Aries 5/23	Aries	Aries
3 AM	Aries	Taurus	Taurus
4 AM	Taurus	Taurus	Taurus; Gemini 6/3
5 AM	Gemini	Gemini	Gemini
6 AM	Gemini	Gemini	Gemini; Cancer 6/2
7 AM	Cancer	Cancer	Cancer
8 AM	Cancer	Cancer	Cancer
9 AM	Cancer; Leo 5/24	Leo	Leo
10 AM	Leo	Leo	Leo
11 AM	Leo	Leo	Virgo
Noon	Virgo	Virgo	Virgo
1 PM	Virgo	Virgo	Virgo
2 PM	Virgo	Libra	Libra
3 PM	Libra	Libra	Libra
4 PM	Libra	Libra; Scorpio 5/25	Scorpio
5 PM	Scorpio	Scorpio	Scorpio
6 PM	Scorpio	Scorpio	Scorpio
7 PM	Scorpio; Sagittarius 5/23	Sagittarius	Sagittarius
8 PM	Sagittarius	Sagittarius	Sagittarius
9 PM	Sagittarius	Sagittarius; Capricorn 5/28	Capricorn
10 PM	Capricorn	Capricorn	Capricorn
11 PM	Capricorn	Aquarius	Aquarius

*Hour of birth given here is for Standard Time in any time zone. If your hour of birth was recorded in Daylight Saving Time, subtract one hour from it and consult that hour in the table above. For example, if you were born at 6 AM. D.S.T., see 5 AM above.

Hour of Birth*	Day of Birth		
	June 5–10	June 11–15	June 16–21
Midnight	Pisces	Pisces	Pisces
1 AM	Pisces; Aries 6/7	Aries	Aries
2 AM	Aries	Taurus	Taurus
3 AM	Taurus	Taurus	Taurus; Gemini 6/18
4 AM	Gemini	Gemini	Gemini
5 AM	Gemini	Gemini	Gemini; Cancer 6/17
6 AM	Cancer	Cancer	Cancer
7 AM	Cancer	Cancer	Cancer
8 AM	Cancer; Leo 6/8	Leo	Leo
9 AM	Leo	Leo	Leo
10 AM	Leo	Leo; Virgo 6/15	Virgo
11 AM	Virgo	Virgo	Virgo
Noon	Virgo	Virgo	Virgo
1 PM	Virgo; Libra 6/7	Libra	Libra
2 PM	Libra	Libra	Libra
3 PM	Libra	Libra; Scorpio 6/14	Scorpio
4 PM	Scorpio	Scorpio	Scorpio
5 PM	Scorpio	Scorpio	Scorpio
6 PM	Scorpio; Sagittarius 6/7	Sagittarius	Sagittarius
7 PM	Sagittarius	Sagittarius	Sagittarius
8 PM	Sagittarius	Sagittarius; Capricorn 6/12	Sagittarius
9 PM	Capricorn	Capricorn	Capricorn
10 PM	Capricorn	Aquarius	Aquarius
11 PM	Aquarius	Aquarius	Pisces

*See note on facing page.

THE PLACE OF ASTROLOGY IN TODAY'S WORLD

Does astrology have a place in the fast-moving, ultra-scientific world we live in today? Can it be justified in a sophisticated society whose outriders are already preparing to step off the moon into the deep space of the planets themselves? Or is it just a hangover of ancient superstition, a psychological dummy for neurotics and dreamers of every historical age?

These are the kind of questions that any inquiring person can be expected to ask when they approach a subject like astrology which goes beyond, but never excludes, the materialistic side of life.

The simple, single answer is that astrology works. It works for many millions of people in the western world alone. In the United States there are 10 million followers and in Europe, an estimated 25 million. America has more than 4000 practicing astrologers, Europe nearly three times as many. Even down-under Australia has its hundreds of thousands of adherents. In the eastern countries, astrology has enormous followings, again, because it has been proved to work. In India, for example, brides and grooms for centuries have been chosen on the basis of their astrological compatibility.

Astrology today is more vital than ever before, more practicable because all over the world the media devotes much space and time to it, more valid because science itself is confirming the precepts of astrological knowledge with every new exciting step. The ordinary person who daily applies astrology intelligently does not have to wonder whether it is true nor believe in it blindly. He can see it working for himself. And, if he can use it—and this book is designed to help the reader to do just that—he can make living a far richer experience, and become a more developed personality and a better person.

Astrology and Relationships

Astrology is the science of relationships. It is not just a study of planetary influences on man and his environment. It is the study of man himself.

We are at the center of our personal universe, of all our relationships. And our happiness or sadness depends on how we act, how we relate to the people and things that surround us. The emotions that we generate have a distinct effect—for better or worse—on the world around us. Our friends and our enemies will confirm this. Just look in the mirror the next time you are angry. In other words, each of us is a kind of sun or planet or star ra-diating our feelings on the environment around us. Our influence on our personal universe, whether loving, helpful, or destructive, varies with our changing moods, expressed through our individual character.

Our personal "radiations" are potent in the way they affect our moods and our ability to control them. But we usually are able to throw off our emotion in some sort of action—we have a good cry, walk it off, or tell someone our troubles—before it can build up too far and make us physically ill. Astrology helps us to understand the universal forces working on us, and through this understanding, we can become more properly adjusted to our surroundings so that we find ourselves coping where others may flounder.

The Challenge of Love

The challenge of love lies in recognizing the difference between infatuation, emotion, sex, and, sometimes, the intentional deceit of the other person. Mankind, with its record of broken marriages, despair, and disillusionment, is obviously not very good at making these distinctions.

Can astrology help?

Yes. In the same way that advance knowledge can usually help in any human situation. And there is probably no situation as human, as poignant, as pathetic and universal, as the failure of man's love.

Love, of course, is not just between man and woman. It involves love of children, parents, home, and friends. But the big problems usually involve the choice of partner.

Astrology has established degrees of compatibility that exist between people born under the various signs of the Zodiac. Because people are individuals, there are numerous variations and modifications. So the astrologer, when approached on mate and marriage matters, makes allowances for them. But the fact remains that some groups of people are suited for each other and some are not, and astrology has expressed this in terms of characteristics we all can study and use as a personal guide.

No matter how much enjoyment and pleasure we find in the different aspects of each other's character, if it is not an overall compatibility, the chances of our finding fulfillment or enduring happiness in each other are pretty hopeless. And astrology can help us to find someone compatible.

Astrology and Science

Closely related to our emotions is the "other side" of our personal universe, our physical welfare. Our body, of course, is largely influenced by things around us over which we have very little control. The phone rings, we hear it. The train runs late. We snag our stocking or cut our face shaving. Our body is under a constant bombardment of events that influence our daily lives to varying degrees.

The question that arises from all this is, what makes each of us act so that we have to involve other people and keep the ball of activity and evolution rolling? This is the question that both science and astrology are involved with. The scientists have attacked it from different angles: anthropology, the study of human evolution as body, mind and response to environment; anatomy, the study of bodily structure; psychology, the science of the human mind; and so on. These studies have produced very impressive classifications and valuable information, but because the approach to the problem is fragmented, so is the result. They remain "branches" of science. Science generally studies effects. It keeps turning up wonderful answers but no lasting solutions. Astrology, on the other hand, approaches the question from the broader viewpoint. Astrology began its inquiry with the totality of human experience and saw it as an effect. It then looked to find the cause, or at least the prime movers, and during thousands of years of observation of man and his *universal* environment came up with the extraordinary principle of planetary influence—or astrology, which, from the Greek, means the science of the stars.

Modern science, as we shall see, has confirmed much of astrology's foundations—most of it unintentionally, some of it reluctantly, but still, indisputably.

It is not difficult to imagine that there must be a connection between outer space and Earth. Even today, scientists are not too sure how our Earth was created, but it is generally agreed that it is only a tiny part of the universe. And as a part of the universe, people on Earth see and feel the influence of heavenly bodies in almost every aspect of our existence. There is no doubt that the Sun has the greatest influence on life on this planet. Without it there would be no life, for without it there would be no warmth, no division into day and night, no cycles of time or season at all. This is clear and easy to see. The influence of the Moon, on the other hand, is more subtle, though no less definite.

There are many ways in which the influence of the Moon manifests itself here on Earth, both on human and animal life. It is a well-known fact, for instance, that the large movements of water on our planet—that is the ebb and flow of the tides—are caused by the

Moon's gravitational pull. Since this is so, it follows that these water movements do not occur only in the oceans, but that all bodies of water are affected, even down to the tiniest puddle.

The human body, too, which consists of about 70 percent water, falls within the scope of this lunar influence. For example the menstrual cycle of most women corresponds to the 28-day lunar month; the period of pregnancy in humans is 273 days, or equal to nine lunar months. Similarly, many illnesses reach a crisis at the change of the Moon, and statistics in many countries have shown that the crime rate is highest at the time of the Full Moon. Even human sexual desire has been associated with the phases of the Moon. But it is in the movement of the tides that we get the clearest demonstration of planetary influence, which leads to the irresistible correspondence between the so-called metaphysical and the physical.

Tide tables are prepared years in advance by calculating the future positions of the Moon. Science has known for a long time that the Moon is the main cause of tidal action. But only in the last few years has it begun to realize the possible extent of this influence on mankind. To begin with, the ocean tides do not rise and fall as we might imagine from our personal observations of them. The Moon as it orbits around Earth sets up a circular wave of attraction which pulls the oceans of the world after it, broadly in an east to west direction. This influence is like a phantom wave crest, a loop of power stretching from pole to pole which passes over and around the Earth like an invisible shadow. It travels with equal effect across the land masses and, as scientists were recently amazed to observe, caused oysters placed in the dark in the middle of the United States where there is no sea to open their shells to receive the nonexistent tide. If the land-locked oysters react to this invisible signal, what effect does it have on us who not so long ago in evolutionary time came out of the sea and still have its salt in our blood and sweat?

Less well known is the fact that the Moon is also the primary force behind the circulation of blood in human beings and animals, and the movement of sap in trees and plants. Agriculturists have established that the Moon has a distinct influence on crops, which explains why for centuries people have planted according to Moon cycles. The habits of many animals, too, are directed by the movement of the Moon. Migratory birds, for instance, depart only at or near the time of the Full Moon. And certain sea creatures, eels in particular, move only in accordance with certain phases of the Moon.

Know Thyself—Why?

In today's fast-changing world, everyone still longs to know what the future holds. It is the one thing that everyone has in common: rich and poor, famous and infamous, all are deeply concerned about tomorrow.

But the key to the future, as every historian knows, lies in the past. This is as true of individual people as it is of nations. You cannot understand your future without first understanding your past, which is simply another way of saying that you must first of all know yourself.

The motto "know thyself" seems obvious enough nowadays, but it was originally put forward as the foundation of wisdom by the ancient Greek philosophers. It was then adopted by the "mystery religions" of the ancient Middle East, Greece, Rome, and is still used in all genuine schools of mind training or mystical discipline, both in those of the East, based on yoga, and those of the West. So it is universally accepted now, and has been through the ages.

But how do you go about discovering what sort of person you are? The first step is usually classification into some sort of system of types. Astrology did this long before the birth of Christ. Psychology has also done it. So has modern medicine, in its way.

One system classifies people according to the source of the impulses they respond to most readily: the muscles, leading to direct bodily action; the digestive organs, resulting in emotion; or the brain and nerves, giving rise to thinking. Another such system says that character is determined by the endocrine glands, and gives us such labels as "pituitary," "thyroid," and "hyperthyroid" types. These different systems are neither contradictory nor mutually exclusive. In fact, they are very often different ways of saying the same thing.

Very popular, useful classifications were devised by Carl Jung, the eminent disciple of Freud. Jung observed among the different faculties of the mind, four which have a predominant influence on character. These four faculties exist in all of us without exception, but not in perfect balance. So when we say, for instance, that someone is a "thinking type," it means that in any situation he or she tries to be rational. Emotion, which may be the opposite of thinking, will be his or her weakest function. This thinking type can be sensible and reasonable, or calculating and unsympathetic. The emotional type, on the other hand, can often be recognized by exaggerated language—everything is either marvelous or terrible—and in extreme cases they even invent dramas and quarrels out of nothing just to make life more interesting.

The other two faculties are intuition and physical sensation. The sensation type does not only care for food and drink, nice clothes and furniture; he or she is also interested in all forms of physical experience. Many scientists are sensation types as are athletes and nature-lovers. Like sensation, intuition is a form of perception and we all possess it. But it works through that part of the mind which is not under conscious control—consequently it sees meanings and connections which are not obvious to thought or emotion. Inventors and original thinkers are always intuitive, but so, too, are superstitious people who see meanings where none exist.

Thus, sensation tells us what is going on in the world, feeling (that is, emotion) tells us how important it is to ourselves, thinking enables us to interpret it and work out what we should do about it, and intuition tells us what it means to ourselves and others. All four faculties are essential, and all are present in every one of us. But some people are guided chiefly by one, others by another. In addition, Jung also observed a division of the human personality into the extrovert and the introvert, which cuts across these four types.

A disadvantage of all these systems of classification is that one cannot tell very easily where to place oneself. Some people are reluctant to admit that they act to please their emotions. So they deceive themselves for years by trying to belong to whichever type they think is the "best." Of course, there is no best; each has its faults and each has its good points.

The advantage of the signs of the Zodiac is that they simplify classification. Not only that, but your date of birth is personal—it is unarguably yours. What better way to know yourself than by going back as far as possible to the very moment of your birth? And this is precisely what your horoscope is all about, as we shall see in the next section.

WHAT IS A HOROSCOPE?

If you had been able to take a picture of the skies at the moment of your birth, that photograph would be your horoscope. Lacking such a snapshot, it is still possible to recreate the picture—and this is at the basis of the astrologer's art. In other words, your horoscope is a representation of the skies with the planets in the exact positions they occupied at the time you were born.

The year of birth tells an astrologer the positions of the distant, slow-moving planets Jupiter, Saturn, Uranus, Neptune, and Pluto. The month of birth indicates the Sun sign, or birth sign as it is commonly called, as well as indicating the positions of the rapidly moving planets Venus, Mercury, and Mars. The day and time of birth will locate the position of our Moon. And the moment—the exact hour and minute—of birth determines the houses through what is called the Ascendant, or Rising sign.

With this information the astrologer consults various tables to calculate the specific positions of the Sun, Moon, and other planets relative to your birthplace at the moment you were born. Then he or she locates them by means of the Zodiac.

The Zodiac

The Zodiac is a band of stars (constellations) in the skies, centered on the Sun's apparent path around the Earth, and is divided into twelve equal segments, or signs. What we are actually dividing up is the Earth's path around the Sun. But from our point of view here on Earth, it seems as if the Sun is making a great circle around our planet in the sky, so we say it is the Sun's apparent path. This twelve-fold division, the Zodiac, is a reference system for the astrologer. At any given moment the planets—and in astrology both the Sun and Moon are considered to be planets—can all be located at a specific point along this path.

Now where in all this are you, the subject of the horoscope? Your character is largely determined by the sign the Sun is in. So that is where the astrologer looks first in your horoscope, at your Sun sign.

The Sun Sign and the Cusp

There are twelve signs in the Zodiac, and the Sun spends approximately one month in each sign. But because of the motion of the Earth around the Sun—the Sun's apparent motion—the dates when the Sun enters and leaves each sign may change from year to year. Some people born near the cusp, or edge, of a sign have difficulty determining which is their Sun sign. But in this book a Table of Cusps is provided for the years 1900 to 2010 (page 5) so you can find out what your true Sun sign is.

Here are the twelve signs of the Zodiac, their ancient zodiacal symbol, and the dates when the Sun enters and leaves each sign for the year 2010. Remember, these dates may change from year to year.

ARIES	Ram	March 20–April 20
TAURUS	Bull	April 20–May 21
GEMINI	Twins	May 21–June 21
CANCER	Crab	June 21–July 22
LEO	Lion	July 22–August 23
VIRGO	Virgin	August 23–September 23
LIBRA	Scales	September 23–October 23
SCORPIO	Scorpion	October 23–November 22
SAGITTARIUS	Archer	November 22–December 21
CAPRICORN	Sea Goat	December 21–January 20
AQUARIUS	Water Bearer	January 20–February 18
PISCES	Fish	February 18–March 20

It is possible to draw significant conclusions and make meaningful predictions based simply on the Sun sign of a person. There are many people who have been amazed at the accuracy of the description of their own character based only on the Sun sign. But an astrologer needs more information than just your Sun sign to interpret the photograph that is your horoscope.

The Rising Sign and the Zodiacal Houses

An astrologer needs the exact time and place of your birth in order to construct and interpret your horoscope. The illustration on the next page shows the flat chart, or natural wheel, an astrologer uses. Note the inner circle of the wheel labeled 1 through 12. These 12 divisions are known as the houses of the Zodiac.

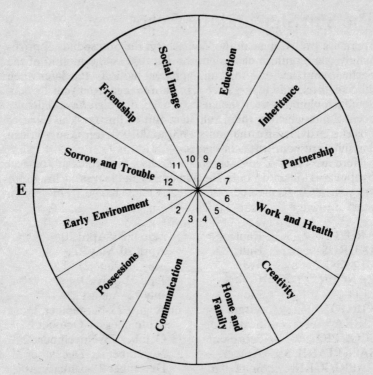

The 1st house always starts from the position marked E, which corresponds to the eastern horizon. The rest of the houses 2 through 12 follow around in a "counterclockwise" direction. The point where each house starts is known as a cusp, or edge.

The cusp, or edge, of the 1st house (point E) is where an astrologer would place your Rising sign, the Ascendant. And, as already noted, the exact time of your birth determines your Rising sign. Let's see how this works.

As the Earth rotates on its axis once every 24 hours, each one of the twelve signs of the Zodiac appears to be "rising" on the horizon, with a new one appearing about every 2 hours. Actually it is the turning of the Earth that exposes each sign to view, but in our astrological work we are discussing apparent motion. This Rising sign marks the Ascendant, and it colors the whole orientation of a horoscope. It indicates the sign governing the 1st house of the chart, and will thus determine which signs will govern all the other houses.

To visualize this idea, imagine two color wheels with twelve divisions superimposed upon each other. For just as the Zodiac is divided into twelve constellations that we identify as the signs, another twelvefold division is used to denote the houses. Now imagine one wheel (the signs) moving slowly while the other wheel (the houses) remains still. This analogy may help you see how the signs keep shifting the "color" of the houses as the Rising sign continues to change every two hours. To simplify things, a Table of Rising Signs has been provided (pages 8–9) for your specific Sun sign.

Once your Rising sign has been placed on the cusp of the 1st house, the signs that govern the rest of the 11 houses can be placed on the chart. In any individual's horoscope the signs do not necessarily correspond with the houses. For example, it could be that a sign covers part of two adjacent houses. It is the interpretation of such variations in an individual's horoscope that marks the professional astrologer.

But to gain a workable understanding of astrology, it is not necessary to go into great detail. In fact, we just need a description of the houses and their meanings, as is shown in the illustration above and in the table below.

THE 12 HOUSES OF THE ZODIAC

1st	Individuality, body appearance, general outlook on life	Personality house
2nd	Finance, possessions, ethical principles, gain or loss	Money house
3rd	Relatives, communication, short journeys, writing, education	Relatives house
4th	Family and home, parental ties, land and property, security	Home house
5th	Pleasure, children, creativity, entertainment, risk	Pleasure house
6th	Health, harvest, hygiene, work and service, employees	Health house
7th	Marriage and divorce, the law, partnerships and alliances	Marriage house
8th	Inheritance, secret deals, sex, death, regeneration	Inheritance house
9th	Travel, sports, study, philosophy, religion	Travel house
10th	Career, social standing, success and honor	Business house
11th	Friendship, social life, hopes and wishes	Friends house
12th	Troubles, illness, secret enemies, hidden agendas	Trouble house

The Planets in the Houses

An astrologer, knowing the exact time and place of your birth, will use tables of planetary motion in order to locate the planets in your horoscope chart. He or she will determine which planet or planets are in which sign and in which house. It is not uncommon, in an individual's horoscope, for there to be two or more planets in the same sign and in the same house.

The characteristics of the planets modify the influence of the Sun according to their natures and strengths.

Sun: Source of life. Basic temperament according to the Sun sign. The conscious will. Human potential.

Moon: Emotions. Moods. Customs. Habits. Changeable. Adaptive. Nurturing.

Mercury: Communication. Intellect. Reasoning power. Curiosity. Short travels.

Venus: Love. Delight. Charm. Harmony. Balance. Art. Beautiful possessions.

Mars: Energy. Initiative. War. Anger. Adventure. Courage. Daring. Impulse.

Jupiter: Luck. Optimism. Generous. Expansive. Opportunities. Protection.

Saturn: Pessimism. Privation. Obstacles. Delay. Hard work. Research. Lasting rewards after long struggle.

Uranus: Fashion. Electricity. Revolution. Independence. Freedom. Sudden changes. Modern science.

Neptune: Sensationalism. Theater. Dreams. Inspiration. Illusion. Deception.

Pluto: Creation and destruction. Total transformation. Lust for power. Strong obsessions.

Superimpose the characteristics of the planets on the functions of the house in which they appear. Express the result through the character of the Sun sign, and you will get the basic idea.

Of course, many other considerations have been taken into account in producing the carefully worked out predictions in this book: the aspects of the planets to each other; their strength according to position and sign; whether they are in a house of exaltation or decline; whether they are natural enemies or not; whether a planet occupies its own sign; the position of a planet in relation to its own house or sign; whether the sign is male or female; whether the sign is a fire, earth, water, or air sign. These are only a few of the colors on the astrologer's pallet which he or she must mix with the inspiration of the artist and the accuracy of the mathematician.

How To Use These Predictions

A person reading the predictions in this book should understand that they are produced from the daily position of the planets for a group of people and are not, of course, individually specialized. To get the full benefit of them our readers should relate the predictions to their own character and circumstances, coordinate them, and draw their own conclusions from them.

If you are a serious observer of your own life, you should find a definite pattern emerging that will be a helpful and reliable guide.

The point is that we always retain our free will. The stars indicate certain directional tendencies but we are not compelled to follow. We can do or not do, and wisdom must make the choice.

We all have our good and bad days. Sometimes they extend into cycles of weeks. It is therefore advisable to study daily predictions in a span ranging from the day before to several days ahead.

Daily predictions should be taken very generally. The word "difficult" does not necessarily indicate a whole day of obstruction or inconvenience. It is a warning to you to be cautious. Your caution will often see you around the difficulty before you are involved. This is the correct use of astrology.

In another section (pages 78–84), detailed information is given about the influence of the Moon as it passes through each of the twelve signs of the Zodiac. There are instructions on how to use the Moon Tables (pages 85–92), which provide Moon Sign Dates throughout the year as well as the Moon's role in health and daily affairs. This information should be used in conjunction with the daily forecasts to give a fuller picture of the astrological trends.

HISTORY OF ASTROLOGY

The origins of astrology have been lost far back in history, but we do know that reference is made to it as far back as the first written records of the human race. It is not hard to see why. Even in primitive times, people must have looked for an explanation for the various happenings in their lives. They must have wanted to know why people were different from one another. And in their search they turned to the regular movements of the Sun, Moon, and stars to see if they could provide an answer.

It is interesting to note that as soon as man learned to use his tools in any type of design, or his mind in any kind of calculation, he turned his attention to the heavens. Ancient cave dwellings reveal dim crescents and circles representative of the Sun and Moon, rulers of day and night. Mesopotamia and the civilization of Chaldea, in itself the foundation of those of Babylonia and Assyria, show a complete picture of astronomical observation and well-developed astrological interpretation.

Humanity has a natural instinct for order. The study of anthropology reveals that primitive people—even as far back as prehistoric times—were striving to achieve a certain order in their lives. They tried to organize the apparent chaos of the universe. They had the desire to attach meaning to things. This demand for order has persisted throughout the history of man. So that observing the regularity of the heavenly bodies made it logical that primitive peoples should turn heavenward in their search for an understanding of the world in which they found themselves so random and alone.

And they did find a significance in the movements of the stars. Shepherds tending their flocks, for instance, observed that when the cluster of stars now known as the constellation Aries was in sight, it was the time of fertility and they associated it with the Ram. And they noticed that the growth of plants and plant life corresponded with different phases of the Moon, so that certain times were favorable for the planting of crops, and other times were not. In this way, there grew up a tradition of seasons and causes connected with the passage of the Sun through the twelve signs of the Zodiac.

Astrology was valued so highly that the king was kept informed of the daily and monthly changes in the heavenly bodies, and the results of astrological studies regarding events of the future. Head astrologers were clearly men of great rank and position, and the office was said to be a hereditary one.

Omens were taken, not only from eclipses and conjunctions of the Moon or Sun with one of the planets, but also from storms and earthquakes. In the eastern civilizations, particularly, the reverence inspired by astrology appears to have remained unbroken since the very earliest days. In ancient China, astrology, astronomy, and religion went hand in hand. The astrologer, who was also an astronomer, was part of the official government service and had his own corner in the Imperial Palace. The duties of the Imperial astrologer, whose office was one of the most important in the land, were clearly defined, as this extract from early records shows:

> This exalted gentleman must concern himself with the stars in the heavens, keeping a record of the changes and movements of the Planets, the Sun and the Moon, in order to examine the movements of the terrestrial world with the object of prognosticating good and bad fortune. He divides the territories of the nine regions of the empire in accordance with their dependence on particular celestial bodies. All the fiefs and principalities are connected with the stars and from this their prosperity or misfortune should be ascertained. He makes prognostications according to the twelve years of the Jupiter cycle of good and evil of the terrestrial world. From the colors of the five kinds of clouds, he determines the coming of floods or droughts, abundance or famine. From the twelve winds, he draws conclusions about the state of harmony of heaven and earth, and takes note of good and bad signs that result from their accord or disaccord. In general, he concerns himself with five kinds of phenomena so as to warn the Emperor to come to the aid of the government and to allow for variations in the ceremonies according to their circumstances.

The Chinese were also keen observers of the fixed stars, giving them such unusual names as Ghost Vehicle, Sun of Imperial Concubine, Imperial Prince, Pivot of Heaven, Twinkling Brilliance, Weaving Girl. But, great astrologers though they may have been, the Chinese lacked one aspect of mathematics that the Greeks applied to astrology—deductive geometry. Deductive geometry was the basis of much classical astrology in and after the time of the Greeks, and this explains the different methods of prognostication used in the East and West.

Down through the ages the astrologer's art has depended, not so much on the uncovering of new facts, though this is important, as on the interpretation of the facts already known. This is the essence of the astrologer's skill.

But why should the signs of the Zodiac have any effect at all on the formation of human character? It is easy to see why people thought they did, and even now we constantly use astrological expressions in our everyday speech. The thoughts of "lucky star," "ill-fated," "star-crossed," "mooning around," are interwoven into the very structure of our language.

Wherever the concept of the Zodiac is understood and used, it could well appear to have an influence on the human character. Does this mean, then, that the human race, in whose civilization the idea of the twelve signs of the Zodiac has long been embedded, is divided into only twelve types? Can we honestly believe that it is really as simple as that? If so, there must be pretty wide ranges of variation within each type. And if, to explain the variation, we call in heredity and environment, experiences in early childhood, the thyroid and other glands, and also the four functions of the mind together with extroversion and introversion, then one begins to wonder if the original classification was worth making at all. No sensible person believes that his favorite system explains everything. But even so, he will not find the system much use at all if it does not even save him the trouble of bothering with the others.

In the same way, if we were to put every person under only one sign of the Zodiac, the system becomes too rigid and unlike life. Besides, it was never intended to be used like that. It may be convenient to have only twelve types, but we know that in practice there is every possible gradation between aggressiveness and timidity, or between conscientiousness and laziness. How, then, do we account for this?

A person born under any given Sun sign can be mainly influenced by one or two of the other signs that appear in their individual horoscope. For instance, famous persons born under the sign of Gemini include Henry VIII, whom nothing and no one could have induced to abdicate, and Edward VIII, who did just that. Obviously, then, the sign Gemini does not fully explain the complete character of either of them.

Again, under the opposite sign, Sagittarius, were both Stalin, who was totally consumed with the notion of power, and Charles V, who freely gave up an empire because he preferred to go into a monastery. And we find under Scorpio many uncompromising characters such as Luther, de Gaulle, Indira Gandhi, and Montgomery, but also Petain, a successful commander whose name later became synonymous with collaboration.

A single sign is therefore obviously inadequate to explain the differences between people; it can only explain resemblances, such as the combativeness of the Scorpio group, or the far-reaching devotion of Charles V and Stalin to their respective ideals—the Christian heaven and the Communist utopia.

But very few people have only one sign in their horoscope chart. In addition to the month of birth, the day and, even more, the hour to the nearest minute if possible, ought to be considered. Without this, it is impossible to have an actual horoscope, for the word horoscope literally means "a consideration of the hour."

The month of birth tells you only which sign of the Zodiac was occupied by the Sun. The day and hour tell you what sign was occupied by the Moon. And the minute tells you which sign was rising on the eastern horizon. This is called the Ascendant, and, as some astrologers believe, it is supposed to be the most important thing in the whole horoscope.

The Sun is said to signify one's heart, that is to say, one's deepest desires and inmost nature. This is quite different from the Moon, which signifies one's superficial way of behaving. When the ancient Romans referred to the Emperor Augustus as a Capricorn, they meant that he had the Moon in Capricorn. Or, to take another example, a modern astrologer would call Disraeli a Scorpion because he had Scorpio Rising, but most people would call him Sagittarius because he had the Sun there. The Romans would have called him Leo because his Moon was in Leo.

So if one does not seem to fit one's birth month, it is always worthwhile reading the other signs, for one may have been born at a time when any of them were rising or occupied by the Moon. It also seems to be the case that the influence of the Sun develops as life goes on, so that the month of birth is easier to guess in people over the age of forty. The young are supposed to be influenced mainly by their Ascendant, the Rising sign, which characterizes the body and physical personality as a whole.

It is nonsense to assume that all people born at a certain time will exhibit the same characteristics, or that they will even behave in the same manner. It is quite obvious that, from the very moment of its birth, a child is subject to the effects of its environment, and that this in turn will influence its character and heritage to a decisive extent. Also to be taken into account are education and economic conditions, which play a very important part in the formation of one's character as well.

People have, in general, certain character traits and qualities which, according to their environment, develop in either a positive or a negative manner. Therefore, selfishness (inherent selfishness, that is) might emerge as unselfishness; kindness and consideration as cruelty and lack of consideration toward others. In the same way, a naturally constructive person may, through frustration, become destructive, and so on. The latent characteristics with which people are born can, therefore, through environment and good or bad training, become something that would appear to be its opposite, and so give the lie to the astrologer's description of their character. But this is not the case. The true character is still there, but it is buried deep beneath these external superficialities.

Careful study of the character traits of various signs of the Zodiac are of immeasurable help, and can render beneficial service to the intelligent person. Undoubtedly, the reader will already have discovered that, while he is able to get on very well with some people, he just "cannot stand" others. The causes sometimes seem inexplicable. At times there is intense dislike, at other times immediate sympathy. And there is, too, the phenomenon of love at first sight, which is also apparently inexplicable. People appear to be either sympathetic or unsympathetic toward each other for no apparent reason.

Now if we look at this in the light of the Zodiac, we find that people born under different signs are either compatible or incompatible with each other. In other words, there are good and bad interrelating factors among the various signs. This does not, of course, mean that humanity can be divided into groups of hostile camps. It would be quite wrong to be hostile or indifferent toward people who happen to be born under an incompatible sign. There is no reason why everybody should not, or cannot, learn to control and adjust their feelings and actions, especially after they are aware of the positive qualities of other people by studying their character analyses, among other things.

Every person born under a certain sign has both positive and negative qualities, which are developed more or less according to our free will. Nobody is entirely good or entirely bad, and it is up to each of us to learn to control ourselves on the one hand and at the same time to endeavor to learn about ourselves and others.

It cannot be emphasized often enough that it is free will that determines whether we will make really good use of our talents and abilities. Using our free will, we can either overcome our failings or allow them to rule us. Our free will enables us to exert sufficient willpower to control our failings so that they do not harm ourselves or others.

Astrology can reveal our inclinations and tendencies. Astrology can tell us about ourselves so that we are able to use our free will to overcome our shortcomings. In this way astrology helps us do our best to become needed and valuable members of society as well as helpmates to our family and our friends. Astrology also can save us a great deal of unhappiness and remorse.

Yet it may seem absurd that an ancient philosophy could be a prop to modern men and women. But below the materialistic surface of modern life, there are hidden streams of feeling and thought. Symbology is reappearing as a study worthy of the scholar; the psychosomatic factor in illness has passed from the writings of the crank to those of the specialist; spiritual healing in all its forms is no longer a pious hope but an accepted phenomenon. And it is into this context that we consider astrology, in the sense that it is an analysis of human types.

Astrology and medicine had a long journey together, and only parted company a couple of centuries ago. There still remain in medical language such astrological terms as "saturnine," "choleric," and "mercurial," used in the diagnosis of physical tendencies. The herbalist, for long the handyman of the medical profession, has been dominated by astrology since the days of the Greeks. Certain herbs traditionally respond to certain planetary influences, and diseases must therefore be treated to ensure harmony between the medicine and the disease.

But the stars are expected to foretell and not only to diagnose.

Astrological forecasting has been remarkably accurate, but often it is wide of the mark. The brave person who cares to predict world events takes dangerous chances. Individual forecasting is less clear cut; it can be a help or a disillusionment. Then we come to the nagging question: if it is possible to foreknow, is it right to foretell? This is a point of ethics on which it is hard to pronounce judgment. The doctor faces the same dilemma if he finds that symptoms of a mortal disease are present in his patient and that he can only prognosticate a steady decline. How much to tell an individual in a crisis is a problem that has perplexed many distinguished scholars. Honest and conscientious astrologers in this modern world, where so many people are seeking guidance, face the same problem.

Five hundred years ago it was customary to call in a learned man who was an astrologer who was probably also a doctor and a philosopher. By his knowledge of astrology, his study of planetary influences, he felt himself qualified to guide those in distress. The world has moved forward at a fantastic rate since then, and yet people are still uncertain of themselves. At first sight it seems fantastic in the light of modern thinking that they turn to the most ancient of all studies, and get someone to calculate a horoscope for them. But is it really so fantastic if you take a second look? For astrology is concerned with tomorrow, with survival. And in a world such as ours, tomorrow and survival are the keywords for the twenty-first century.

SPECIAL OVERVIEW 2011–2020

The second decade of the twenty-first century opens on major planetary shifts that set the stage for challenge, opportunity, and change. The personal planets—notably Jupiter and Saturn—and the generational planets—Uranus, Neptune, and Pluto—have all moved forward into new signs of the zodiac. These fresh planetary influences act to shape unfolding events and illuminate pathways to the future.

Jupiter, the big planet that attracts luck, spends about one year in each zodiacal sign. It takes approximately twelve years for Jupiter to travel through all twelve signs of the zodiac in order to complete a cycle. In 2011 a new Jupiter cycle is initiated with Jupiter transiting Aries, the first sign of the zodiac. As each year progresses over the course of the decade, Jupiter moves forward into the next sign, following the natural progression of the zodiac. Jupiter visits Taurus in 2012, Gemini in 2013, Cancer in 2014, Leo in 2015, Virgo in 2016, Libra in 2017, Scorpio in 2018, Sagittarius in 2019, Capricorn in 2020. Then in late December 2020 Jupiter enters Aquarius just two weeks before the decade closes. Jupiter's vibrations are helpful and fruitful, a source of good luck and a protection against bad luck. Opportunity swells under Jupiter's powerful rays. Learning takes leaps of faith.

Saturn, the beautiful planet of reason and responsibility, spends about two and a half years in each zodiacal sign. A complete Saturn cycle through all twelve signs of the zodiac takes about twenty-nine to thirty years. Saturn is known as the lawgiver: setting boundaries and codes of conduct, urging self-discipline and structure within a creative framework. The rule of law, the role of government, the responsibility of the individual are all sourced from Saturn. Saturn gives as it takes. Once a lesson is learned, Saturn's reward is just and full.

Saturn transits Libra throughout 2011 until early autumn of 2012. Here Saturn seeks to harmonize, to balance, to bring order out of chaos. Saturn in Libra ennobles the artist, the judge, the high-minded, the honest. Saturn next visits Scorpio from autumn 2012 until late December 2014. With Saturn in Scorpio, tactic and strategy combine to get workable solutions and desired results. Saturn's problem-solving tools here can harness dynamic energy for the common good. Saturn in Sagittarius, an idealistic and humanistic transit that stretches from December 2014 into the last day of autumn 2017, promotes activism over mere dogma and debate. Saturn in Sagittarius can be a driving force for good. Saturn tours Capricorn, the sign that Saturn rules, from the first day of winter 2017 into early spring 2020. Saturn in Capricorn is a consolidating transit, bringing things forth and into fruition. Here a plan can be made right, made whole, then launched for success. Saturn starts to visit Aquarius, a sign that Saturn corules and a very good sign for Saturn to visit, in the very last year of the decade. Saturn in Aquarius fosters team spirit, the unity of effort amid diversity. The transit of Saturn in Aquarius until early 2023 represents a period of enlightened activism and unprecedented growth.

Uranus, Neptune, and Pluto spend more than several years in each sign. They produce the differences in attitude, belief, behavior, and taste that distinguish one generation from another—and so are called the generational planets.

Uranus, planet of innovation and surprise, is known as the awakener. Uranus spends seven to eight years in each sign. Uranus started a new cycle when it entered Aries, the first sign of the zodiac, in May 2010. Uranus tours Aries until May 2018. Uranus in Aries accents originality, freedom, independence, unpredictability. There can be a start-stop quality to undertakings given this transit. Despite contradiction and confrontation, significant invention and productivity mark this transit. Uranus next visits Taurus through the end of the decade into 2026. Strategic thinking and timely action characterize the transit of Uranus in Taurus. Here intuition is backed up by common sense, leading to fresh discoveries upon which new industries can be built.

Neptune spends about fourteen years in each sign. Neptune, the visionary planet, enters Pisces, the sign Neptune rules and the final sign of the zodiac, in early April 2011. Neptune journeys through Pisces until 2026 to complete the Neptune cycle of visiting all twelve zodiacal signs. Neptune's tour of Pisces ushers in a long period of great potentiality: universal understanding, universal good, universal love, universal generosity, universal forgiveness—the universal spirit affects all. Neptune in Pisces can oversee the fruition of such noble aims as human rights for all and liberation from all forms of tyranny. Neptune in Pisces is a pervasive influence that changes concepts, consciences, attitudes, actions. The impact of Neptune in Pisces is to illuminate and to inspire.

Pluto, dwarf planet of beginnings and endings, entered the earthy sign of Capricorn in 2008 and journeys there for sixteen years into late 2024. Pluto in Capricorn over the course of this extensive visit has the capacity to change the landscape as well as the humanscape. The transforming energy of Pluto combines with the persevering power of Capricorn to give depth and character to potential change. Pluto in Capricorn brings focus and cohesion to disparate, diverse creativities. As new forms arise and take root, Pluto in Capricorn organizes the rebuilding process. Freedom versus limitation, freedom versus authority is in the framework during this transit. Reasonableness struggles with recklessness to solve divisive issues. Pluto in Capricorn teaches important lessons about adversity, and the lessons will be learned.

THE SIGNS OF THE ZODIAC

Dominant Characteristics

Aries: March 21–April 20

The Positive Side of Aries

The Aries has many positive points to his character. People born under this first sign of the Zodiac are often quite strong and enthusiastic. On the whole, they are forward-looking people who are not easily discouraged by temporary setbacks. They know what they want out of life and they go out after it. Their personalities are strong. Others are usually quite impressed by the Ram's way of doing things. Quite often they are sources of inspiration for others traveling the same route. Aries men and women have a special zest for life that can be contagious; for others, they are a fine example of how life should be lived.

The Aries person usually has a quick and active mind. He is imaginative and inventive. He enjoys keeping busy and active. He generally gets along well with all kinds of people. He is interested in mankind, as a whole. He likes to be challenged. Some would say he thrives on opposition, for it is when he is set against that he often does his best. Getting over or around obstacles is a challenge he generally enjoys. All in all, Aries is quite positive and young-thinking. He likes to keep abreast of new things that are happening in the world. Aries are often fond of speed. They like things to be done quickly, and this sometimes aggravates their slower colleagues and associates.

The Aries man or woman always seems to remain young. Their whole approach to life is youthful and optimistic. They never say die, no matter what the odds. They may have an occasional setback, but it is not long before they are back on their feet again.

The Negative Side of Aries

Everybody has his less positive qualities—and Aries is no exception. Sometimes the Aries man or woman is not very tactful in communicating with others; in his hurry to get things done he is apt to be a little callous or inconsiderate. Sensitive people are likely to find him somewhat sharp-tongued in some situations. Often in his eagerness to get the show on the road, he misses the mark altogether and cannot achieve his aims.

At times Aries can be too impulsive. He can occasionally be stubborn and refuse to listen to reason. If things do not move quickly enough to suit the Aries man or woman, he or she is apt to become rather nervous or irritable. The uncultivated Aries is not unfamiliar with moments of doubt and fear. He is capable of being destructive if he does not get his way. He can overcome some of his emotional problems by steadily trying to express himself as he really is, but this requires effort.

Taurus: April 21–May 20

The Positive Side of Taurus

The Taurus person is known for his ability to concentrate and for his tenacity. These are perhaps his strongest qualities. The Taurus man or woman generally has very little trouble in getting along with others; it's his nature to be helpful toward people in need. He can always be depended on by his friends, especially those in trouble.

Taurus generally achieves what he wants through his ability to persevere. He never leaves anything unfinished but works on something until it has been completed. People can usually take him at his word; he is honest and forthright in most of his dealings. The Taurus person has a good chance to make a success of his life because of his many positive qualities. The Taurus who aims high seldom falls short of his mark. He learns well by experience. He is thorough and does not believe in shortcuts of any kind. The Bull's thoroughness pays off in the end, for through his deliberateness he learns how to rely on himself and what he has learned. The Taurus person tries to get along with others, as a rule. He is not overly critical

and likes people to be themselves. He is a tolerant person and enjoys peace and harmony—especially in his home life.

Taurus is usually cautious in all that he does. He is not a person who believes in taking unnecessary risks. Before adopting any one line of action, he will weigh all of the pros and cons. The Taurus person is steadfast. Once his mind is made up it seldom changes. The person born under this sign usually is a good family person—reliable and loving.

The Negative Side of Taurus

Sometimes the Taurus man or woman is a bit too stubborn. He won't listen to other points of view if his mind is set on something. To others, this can be quite annoying. Taurus also does not like to be told what to do. He becomes rather angry if others think him not too bright. He does not like to be told he is wrong, even when he is. He dislikes being contradicted.

Some people who are born under this sign are very suspicious of others—even of those persons close to them. They find it difficult to trust people fully. They are often afraid of being deceived or taken advantage of. The Bull often finds it difficult to forget or forgive. His love of material things sometimes makes him rather avaricious and petty.

Gemini: May 21–June 20

The Positive Side of Gemini

The person born under this sign of the Heavenly Twins is usually quite bright and quick-witted. Some of them are capable of doing many different things. The Gemini person very often has many different interests. He keeps an open mind and is always anxious to learn new things.

Gemini is often an analytical person. He is a person who enjoys making use of his intellect. He is governed more by his mind than by his emotions. He is a person who is not confined to one view; he can often understand both sides to a problem or question. He knows how to reason, how to make rapid decisions if need be.

He is an adaptable person and can make himself at home almost anywhere. There are all kinds of situations he can adapt to. He is a person who seldom doubts himself; he is sure of his talents and his ability to think and reason. Gemini is generally most satisfied when he is in a situation where he can make use of his intellect. Never short of imagination, he often has strong talents for invention. He is rather a modern person when it comes to life; Gemini almost always moves along with the times—perhaps that is why he remains so youthful throughout most of his life.

Literature and art appeal to the person born under this sign. Creativity in almost any form will interest and intrigue the Gemini man or woman.

The Gemini is often quite charming. A good talker, he often is the center of attraction at any gathering. People find it easy to like a person born under this sign because he can appear easygoing and usually has a good sense of humor.

The Negative Side of Gemini

Sometimes the Gemini person tries to do too many things at one time—and as a result, winds up finishing nothing. Some Twins are easily distracted and find it rather difficult to concentrate on one thing for too long a time. Sometimes they give in to trifling fancies and find it rather boring to become too serious about any one thing. Some of them are never dependable, no matter what they promise.

Although the Gemini man or woman often appears to be well-versed on many subjects, this is sometimes just a veneer. His knowledge may be only superficial, but because he speaks so well he gives people the impression of erudition. Some Geminis are sharp-tongued and inconsiderate; they think only of themselves and their own pleasure.

Cancer: June 21–July 20

The Positive Side of Cancer

The Moon Child's most positive point is his understanding nature. On the whole, he is a loving and sympathetic person. He would never go out of his way to hurt anyone. The Cancer man or woman is often very kind and tender; they give what they can to others. They hate to see others suffering and will do what they can to help someone in less fortunate circumstances than themselves. They are often very concerned about the world. Their interest in people generally goes beyond that of just their own families and close friends; they have a deep sense of community and respect humanitarian values. The Moon Child means what he says, as a rule; he is honest about his feelings.

The Cancer man or woman is a person who knows the art of patience. When something seems difficult, he is willing to wait until the situation becomes manageable again. He is a person who knows how to bide his time. Cancer knows how to concentrate on one thing at a time. When he has made his mind up he generally sticks with what he does, seeing it through to the end.

Cancer is a person who loves his home. He enjoys being surrounded by familiar things and the people he loves. Of all the signs, Cancer is the most maternal. Even the men born under this sign often have a motherly or protective quality about them. They like to take care of people in their family—to see that they are well loved and well provided for. They are usually loyal and faithful. Family ties mean a lot to the Cancer man or woman. Parents and in-laws are respected and loved. Young Cancer responds very well to adults who show faith in him. The Moon Child has a strong sense of tradition. He is very sensitive to the moods of others.

The Negative Side of Cancer

Sometimes Cancer finds it rather hard to face life. It becomes too much for him. He can be a little timid and retiring, when things don't go too well. When unfortunate things happen, he is apt to just shrug and say, "Whatever will be will be." He can be fatalistic to a fault. The uncultivated Cancer is a bit lazy. He doesn't have very much ambition. Anything that seems a bit difficult he'll gladly leave to others. He may be lacking in initiative. Too sensitive, when he feels he's been injured, he'll crawl back into his shell and nurse his imaginary wounds. The immature Moon Child often is given to crying when the smallest thing goes wrong.

Some Cancers find it difficult to enjoy themselves in environments outside their homes. They make heavy demands on others, and need to be constantly reassured that they are loved. Lacking such reassurance, they may resort to sulking in silence.

Leo: July 21–August 21

The Positive Side of Leo

Often Leos make good leaders. They seem to be good organizers and administrators. Usually they are quite popular with others. Whatever group it is that they belong to, the Leo man or woman is almost sure to be or become the leader. Loyalty, one of the Lion's noblest traits, enables him or her to maintain this leadership position.

Leo is generous most of the time. It is his best characteristic. He or she likes to give gifts and presents. In making others happy, the Leo person becomes happy himself. He likes to splurge when spending money on others. In some instances it may seem that the Lion's generosity knows no boundaries. A hospitable person, the Leo man or woman is very fond of welcoming people to his house and entertaining them. He is never short of company.

Leo has plenty of energy and drive. He enjoys working toward some specific goal. When he applies himself correctly, he gets what he wants most often. The Leo person is almost never unsure of himself. He has plenty of confidence and aplomb. He is a person who is direct in almost everything he does. He has a quick mind and can make a decision in a very short time.

He usually sets a good example for others because of his ambitious manner and positive ways. He knows how to stick to something once he's started. Although Leo may be good at making a joke, he is not superficial or glib. He is a loving person, kind and thoughtful.

There is generally nothing small or petty about the Leo man or woman. He does what he can for those who are deserving. He is a person others can rely upon at all times. He means what he says. An honest person, generally speaking, he is a friend who is valued and sought out.

The Negative Side of Leo

Leo, however, does have his faults. At times, he can be just a bit too arrogant. He thinks that no one deserves a leadership position except him. Only he is capable of doing things well. His opinion of himself is often much too high. Because of his conceit, he is sometimes rather unpopular with a good many people. Some Leos are too materialistic; they can only think in terms of money and profit.

Some Leos enjoy lording it over others—at home or at their place of business. What is more, they feel they have the right to. Egocentric to an impossible degree, this sort of Leo cares little about how others think or feel. He can be rude and cutting.

Virgo: August 22–September 22

The Positive Side of Virgo

The person born under the sign of Virgo is generally a busy person. He knows how to arrange and organize things. He is a good planner. Above all, he is practical and is not afraid of hard work.

Often called the sign of the Harvester, Virgo knows how to attain what he desires. He sticks with something until it is finished. He never shirks his duties, and can always be depended upon. The Virgo person can be thoroughly trusted at all times.

The man or woman born under this sign tries to do everything to perfection. He doesn't believe in doing anything halfway. He always aims for the top. He is the sort of a person who is always learning and constantly striving to better himself—not because he wants more money or glory, but because it gives him a feeling of accomplishment.

The Virgo man or woman is a very observant person. He is sensitive to how others feel, and can see things below the surface of a situation. He usually puts this talent to constructive use.

It is not difficult for the Virgo to be open and earnest. He believes in putting his cards on the table. He is never secretive or underhanded. He's as good as his word. The Virgo person is generally plainspoken and down to earth. He has no trouble in expressing himself.

The Virgo person likes to keep up to date on new developments in his particular field. Well-informed, generally, he sometimes has a keen interest in the arts or literature. What he knows, he knows well. His ability to use his critical faculties is well-developed and sometimes startles others because of its accuracy.

Virgos adhere to a moderate way of life; they avoid excesses. Virgo is a responsible person and enjoys being of service.

The Negative Side of Virgo

Sometimes a Virgo person is too critical. He thinks that only he can do something the way it should be done. Whatever anyone else does is inferior. He can be rather annoying in the way he quibbles over insignificant details. In telling others how things should be done, he can be rather tactless and mean.

Some Virgos seem rather emotionless and cool. They feel emotional involvement is beneath them. They are sometimes too tidy, too neat. With money they can be rather miserly. Some Virgos try to force their opinions and ideas on others.

Libra: September 23–October 22

The Positive Side of Libra

Libras love harmony. It is one of their most outstanding character traits. They are interested in achieving balance; they admire beauty and grace in things as well as in people. Generally speaking, they are kind and considerate people. Libras are usually very sympathetic. They go out of their way not to hurt another person's feelings. They are outgoing and do what they can to help those in need.

People born under the sign of Libra almost always make good friends. They are loyal and amiable. They enjoy the company of others. Many of them are rather moderate in their views; they believe in keeping an open mind, however, and weighing both sides of an issue fairly before making a decision.

Alert and intelligent, Libra, often known as the Lawgiver, is always fair-minded and tries to put himself in the position of the other person. They are against injustice; quite often they take up for the underdog. In most of their social dealings, they try to be tactful and kind. They dislike discord and bickering, and most Libras strive for peace and harmony in all their relationships.

The Libra man or woman has a keen sense of beauty. They appreciate handsome furnishings and clothes. Many of them are artistically inclined. Their taste is usually impeccable. They know how to use color. Their homes are almost always attractively arranged and inviting. They enjoy entertaining people and see to it that their guests always feel at home and welcome.

Libra gets along with almost everyone. He is well-liked and socially much in demand.

The Negative Side of Libra

Some people born under this sign tend to be rather insincere. So eager are they to achieve harmony in all relationships that they will even go so far as to lie. Many of them are escapists. They find facing the truth an ordeal and prefer living in a world of make-believe.

In a serious argument, some Libras give in rather easily even when they know they are right. Arguing, even about something they believe in, is too unsettling for some of them.

Libras sometimes care too much for material things. They enjoy possessions and luxuries. Some are vain and tend to be jealous.

Scorpio: October 23–November 22

The Positive Side of Scorpio

The Scorpio man or woman generally knows what he or she wants out of life. He is a determined person. He sees something through to the end. Scorpio is quite sincere, and seldom says anything he doesn't mean. When he sets a goal for himself he tries to go about achieving it in a very direct way.

The Scorpion is brave and courageous. They are not afraid of hard work. Obstacles do not frighten them. They forge ahead until they achieve what they set out for. The Scorpio man or woman has a strong will.

Although Scorpio may seem rather fixed and determined, inside he is often quite tender and loving. He can care very much for others. He believes in sincerity in all relationships. His feelings about someone tend to last; they are profound and not superficial.

The Scorpio person is someone who adheres to his principles no matter what happens. He will not be deterred from a path he believes to be right.

Because of his many positive strengths, the Scorpion can often achieve happiness for himself and for those that he loves.

He is a constructive person by nature. He often has a deep understanding of people and of life, in general. He is perceptive and unafraid. Obstacles often seem to spur him on. He is a positive person who enjoys winning. He has many strengths and resources; challenge of any sort often brings out the best in him.

The Negative Side of Scorpio

The Scorpio person is sometimes hypersensitive. Often he imagines injury when there is none. He feels that others do not bother to recognize him for his true worth. Sometimes he is given to excessive boasting in order to compensate for what he feels is neglect.

Scorpio can be proud, arrogant, and competitive. They can be sly when they put their minds to it and they enjoy outwitting persons or institutions noted for their cleverness.

Their tactics for getting what they want are sometimes devious and ruthless. They don't care too much about what others may think. If they feel others have done them an injustice, they will do their best to seek revenge. The Scorpion often has a sudden, violent temper; and this person's interest in sex is sometimes quite unbalanced or excessive.

Sagittarius: November 23–December 20

The Positive Side of Sagittarius

People born under this sign are honest and forthright. Their approach to life is earnest and open. Sagittarius is often quite adult in his way of seeing things. They are broad-minded and tolerant people. When dealing with others the person born under the sign of the Archer is almost always open and forthright. He doesn't believe in deceit or pretension. His standards are high. People who associate with Sagittarius generally admire and respect his tolerant viewpoint.

The Archer trusts others easily and expects them to trust him. He is never suspicious or envious and almost always thinks well of others. People always enjoy his company because he is so friendly and easygoing. The Sagittarius man or woman is often good-humored. He can always be depended upon by his friends, family, and co-workers.

The person born under this sign of the Zodiac likes a good joke every now and then. Sagittarius is eager for fun and laughs, which makes him very popular with others.

A lively person, he enjoys sports and outdoor life. The Archer is fond of animals. Intelligent and interesting, he can begin an animated conversation with ease. He likes exchanging ideas and discussing various views.

He is not selfish or proud. If someone proposes an idea or plan

that is better than his, he will immediately adopt it. Imaginative yet practical, he knows how to put ideas into practice.

The Archer enjoys sport and games, and it doesn't matter if he wins or loses. He is a forgiving person, and never sulks over something that has not worked out in his favor.

He is seldom critical, and is almost always generous.

The Negative Side of Sagittarius

Some Sagittarius are restless. They take foolish risks and seldom learn from the mistakes they make. They don't have heads for money and are often mismanaging their finances. Some of them devote much of their time to gambling.

Some are too outspoken and tactless, always putting their feet in their mouths. They hurt others carelessly by being honest at the wrong time. Sometimes they make promises which they don't keep. They don't stick close enough to their plans and go from one failure to another. They are undisciplined and waste a lot of energy.

Capricorn: December 21–January 19

The Positive Side of Capricorn

The person born under the sign of Capricorn, known variously as the Mountain Goat or Sea Goat, is usually very stable and patient. He sticks to whatever tasks he has and sees them through. He can always be relied upon and he is not averse to work.

An honest person, Capricorn is generally serious about whatever he does. He does not take his duties lightly. He is a practical person and believes in keeping his feet on the ground.

Quite often the person born under this sign is ambitious and knows how to get what he wants out of life. The Goat forges ahead and never gives up his goal. When he is determined about something, he almost always wins. He is a good worker—a hard worker. Although things may not come easy to him, he will not complain, but continue working until his chores are finished.

He is usually good at business matters and knows the value of

money. He is not a spendthrift and knows how to put something away for a rainy day; he dislikes waste and unnecessary loss.

Capricorn knows how to make use of his self-control. He can apply himself to almost anything once he puts his mind to it. His ability to concentrate sometimes astounds others. He is diligent and does well when involved in detail work.

The Capricorn man or woman is charitable, generally speaking, and will do what is possible to help others less fortunate. As a friend, he is loyal and trustworthy. He never shirks his duties or responsibilities. He is self-reliant and never expects too much of the other fellow. He does what he can on his own. If someone does him a good turn, then he will do his best to return the favor.

The Negative Side of Capricorn

Like everyone, Capricorn, too, has faults. At times, the Goat can be overcritical of others. He expects others to live up to his own high standards. He thinks highly of himself and tends to look down on others.

His interest in material things may be exaggerated. The Capricorn man or woman thinks too much about getting on in the world and having something to show for it. He may even be a little greedy.

He sometimes thinks he knows what's best for everyone. He is too bossy. He is always trying to organize and correct others. He may be a little narrow in his thinking.

Aquarius: January 20–February 18

The Positive Side of Aquarius

The Aquarius man or woman is usually very honest and forthright. These are his two greatest qualities. His standards for himself are generally very high. He can always be relied upon by others. His word is his bond.

Aquarius is perhaps the most tolerant of all the Zodiac personalities. He respects other people's beliefs and feels that everyone is entitled to his own approach to life.

He would never do anything to injure another's feelings. He is never unkind or cruel. Always considerate of others, the Water Bearer is always willing to help a person in need. He feels a very strong tie between himself and all the other members of mankind.

The person born under this sign, called the Water Bearer, is almost always an individualist. He does not believe in teaming up with the masses, but prefers going his own way. His ideas about life and mankind are often quite advanced. There is a saying to the effect that the average Aquarius is fifty years ahead of his time.

Aquarius is community-minded. The problems of the world concern him greatly. He is interested in helping others no matter what part of the globe they live in. He is truly a humanitarian sort. He likes to be of service to others.

Giving, considerate, and without prejudice, Aquarius have no trouble getting along with others.

The Negative Side of Aquarius

Aquarius may be too much of a dreamer. He makes plans but seldom carries them out. He is rather unrealistic. His imagination has a tendency to run away with him. Because many of his plans are impractical, he is always in some sort of a dither.

Others may not approve of him at all times because of his unconventional behavior. He may be a bit eccentric. Sometimes he is so busy with his own thoughts that he loses touch with the realities of existence.

Some Aquarius feel they are more clever and intelligent than others. They seldom admit to their own faults, even when they are quite apparent. Some become rather fanatic in their views. Their criticism of others is sometimes destructive and negative.

Pisces: February 19–March 20

The Positive Side of Pisces

Known as the sign of the Fishes, Pisces has a sympathetic nature. Kindly, he is often dedicated in the way he goes about helping others. The sick and the troubled often turn to him for advice and assistance. Possessing keen intuition, Pisces can easily understand people's deepest problems.

He is very broad-minded and does not criticize others for their faults. He knows how to accept people for what they are. On the whole, he is a trustworthy and earnest person. He is loyal to his friends

and will do what he can to help them in time of need. Generous and good-natured, he is a lover of peace; he is often willing to help others solve their differences. People who have taken a wrong turn in life often interest him and he will do what he can to persuade them to rehabilitate themselves.

He has a strong intuitive sense and most of the time he knows how to make it work for him. Pisces is unusually perceptive and often knows what is bothering someone before that person, himself, is aware of it. The Pisces man or woman is an idealistic person, basically, and is interested in making the world a better place in which to live. Pisces believes that everyone should help each other. He is willing to do more than his share in order to achieve cooperation with others.

The person born under this sign often is talented in music or art. He is a receptive person; he is able to take the ups and downs of life with philosophic calm.

The Negative Side of Pisces

Some Pisces are often depressed; their outlook on life is rather glum. They may feel that they have been given a bad deal in life and that others are always taking unfair advantage of them. Pisces sometimes feel that the world is a cold and cruel place. The Fishes can be easily discouraged. The Pisces man or woman may even withdraw from the harshness of reality into a secret shell of his own where he dreams and idles away a good deal of his time.

Pisces can be lazy. He lets things happen without giving the least bit of resistance. He drifts along, whether on the high road or on the low. He can be lacking in willpower.

Some Pisces people seek escape through drugs or alcohol. When temptation comes along they find it hard to resist. In matters of sex, they can be rather permissive.

Sun Sign Personalities

ARIES: Hans Christian Andersen, Pearl Bailey, Marlon Brando, Wernher Von Braun, Charlie Chaplin, Joan Crawford, Da Vinci, Bette Davis, Doris Day, W.C. Fields, Alec Guinness, Adolf Hitler, William Holden, Thomas Jefferson, Nikita Khrushchev, Elton John, Arturo Toscanini, J.P. Morgan, Paul Robeson, Gloria Steinem, Sarah Vaughn, Vincent van Gogh, Tennessee Williams

TAURUS: Fred Astaire, Charlotte Brontë, Carol Burnett, Irving Berlin, Bing Crosby, Salvador Dali, Tchaikovsky, Queen Elizabeth II, Duke Ellington, Ella Fitzgerald, Henry Fonda, Sigmund Freud, Orson Welles, Joe Louis, Lenin, Karl Marx, Golda Meir, Eva Peron, Bertrand Russell, Shakespeare, Kate Smith, Benjamin Spock, Barbra Streisand, Shirley Temple, Harry Truman

GEMINI: Ruth Benedict, Josephine Baker, Rachel Carson, Carlos Chavez, Walt Whitman, Bob Dylan, Ralph Waldo Emerson, Judy Garland, Paul Gauguin, Allen Ginsberg, Benny Goodman, Bob Hope, Burl Ives, John F. Kennedy, Peggy Lee, Marilyn Monroe, Joe Namath, Cole Porter, Laurence Olivier, Harriet Beecher Stowe, Queen Victoria, John Wayne, Frank Lloyd Wright

CANCER: "Dear Abby," Lizzie Borden, David Brinkley, Yul Brynner, Pearl Buck, Marc Chagall, Princess Diana, Babe Didrikson, Mary Baker Eddy, Henry VIII, John Glenn, Ernest Hemingway, Lena Horne, Oscar Hammerstein, Helen Keller, Ann Landers, George Orwell, Nancy Reagan, Rembrandt, Richard Rodgers, Ginger Rogers, Rubens, Jean-Paul Sartre, O.J. Simpson

LEO: Neil Armstrong, James Baldwin, Lucille Ball, Emily Brontë, Wilt Chamberlain, Julia Child, William J. Clinton, Cecil B. De Mille, Ogden Nash, Amelia Earhart, Edna Ferber, Arthur Goldberg, Alfred Hitchcock, Mick Jagger, George Meany, Annie Oakley, George Bernard Shaw, Napoleon, Jacqueline Onassis, Henry Ford, Francis Scott Key, Andy Warhol, Mae West, Orville Wright

VIRGO: Ingrid Bergman, Warren Burger, Maurice Chevalier, Agatha Christie, Sean Connery, Lafayette, Peter Falk, Greta Garbo, Althea Gibson, Arthur Godfrey, Goethe, Buddy Hackett, Michael Jackson, Lyndon Johnson, D.H. Lawrence, Sophia Loren, Grandma Moses, Arnold Palmer, Queen Elizabeth I, Walter Reuther, Peter Sellers, Lily Tomlin, George Wallace

LIBRA: Brigitte Bardot, Art Buchwald, Truman Capote, Dwight D. Eisenhower, William Faulkner, F. Scott Fitzgerald, Gandhi, George Gershwin, Micky Mantle, Helen Hayes, Vladimir Horowitz, Doris Lessing, Martina Navratalova, Eugene O'Neill, Luciano Pavarotti, Emily Post, Eleanor Roosevelt, Bruce Springsteen, Margaret Thatcher, Gore Vidal, Barbara Walters, Oscar Wilde

SCORPIO: Vivien Leigh, Richard Burton, Art Carney, Johnny Carson, Billy Graham, Grace Kelly, Walter Cronkite, Marie Curie, Charles de Gaulle, Linda Evans, Indira Gandhi, Theodore Roosevelt, Rock Hudson, Katherine Hepburn, Robert F. Kennedy, Billie Jean King, Martin Luther, Georgia O'Keeffe, Pablo Picasso, Jonas Salk, Alan Shepard, Robert Louis Stevenson

SAGITTARIUS: Jane Austen, Louisa May Alcott, Woody Allen, Beethoven, Willy Brandt, Mary Martin, William F. Buckley, Maria Callas, Winston Churchill, Noel Coward, Emily Dickinson, Walt Disney, Benjamin Disraeli, James Doolittle, Kirk Douglas, Chet Huntley, Jane Fonda, Chris Evert Lloyd, Margaret Mead, Charles Schulz, John Milton, Frank Sinatra, Steven Spielberg

CAPRICORN: Muhammad Ali, Isaac Asimov, Pablo Casals, Dizzy Dean, Marlene Dietrich, James Farmer, Ava Gardner, Barry Goldwater, Cary Grant, J. Edgar Hoover, Howard Hughes, Joan of Arc, Gypsy Rose Lee, Martin Luther King, Jr., Rudyard Kipling, Mao Tse-tung, Richard Nixon, Gamal Nasser, Louis Pasteur, Albert Schweitzer, Stalin, Benjamin Franklin, Elvis Presley

AQUARIUS: Marian Anderson, Susan B. Anthony, Jack Benny, John Barrymore, Mikhail Baryshnikov, Charles Darwin, Charles Dickens, Thomas Edison, Clark Gable, Jascha Heifetz, Abraham Lincoln, Yehudi Menuhin, Mozart, Jack Nicklaus, Ronald Reagan, Jackie Robinson, Norman Rockwell, Franklin D. Roosevelt, Gertrude Stein, Charles Lindbergh, Margaret Truman

PISCES: Edward Albee, Harry Belafonte, Alexander Graham Bell, Chopin, Adelle Davis, Albert Einstein, Golda Meir, Jackie Gleason, Winslow Homer, Edward M. Kennedy, Victor Hugo, Mike Mansfield, Michelangelo, Edna St. Vincent Millay, Liza Minelli, John Steinbeck, Linus Pauling, Ravel, Renoir, Diana Ross, William Shirer, Elizabeth Taylor, George Washington

The Signs and Their Key Words

		POSITIVE	NEGATIVE
ARIES	self	courage, initiative, pioneer instinct	brash rudeness, selfish impetuosity
TAURUS	money	endurance, loyalty, wealth	obstinacy, gluttony
GEMINI	mind	versatility	capriciousness, unreliability
CANCER	family	sympathy, homing instinct	clannishness, childishness
LEO	children	love, authority, integrity	egotism, force
VIRGO	work	purity, industry, analysis	faultfinding, cynicism
LIBRA	marriage	harmony, justice	vacillation, superficiality
SCORPIO	sex	survival, regeneration	vengeance, discord
SAGITTARIUS	travel	optimism, higher learning	lawlessness
CAPRICORN	career	depth	narrowness, gloom
AQUARIUS	friends	human fellowship, genius	perverse unpredictability
PISCES	confinement	spiritual love, universality	diffusion, escapism

The Elements and Qualities of The Signs

Every sign has both an *element* and a *quality* associated with it. The element indicates the basic makeup of the sign, and the quality describes the kind of activity associated with each.

Element	Sign	Quality	Sign
FIRE	ARIES LEO SAGITTARIUS	CARDINAL	ARIES LIBRA CANCER CAPRICORN
EARTH	TAURUS VIRGO CAPRICORN	FIXED	TAURUS LEO SCORPIO AQUARIUS
AIR	GEMINI LIBRA AQUARIUS		
WATER	CANCER SCORPIO PISCES	MUTABLE	GEMINI VIRGO SAGITTARIUS PISCES

Signs can be grouped together according to their element and quality. Signs of the same element share many basic traits in common. They tend to form stable configurations and ultimately harmonious relationships. Signs of the same quality are often less harmonious, but they share many dynamic potentials for growth as well as profound fulfillment.

Further discussion of each of these sign groupings is provided on the following pages.

The Fire Signs

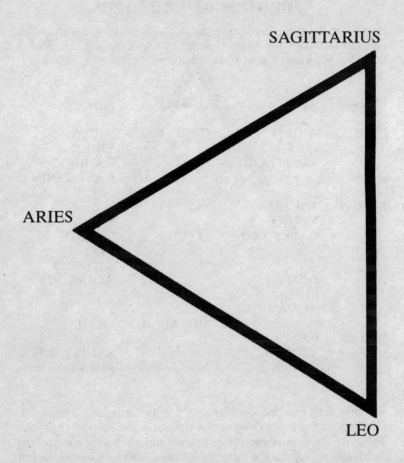

This is the fire group. On the whole these are emotional, volatile types, quick to anger, quick to forgive. They are adventurous, powerful people and act as a source of inspiration for everyone. They spark into action with immediate exuberant impulses. They are intelligent, self-involved, creative, and idealistic. They all share a certain vibrancy and glow that outwardly reflects an inner flame and passion for living.

The Earth Signs

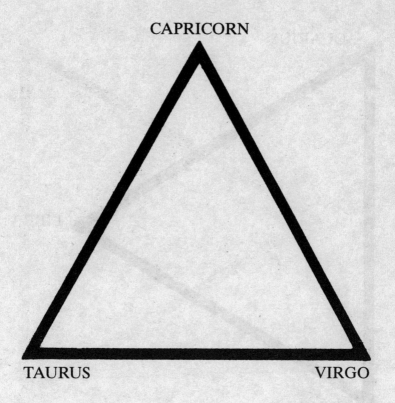

CAPRICORN

TAURUS   VIRGO

This is the earth group. They are in constant touch with the material world and tend to be conservative. Although they are all capable of spartan self-discipline, they are earthy, sensual people who are stimulated by the tangible, elegant, and luxurious. The thread of their lives is always practical, but they do fantasize and are often attracted to dark, mysterious, emotional people. They are like great cliffs overhanging the sea, forever married to the ocean but always resisting erosion from the dark, emotional forces that thunder at their feet.

The Air Signs

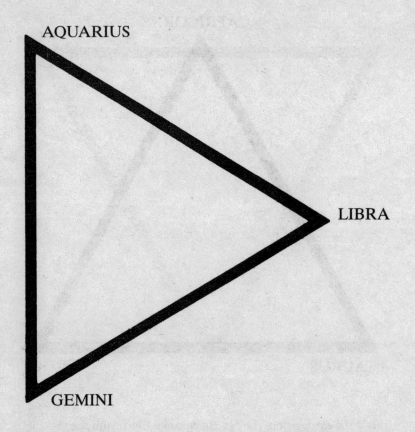

This is the air group. They are light, mental creatures desirous of contact, communication, and relationship. They are involved with people and the forming of ties on many levels. Original thinkers, they are the bearers of human news. Their language is their sense of word, color, style, and beauty. They provide an atmosphere suitable and pleasant for living. They add change and versatility to the scene, and it is through them that we can explore new territory of human intelligence and experience.

The Water Signs

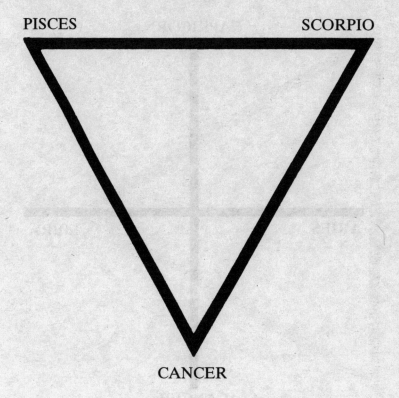

PISCES   SCORPIO

CANCER

This is the water group. Through the water people, we are all joined together on emotional, nonverbal levels. They are silent, mysterious types whose magic hypnotizes even the most determined realist. They have uncanny perceptions about people and are as rich as the oceans when it comes to feeling, emotion, or imagination. They are sensitive, mystical creatures with memories that go back beyond time. Through water, life is sustained. These people have the potential for the depths of darkness or the heights of mysticism and art.

The Cardinal Signs

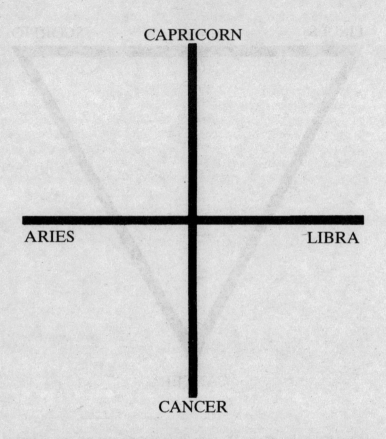

CAPRICORN

ARIES   LIBRA

CANCER

Put together, this is a clear-cut picture of dynamism, activity, tremendous stress, and remarkable achievement. These people know the meaning of great change since their lives are often characterized by significant crises and major successes. This combination is like a simultaneous storm of summer, fall, winter, and spring. The danger is chaotic diffusion of energy; the potential is irrepressible growth and victory.

The Fixed Signs

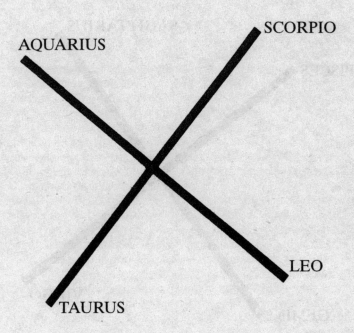

Fixed signs are always establishing themselves in a given place or area of experience. Like explorers who arrive and plant a flag, these people claim a position from which they do not enjoy being deposed. They are staunch, stalwart, upright, trusty, honorable people, although their obstinacy is well-known. Their contribution is fixity, and they are the angels who support our visible world.

The Mutable Signs

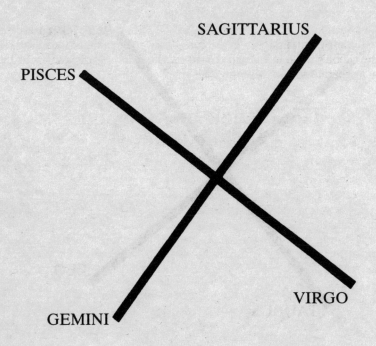

Mutable people are versatile, sensitive, intelligent, nervous, and deeply curious about life. They are the translators of all energy. They often carry out or complete tasks initiated by others. Combinations of these signs have highly developed minds; they are imaginative and jumpy and think and talk a lot. At worst their lives are a Tower of Babel. At best they are adaptable and ready creatures who can assimilate one kind of experience and enjoy it while anticipating coming changes.

THE PLANETS
OF THE SOLAR SYSTEM

This section describes the planets of the solar system. In astrology, both the Sun and the Moon are considered to be planets. Because of the Moon's influence in our day-to-day lives, the Moon is described in a separate section following this one.

The Planets and the Signs They Rule

The signs of the Zodiac are linked to the planets in the following way. Each sign is governed or ruled by one or more planets. No matter where the planets are located in the sky at any given moment, they still rule their respective signs, and when they travel through the signs they rule, they have special dignity and their effects are stronger.

Following is a list of the planets and the signs they rule. After looking at the list, read the definitions of the planets and see if you can determine how the planet ruling *your* Sun sign has affected your life.

SIGNS	RULING PLANETS
Aries	Mars, Pluto
Taurus	Venus
Gemini	Mercury
Cancer	Moon
Leo	Sun
Virgo	Mercury
Libra	Venus
Scorpio	Mars, Pluto
Sagittarius	Jupiter
Capricorn	Saturn
Aquarius	Saturn, Uranus
Pisces	Jupiter, Neptune

Characteristics of the Planets

The following pages give the meaning and characteristics of the planets of the solar system. They all travel around the Sun at different speeds and different distances. Taken with the Sun, they all distribute individual intelligence and ability throughout the entire chart.

The planets modify the influence of the Sun in a chart according to their own particular natures, strengths, and positions. Their positions must be calculated for each year and day, and their function and expression in a horoscope will change as they move from one area of the Zodiac to another.

We start with a description of the sun.

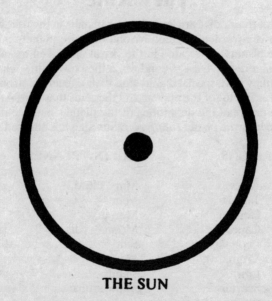

THE SUN

SUN

This is the center of existence. Around this flaming sphere all the planets revolve in endless orbits. Our star is constantly sending out its beams of light and energy without which no life on Earth would be possible. In astrology it symbolizes everything we are trying to become, the center around which all of our activity in life will always revolve. It is the symbol of our basic nature and describes the natural and constant thread that runs through everything that we do from birth to death on this planet.

To early astrologers, the Sun seemed to be another planet because it crossed the heavens every day, just like the rest of the bodies in the sky.

It is the only star near enough to be seen well—it is, in fact, a dwarf star. Approximately 860,000 miles in diameter, it is about ten times as wide as the giant planet Jupiter. The next nearest star is nearly 300,000 times as far away, and if the Sun were located as far away as most of the bright stars, it would be too faint to be seen without a telescope.

Everything in the horoscope ultimately revolves around this singular body. Although other forces may be prominent in the charts of some individuals, still the Sun is the total nucleus of being and symbolizes the complete potential of every human being alive. It is vitality and the life force. Your whole essence comes from the position of the Sun.

You are always trying to express the Sun according to its position by house and sign. Possibility for all development is found in the Sun, and it marks the fundamental character of your personal radiations all around you.

It is the symbol of strength, vigor, wisdom, dignity, ardor, and generosity, and the ability for a person to function as a mature individual. It is also a creative force in society. It is consciousness of the gift of life.

The underdeveloped solar nature is arrogant, pushy, undependable, and proud, and is constantly using force.

MERCURY

Mercury is the planet closest to the Sun. It races around our star, gathering information and translating it to the rest of the system. Mercury represents your capacity to understand the desires of your own will and to translate those desires into action.

In other words it is the planet of mind and the power of communication. Through Mercury we develop an ability to think, write, speak, and observe—to become aware of the world around us. It colors our attitudes and vision of the world, as well as our capacity to communicate our inner responses to the outside world. Some people who have serious disabilities in their power of verbal communication have often wrongly been described as people lacking intelligence.

Although this planet (and its position in the horoscope) indicates your power to communicate your thoughts and perceptions to the world, intelligence is something deeper. Intelligence is distributed throughout all the planets. It is the relationship of the planets to each other that truly describes what we call intelligence. Mercury rules speaking, language, mathematics, draft and design, students, messengers, young people, offices, teachers, and any pursuits where the mind of man has wings.

VENUS

Venus is beauty. It symbolizes the harmony and radiance of a rare and elusive quality: beauty itself. It is refinement and delicacy, softness and charm. In astrology it indicates grace, balance, and the aesthetic sense. Where Venus is we see beauty, a gentle drawing in of energy and the need for satisfaction and completion. It is a special touch that finishes off rough edges. It is sensitivity, and affection, and it is always the place for that other elusive phenomenon: love. Venus describes our sense of what is beautiful and loving. Poorly developed, it is vulgar, tasteless, and self-indulgent. But its ideal is the flame of spiritual love—Aphrodite, goddess of love, and the sweetness and power of personal beauty.

MARS

Mars is raw, crude energy. The planet next to Earth but outward from the Sun is a fiery red sphere that charges through the horoscope with force and fury. It represents the way you reach out for new adventure and new experience. It is energy and drive, initiative, courage, and daring. It is the power to start something and see it through. It can be thoughtless, cruel and wild, angry and hostile, causing cuts, burns, scalds, and wounds. It can stab its way through a chart, or it can be the symbol of healthy spirited adventure, well-channeled constructive power to begin and keep up the drive. If you have trouble starting things, if you lack the get-up-and-go to start the ball rolling, if you lack aggressiveness and self-confidence, chances are there's another planet influencing your Mars. Mars rules soldiers, butchers, surgeons, salesmen—any field that requires daring, bold skill, operational technique, or self-promotion.

JUPITER

This is the largest planet of the solar system. Scientists have recently learned that Jupiter reflects more light than it receives from the Sun. In a sense it is like a star itself. In astrology it rules good luck and good cheer, health, wealth, optimism, happiness, success, and joy. It is the symbol of opportunity and always opens the way for new possibilities in your life. It rules exuberance, enthusiasm, wisdom, knowledge, generosity, and all forms of expansion in general. It rules actors, statesmen, clerics, professional people, religion, publishing, and the distribution of many people over large areas.

Sometimes Jupiter makes you think you deserve everything, and you become sloppy, wasteful, careless and rude, prodigal and lawless, in the illusion that nothing can ever go wrong. Then there is the danger of overconfidence, exaggeration, undependability, and overindulgence.

Jupiter is the minimization of limitation and the emphasis on spirituality and potential. It is the thirst for knowledge and higher learning.

SATURN

Saturn circles our system in dark splendor with its mysterious rings, forcing us to be awakened to whatever we have neglected in the past. It will present real puzzles and problems to be solved, causing delays, obstacles, and hindrances. By doing so, Saturn stirs our own sensitivity to those areas where we are laziest.

Here we must patiently develop *method*, and only through painstaking effort can our ends be achieved. It brings order to a horoscope and imposes reason just where we are feeling least reasonable. By creating limitations and boundary, Saturn shows the consequences of being human and demands that we accept the changing cycles inevitable in human life. Saturn rules time, old age, and sobriety. It can bring depression, gloom, jealousy, and greed, or serious acceptance of responsibilities out of which success will develop. With Saturn there is nothing to do but face facts. It rules laborers, stones, granite, rocks, and crystals of all kinds.

THE OUTER PLANETS:
URANUS, NEPTUNE, PLUTO

Uranus, Neptune, Pluto are the outer planets. They liberate human beings from cultural conditioning, and in that sense are the law-breakers. In early times it was thought that Saturn was the last planet of the system—the outer limit beyond which we could never go. The discovery of the next three planets ushered in new phases of human history, revolution, and technology.

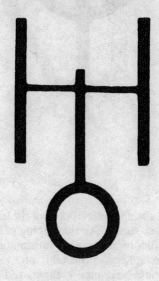

URANUS

Uranus rules unexpected change, upheaval, revolution. It is the symbol of total independence and asserts the freedom of an individual from all restriction and restraint. It is a breakthrough planet and indicates talent, originality, and genius in a horoscope. It usually causes last-minute reversals and changes of plan, unwanted separations, accidents, catastrophes, and eccentric behavior. It can add irrational rebelliousness and perverse bohemianism to a personality or a streak of unaffected brilliance in science and art. It rules technology, aviation, and all forms of electrical and electronic advancement. It governs great leaps forward and topsy-turvy situations, and *always* turns things around at the last minute. Its effects are difficult to predict, since it rules sudden last-minute decisions and events that come like lightning out of the blue.

NEPTUNE

Neptune dissolves existing reality the way the sea erodes the cliffs beside it. Its effects are subtle like the ringing of a buoy's bell in the fog. It suggests a reality higher than definition can usually describe. It awakens a sense of higher responsibility often causing guilt, worry, anxieties, or delusions. Neptune is associated with all forms of escape and can make things seem a certain way so convincingly that you are absolutely sure of something that eventually turns out to be quite different.

It is the planet of illusion and therefore governs the invisible realms that lie beyond our ordinary minds, beyond our simple factual ability to prove what is "real." Treachery, deceit, disillusionment, and disappointment are linked to Neptune. It describes a vague reality that promises eternity and the divine, yet in a manner so complex that we cannot really fathom it at all. At its worst Neptune is a cheap intoxicant; at its best it is the poetry, music, and inspiration of the higher planes of spiritual love. It has dominion over movies, photographs, and much of the arts.

PLUTO

Pluto lies at the outpost of our system and therefore rules finality in a horoscope—the final closing of chapters in your life, the passing of major milestones and points of development from which there is no return. It is a final wipeout, a closeout, an evacuation. It is a distant, subtle but powerful catalyst in all transformations that occur. It creates, destroys, then recreates. Sometimes Pluto starts its influence with a minor event or insignificant incident that might even go unnoticed. Slowly but surely, little by little, everything changes, until at last there has been a total transformation in the area of your life where Pluto has been operating. It rules mass thinking and the trends that society first rejects, then adopts, and finally outgrows.

Pluto rules the dead and the underworld—all the powerful forces of creation and destruction that go on all the time beneath, around, and above us. It can bring a lust for power with strong obsessions.

It is the planet that rules the metamorphosis of the caterpillar into a butterfly, for it symbolizes the capacity to change totally and forever a person's lifestyle, way of thought, and behavior.

THE MOON IN EACH SIGN

The Moon is the nearest planet to the Earth. It exerts more observable influence on us from day to day than any other planet. The effect is very personal, very intimate, and if we are not aware of how it works it can make us quite unstable in our ideas. And the annoying thing is that at these times we often see our own instability but can do nothing about it. A knowledge of what can be expected may help considerably. We can then be prepared to stand strong against the Moon's negative influences and use its positive ones to help us to get ahead. Who has not heard of going with the tide?

The Moon reflects, has no light of its own. It reflects the Sun—the life giver—in the form of vital movement. The Moon controls the tides, the blood rhythm, the movement of sap in trees and plants. Its nature is inconstancy and change so it signifies our moods, our superficial behavior—walking, talking, and especially thinking. Being a true reflector of other forces, the Moon is cold, watery like the surface of a still lake, brilliant and scintillating at times, but easily ruffled and disturbed by the winds of change.

The Moon takes about 27⅓ days to make a complete transit of the Zodiac. It spends just over 2¼ days in each sign. During that time it reflects the qualities, energies, and characteristics of the sign and, to a degree, the planet which rules the sign. When the Moon in its transit occupies a sign incompatible with our own birth sign, we can expect to feel a vague uneasiness, perhaps a touch of irritableness. We should not be discouraged nor let the feeling get us down, or, worse still, allow ourselves to take the discomfort out on others. Try to remember that the Moon has to change signs within 55 hours and, provided you are not physically ill, your mood will probably change with it. It is amazing how frequently depression lifts with the shift in the Moon's position. And, of course, when the Moon is transiting a sign compatible or sympathetic to yours, you will probably feel some sort of stimulation or just be plain happy to be alive.

In the horoscope, the Moon is such a powerful indicator that competent astrologers often use the sign it occupied at birth as the birth sign of the person. This is done particularly when the Sun is on the cusp, or edge, of two signs. Most experienced astrologers, however, coordinate both Sun and Moon signs by reading and confirming from one to the other and secure a far more accurate and personalized analysis.

For these reasons, the Moon tables which follow this section (see pages 86–92) are of great importance to the individual. They show the days and the exact times the Moon will enter each sign of the Zodiac for the year. Remember, you have to adjust the indicated times to local time. The corrections, already calculated for most of the main cities, are at the beginning of the tables. What follows now is a guide to the influences that will be reflected to the Earth by the Moon while it transits each of the twelve signs. The influence is at its peak about 26 hours after the Moon enters a sign. As you read the daily forecast, check the Moon sign for any given day and glance back at this guide.

MOON IN ARIES

This is a time for action, for reaching out beyond the usual self-imposed limitations and faint-hearted cautions. If you have plans in your head or on your desk, put them into practice. New ventures, applications, new jobs, new starts of any kind—all have a good chance of success. This is the period when original and dynamic impulses are being reflected onto Earth. Such energies are extremely vital and favor the pursuit of pleasure and adventure in practically every form. Sick people should feel an improvement. Those who are well will probably find themselves exuding confidence and optimism. People fond of physical exercise should find their bodies growing with tone and well-being. Boldness, strength, determination should character-ize most of your activities with a readiness to face up to old chal-lenges. Yesterday's problems may seem petty and exaggerated—so deal with them. Strike out alone. Self-reliance will attract others to you. This is a good time for making friends. Business and marriage partners are more likely to be impressed with the man and woman of action. Opposition will be overcome or thrown aside with much less effort than usual. CAUTION: Be dominant but not domineering.

MOON IN TAURUS

The spontaneous, action-packed person of yesterday gives way to the cautious, diligent, hardworking "thinker." In this period ideas will probably be concentrated on ways of improving finances. A great deal of time may be spent figuring out and going over schemes and plans. It is the right time to be careful with detail. People will find them-selves working longer than usual at their desks. Or devoting more time to serious thought about the future. A strong desire to put order into business and financial arrangements may cause extra work. Loved ones may complain of being neglected and may fail to appreciate that your efforts are for their ultimate benefit. Your desire for system may extend to criticism of arrangements in the home and lead to minor upsets. Health may be affected through overwork. Try to secure a reasonable amount of rest and relaxation, although the tendency will be to "keep going" despite good advice. Work done conscientiously in this period should result in a solid contribution to your future security. CAUTION: Try not to be as serious with people as the work you are engaged in.

MOON IN GEMINI
The humdrum of routine and too much work should suddenly end. You are likely to find yourself in an expansive, quicksilver world of change and self-expression. Urges to write, to paint, to experience the freedom of some sort of artistic outpouring, may be very strong. Take full advantage of them. You may find yourself finishing something you began and put aside long ago. Or embarking on something new which could easily be prompted by a chance meeting, a new acquaintance, or even an advertisement. There may be a yearning for a change of scenery, the feeling to visit another country (not too far away), or at least to get away for a few days. This may result in short, quick journeys. Or, if you are planning a single visit, there may be some unexpected changes or detours on the way. Familiar activities will seem to give little satisfaction unless they contain a fresh element of excitement or expectation. The inclination will be toward untried pursuits, particularly those that allow you to express your inner nature. The accent is on new faces, new places. CAUTION: Do not be too quick to commit yourself emotionally.

MOON IN CANCER
Feelings of uncertainty and vague insecurity are likely to cause problems while the Moon is in Cancer. Thoughts may turn frequently to the warmth of the home and the comfort of loved ones. Nostalgic impulses could cause you to bring out old photographs and letters and reflect on the days when your life seemed to be much more rewarding and less demanding. The love and understanding of parents and family may be important, and, if it is not forthcoming, you may have to fight against bouts of self-pity. The cordiality of friends and the thought of good times with them that are sure to be repeated will help to restore you to a happier frame of mind. The desire to be alone may follow minor setbacks or rebuffs at this time, but solitude is unlikely to help. Better to get on the telephone or visit someone. This period often causes peculiar dreams and upsurges of imagina-

tive thinking which can be helpful to authors of occult and mystical works. Preoccupation with the personal world of simple human needs can overshadow any material strivings. CAUTION: Do not spend too much time thinking—seek the company of loved ones or close friends.

MOON IN LEO

New horizons of exciting and rather extravagant activity open up. This is the time for exhilarating entertainment, glamorous and lavish parties, and expensive shopping sprees. Any merrymaking that relies upon your generosity as a host has every chance of being a spectacular success. You should find yourself right in the center of the fun, either as the life of the party or simply as a person whom happy people like to be with. Romance thrives in this heady atmosphere and friendships are likely to explode unexpectedly into serious attachments. Children and younger people should be attracted to you and you may find yourself organizing a picnic or a visit to a fun-fair, the movies, or the beach. The sunny company and vitality of youthful companions should help you to find some unsuspected energy. In career, you could find an opening for promotion or advancement. This should be the time to make a direct approach. The period favors those engaged in original research. CAUTION: Bask in popularity, not in flattery.

MOON IN VIRGO

Off comes the party cap and out steps the busy, practical worker. He wants to get his personal affairs straight, to rearrange them, if necessary, for more efficiency, so he will have more time for more work. He clears up his correspondence, pays outstanding bills, makes numerous phone calls. He is likely to make inquiries, or sign up for some new insurance and put money into gilt-edged investment. Thoughts probably revolve around the need for future security—to tie up loose ends and clear the decks. There may be a tendency to be "finicky," to interfere in the routine of others, particularly friends and family members. The motive may be a genuine desire to help with suggestions for updating or streamlining their affairs, but these will probably not be welcomed. Sympathy may be felt for less fortunate sections of the community and a flurry of some sort of voluntary service is likely. This may be accompanied by strong feelings of responsibility on several fronts and health may suffer from extra efforts made. CAUTION: Everyone may not want your help or advice.

MOON IN LIBRA

These are days of harmony and agreement and you should find yourself at peace with most others. Relationships tend to be smooth and sweet-flowing. Friends may become closer and bonds deepen in

mutual understanding. Hopes will be shared. Progress by cooperation could be the secret of success in every sphere. In business, established partnerships may flourish and new ones get off to a good start.
Acquaintances could discover similar interests that lead to congenial
discussions and rewarding exchanges of some sort. Love, as a unify-
ing force, reaches its optimum. Marriage partners should find accord.
Those who wed at this time face the prospect of a happy union.
Cooperation and tolerance are felt to be stronger than dissension
and impatience. The argumentative are not quite so loud in their bel-
lowings, nor as inflexible in their attitudes. In the home, there should
be a greater recognition of the other point of view and a readiness to
put the wishes of the group before selfish insistence. This is a favorable
time to join an art group. CAUTION: Do not be too independent—let
others help you if they want to.

MOON IN SCORPIO

Driving impulses to make money and to economize are likely to
cause upsets all around. No area of expenditure is likely to be spared
the ax, including the household budget. This is a time when the desire
to cut down on extravagance can become near fanatical. Care must
be exercised to try to keep the aim in reasonable perspective. Others
may not feel the same urgent need to save and may retaliate. There is
a danger that possessions of sentimental value will be sold to realize
cash for investment. Buying and selling of stock for quick profit is
also likely. The attention turns to organizing, reorganizing, tidying up
at home and at work. Neglected jobs could suddenly be done with
great bursts of energy. The desire for solitude may intervene. Self-
searching thoughts could disturb. The sense of invisible and mysterious energies in play could cause some excitability. The reassurance of
loves ones may help. CAUTION: Be kind to the people you love.

MOON IN SAGITTARIUS

These are days when you are likely to be stirred and elevated by discussions and reflections of a religious and philosophical nature. Ideas
of faraway places may cause unusual response and excitement. A
decision may be made to visit someone overseas, perhaps a person
whose influence was important to your earlier character development. There could be a strong resolution to get away from present
intellectual patterns, to learn new subjects, and to meet more interesting people. The superficial may be rejected in all its forms. An
impatience with old ideas and unimaginative contacts could lead to
a change of companions and interests. There may be an upsurge of
religious feeling and metaphysical inquiry. Even a new insight into
the significance of astrology and other occult studies is likely under
the curious stimulus of the Moon in Sagittarius. Physically, you may

express this need for fundamental change by spending more time outdoors: sports, gardening, long walks appeal. CAUTION: Try to channel any restlessness into worthwhile study.

MOON IN CAPRICORN

Life in these hours may seem to pivot around the importance of gaining prestige and honor in the career, as well as maintaining a spotless reputation. Ambitious urges may be excessive and could be accompanied by quite acquisitive drives for money. Effort should be directed along strictly ethical lines where there is no possibility of reproach or scandal. All endeavors are likely to be characterized by great earnestness, and an air of authority and purpose which should impress those who are looking for leadership or reliability. The desire to conform to accepted standards may extend to sharp criticism of family members. Frivolity and unconventional actions are unlikely to amuse while the Moon is in Capricorn. Moderation and seriousness are the orders of the day. Achievement and recognition in this period could come through community work or organizing for the benefit of some amateur group. CAUTION: Dignity and esteem are not always self-awarded.

MOON IN AQUARIUS

Moon in Aquarius is in the second last sign of the Zodiac where ideas can become disturbingly fine and subtle. The result is often a mental "no-man's land" where imagination cannot be trusted with the same certitude as other times. The dangers for the individual are the extremes of optimism and pessimism. Unless the imagination is held in check, situations are likely to be misread, and rosy conclusions drawn where they do not exist. Consequences for the unwary can be costly in career and business. Best to think twice and not speak or act until you think again. Pessimism can be a cruel self-inflicted penalty for delusion at this time. Between the two extremes are strange areas of self-deception which, for example, can make the selfish person think he is actually being generous. Eerie dreams which resemble the reality and even seem to continue into the waking state are also possible. CAUTION: Look for the fact and not just for the image in your mind.

MOON IN PISCES

Everything seems to come to the surface now. Memory may be crystal clear, throwing up long-forgotten information which could be valuable in the career or business. Flashes of clairvoyance and intuition are possible along with sudden realizations of one's own nature, which may be used for self-improvement. A talent, never before suspected, may be discovered. Qualities not evident before in friends and marriage partners are likely to be noticed. As this is a period in which the truth seems to emerge, the discovery of false characteristics is likely to lead to disenchantment or a shift in attachments. However, when qualities are accepted, it should lead to happiness and deeper feeling. Surprise solutions could bob up for old problems. There may be a public announcement of the solving of a crime or mystery. People with secrets may find someone has "guessed" correctly. The secrets of the soul or the inner self also tend to reveal themselves. Religious and philosophical groups may make some interesting discoveries. CAUTION: Not a time for activities that depend on secrecy.

NOTE: When you read your daily forecasts, use the Moon Sign Dates that are provided in the following section of Moon Tables. Then you may want to glance back here for the Moon's influence in a given sign.

MOON TABLES

CORRECTION FOR NEW YORK TIME, FIVE HOURS
WEST OF GREENWICH

Atlanta, Boston, Detroit, Miami, Washington, Montreal,
  Ottawa, Quebec, Bogota, Havana, Lima, Santiago . . . Same time
Chicago, New Orleans, Houston, Winnipeg, Churchill,
  Mexico City .... Deduct 1 hour
Albuquerque, Denver, Phoenix, El Paso, Edmonton,
  Helena .... Deduct 2 hours
Los Angeles, San Francisco, Reno, Portland,
  Seattle, Vancouver .... Deduct 3 hours
Honolulu, Anchorage, Fairbanks, Kodiak .... Deduct 5 hours
Nome, Samoa, Tonga, Midway .... Deduct 6 hours
Halifax, Bermuda, San Juan, Caracas, La Paz,
  Barbados .... Add 1 hour
St. John's, Brasilia, Rio de Janeiro, Sao Paulo,
  Buenos Aires, Montevideo .... Add 2 hours
Azores, Cape Verde Islands .... Add 3 hours
Canary Islands, Madeira, Reykjavik .... Add 4 hours
London, Paris, Amsterdam, Madrid, Lisbon,
  Gibraltar, Belfast, Raba .... Add 5 hours
Frankfurt, Rome, Oslo, Stockholm, Prague,
  Belgrade .... Add 6 hours
Bucharest, Beirut, Tel Aviv, Athens, Istanbul, Cairo,
  Alexandria, Cape Town, Johannesburg .... Add 7 hours
Moscow, Leningrad, Baghdad, Dhahran,
  Addis Ababa, Nairobi, Teheran, Zanzibar .... Add 8 hours
Bombay, Calcutta, Sri Lanka .... Add 10½
Hong Kong, Shanghai, Manila, Peking, Perth .... Add 13 hours
Tokyo, Okinawa, Darwin, Pusan .... Add 14 hours
Sydney, Melbourne, Port Moresby, Guam .... Add 15 hours
Auckland, Wellington, Suva, Wake .... Add 17 hours

2010 MOON SIGN DATES— NEW YORK TIME

JANUARY
Day Moon Enters

1. Leo — 9:42 pm
2. Leo
3. Virgo — 9:54 pm
4. Virgo
5. Libra — 11:59 pm
6. Libra
7. Libra
8. Scorp. — 5:01 am
9. Scorp.
10. Sagitt. — 1:11 pm
11. Sagitt.
12. Capric. 11:55 pm
13. Capric.
14. Capric.
15. Aquar. 12:18 pm
16. Aquar.
17. Aquar.
18. Pisces — 1:18 am
19. Pisces
20. Aries — 1:37 pm
21. Aries
22. Taurus 11:41 pm
23. Taurus
24. Taurus
25. Gemini 6:12 am
26. Gemini
27. Cancer 9:02 am
28. Cancer
29. Leo — 9:11 am
30. Leo
31. Virgo — 8:24 am

FEBRUARY
Day Moon Enters

1. Virgo
2. Libra — 8:43 am
3. Libra
4. Scorp. 11:57 am
5. Scorp.
6. Sagitt. — 7:05 pm
7. Sagitt.
8. Sagitt.
9. Capric. 5:45 am
10. Capric.
11. Aquar. 6:25 pm
12. Aquar.
13. Aquar.
14. Pisces — 7:24 am
15. Pisces
16. Aries — 7:31 pm
17. Aries
18. Aries
19. Taurus 5:56 am
20. Taurus
21. Gemini 1:48 pm
22. Gemini
23. Cancer 6:30 pm
24. Cancer
25. Leo — 8:09 pm
26. Leo
27. Virgo — 7:53 pm
28. Virgo

MARCH
Day Moon Enters

1. Libra — 7:32 pm
2. Libra
3. Scorp. — 9:12 pm
4. Scorp.
5. Scorp.
6. Sagitt. — 1:37 am
7. Sagitt.
8. Capric. 12:14 pm
9. Capric.
10. Capric.
11. Aquar. 12:43 am
12. Aquar.
13. Pisces — 1:45 pm
14. Pisces
15. Pisces
16. Aries — 1:33 am
17. Aries
18. Taurus 11:30 am
19. Taurus
20. Gemini 7:29 pm
21. Gemini
22. Gemini
23. Cancer 1:17 am
24. Cancer
25. Leo — 4:40 am
26. Leo
27. Virgo — 5:58 am
28. Virgo
29. Libra — 6:22 am
30. Libra
31. Scorp. — 7:42 am

Daylight saving time to be considered where applicable.

2010 MOON SIGN DATES—
NEW YORK TIME

APRIL		MAY		JUNE	
Day Moon Enters		**Day Moon Enters**		**Day Moon Enters**	
1. Scorp.		1. Sagitt.		1. Aquar.	12:09 am
2. Sagitt.	11:54 am	2. Capric.	5:01 am	2. Aquar.	
3. Sagitt.		3. Capric.		3. Pisces	12:35 pm
4. Capric.	8:08 pm	4. Aquar.	3:53 pm	4. Pisces	
5. Capric.		5. Aquar.		5. Pisces	
6. Capric.		6. Aquar.		6. Aries	12:51 am
7. Aquar.	7:52 am	7. Pisces	4:35 am	7. Aries	
8. Aquar.		8. Pisces		8. Taurus	10:42 am
9. Pisces	8:49 pm	9. Aries	4:30 pm	9. Taurus	
10. Pisces		10. Aries		10. Gemini	5:12 pm
11. Pisces		11. Aries		11. Gemini	
12. Aries	8:32 am	12. Taurus	1:49 am	12. Cancer	8:51 pm
13. Aries		13. Taurus		13. Cancer	
14. Taurus	5:56 pm	14. Gemini	8:19 am	14. Leo	10:55 pm
15. Taurus		15. Gemini		15. Leo	
16. Taurus		16. Cancer	12:47 pm	16. Leo	
17. Gemini	1:09 am	17. Cancer		17. Virgo	12:42 am
18. Gemini		18. Leo	4:07 pm	18. Virgo	
19. Cancer	6:40 am	19. Leo		19. Libra	3:14 am
20. Cancer		20. Virgo	6:59 pm	20. Libra	
21. Leo	10:43 am	21. Virgo		21. Scorp.	7:15 am
22. Leo		22. Libra	9:51 pm	22. Scorp.	
23. Virgo	1:25 pm	23. Libra		23. Sagitt.	1:11 pm
24. Virgo		24. Libra		24. Sagitt.	
25. Libra	3:18 pm	25. Scorp.	1:18 am	25. Capric.	9:22 pm
26. Libra		26. Scorp.		26. Capric.	
27. Scorp.	5:30 pm	27. Sagitt.	6:17 am	27. Capric.	
28. Scorp.		28. Sagitt.		28. Aquar.	7:53 am
29. Sagitt.	9:37 pm	29. Capric.	1:45 pm	29. Aquar.	
30. Sagitt.		30. Capric.		30. Pisces	8:11 pm
		31. Capric.			

Daylight saving time to be considered where applicable.

2010 MOON SIGN DATES—
NEW YORK TIME

JULY Day Moon Enters		AUGUST Day Moon Enters		SEPTEMBER Day Moon Enters	
1. Pisces		1. Aries		1. Gemini	
2. Pisces		2. Taurus	3:14 am	2. Gemini	
3. Aries	8:45 am	3. Taurus		3. Cancer	1:52 am
4. Aries		4. Gemini	11:55 am	4. Cancer	
5. Taurus	7:30 pm	5. Gemini		5. Leo	4:46 am
6. Taurus		6. Cancer	4:51 pm	6. Leo	
7. Taurus		7. Cancer		7. Virgo	4:54 am
8. Gemini	2:52 am	8. Leo	6:24 pm	8. Virgo	
9. Gemini		9. Leo		9. Libra	4:02 am
10. Cancer	6:39 am	10. Virgo	6:02 pm	10. Libra	
11. Cancer		11. Virgo		11. Scorp.	4:22 am
12. Leo	7:55 am	12. Libra	5:44 pm	12. Scorp.	
13. Leo		13. Libra		13. Sagitt.	7:53 am
14. Virgo	8:16 am	14. Scorp.	7:27 pm	14. Sagitt.	
15. Virgo		15. Scorp.		15. Capric.	3:31 pm
16. Libra	9:25 am	16. Scorp.		16. Capric.	
17. Libra		17. Sagitt.	12:35 am	17. Capric.	
18. Scorp.	12:43 pm	18. Sagitt.		18. Aquar.	2:36 am
19. Scorp.		19. Capric.	9:18 am	19. Aquar.	
20. Sagitt.	6:50 pm	20. Capric.		20. Pisces	3:16 pm
21. Sagitt.		21. Aquar.	8:38 pm	21. Pisces	
22. Sagitt.		22. Aquar.		22. Pisces	
23. Capric.	3:40 am	23. Aquar.		23. Aries	3:48 am
24. Capric.		24. Pisces	9:12 am	24. Aries	
25. Aquar.	2:39 pm	25. Pisces		25. Taurus	3:18 pm
26. Aquar.		26. Aries	9:50 pm	26. Taurus	
27. Aquar.		27. Aries		27. Taurus	
28. Pisces	3:01 am	28. Aries		28. Gemini	1:12 am
29. Pisces		29. Taurus	9:36 am	29. Gemini	
30. Aries	3:43 pm	30. Taurus		30. Cancer	8:47 am
31. Aries		31. Gemini	7:20 pm		

Daylight saving time to be considered where applicable.

2010 MOON SIGN DATES—
NEW YORK TIME

OCTOBER Day Moon Enters		NOVEMBER Day Moon Enters		DECEMBER Day Moon Enters	
1. Cancer		1. Virgo		1. Libra	
2. Leo	1:22 pm	2. Virgo		2. Scorp.	9:45 am
3. Leo		3. Libra	12:20 am	3. Scorp.	
4. Virgo	3:01 pm	4. Libra		4. Sagitt.	1:00 pm
5. Virgo		5. Scorp.	1:17 am	5. Sagitt.	
6. Libra	2:53 pm	6. Scorp.		6. Capric.	6:17 pm
7. Libra		7. Sagitt.	3:29 am	7. Capric.	
8. Scorp.	2:53 pm	8. Sagitt.		8. Capric.	
9. Scorp.		9. Capric.	8:38 am	9. Aquar.	2:32 am
10. Sagitt.	5:10 pm	10. Capric.		10. Aquar.	
11. Sagitt.		11. Aquar.	5:33 pm	11. Pisces	1:42 pm
12. Capric.	11:18 pm	12. Aquar.		12. Pisces	
13. Capric.		13. Aquar.		13. Pisces	
14. Capric.		14. Pisces	5:25 am	14. Aries	2:16 am
15. Aquar.	9:25 am	15. Pisces		15. Aries	
16. Aquar.		16. Aries	6:00 pm	16. Taurus	1:50 pm
17. Pisces	9:53 pm	17. Aries		17. Taurus	
18. Pisces		18. Aries		18. Gemini	10:38 pm
19. Pisces		19. Taurus	5:05 am	19. Gemini	
20. Aries	10:24 am	20. Taurus		20. Gemini	
21. Aries		21. Gemini	1:47 pm	21. Cancer	4:23 am
22. Taurus	9:31 pm	22. Gemini		22. Cancer	
23. Taurus		23. Cancer	8:15 pm	23. Leo	7:52 am
24. Taurus		24. Cancer		24. Leo	
25. Gemini	6:49 am	25. Cancer		25. Virgo	10:15 am
26. Gemini		26. Leo	1:02 am	26. Virgo	
27. Cancer	2:15 pm	27. Leo		27. Libra	12:39 pm
28. Cancer		28. Virgo	4:35 am	28. Libra	
29. Leo	7:40 pm	29. Virgo		29. Scorp.	3:51 pm
30. Leo		30. Libra	7:16 am	30. Scorp.	
31. Virgo	10:52 pm			31. Sagitt.	8:22 pm

Daylight saving time to be considered where applicable.

2010 PHASES OF THE MOON—
NEW YORK TIME

New Moon	First Quarter	Full Moon	Last Quarter
Dec. 15 ('09)	Dec. 24 ('09)	Dec. 31 ('09)	Jan. 7
Jan. 15	Jan. 23	Jan. 30	Feb. 5
Feb. 13	Feb. 21	Feb. 28	March 7
March 15	March 23	March 29	April 6
April 14	April 21	April 28	May 5
May 13	May 20	May 27	June 4
June 12	June 18	June 26	July 4
July 11	July 18	July 25	August 3
August 9	August 16	August 24	Sept. 1
Sept. 8	Sept. 15	Sept. 23	Sept. 30
Oct. 7	Oct. 14	Oct. 22	Oct. 30
Nov. 6	Nov. 13	Nov. 21	Nov. 28
Dec. 5	Dec. 13	Dec. 21	Dec. 27

Each phase of the Moon lasts approximately seven to eight days, during which the Moon's shape gradually changes as it comes out of one phase and goes into the next.

There will be a solar eclipse during the New Moon phase on January 15 and July 11.

There will be a lunar eclipse during the Full Moon phase on June 26 and December 21.

2010 FISHING GUIDE

	Good	Best
January	3-4-16-28-29-30-31	2-6-23-27
February	1-2-13-21-26-27-28	5-25
March	1-7-15-27-28-29	2-3-24-30-31
April	13-22-24-29	1-2-3-8-26-27-28
May	1-7-14-20-27-28-29	25-26-30
June	12-24-25-28-29	4-19-26-27
July	4-22-26-27	11-17-23-24-28
August	10-16-21-22-23-27-28	3-24-25
September	1-8-14-19-20-23-24-25	21-22-26
October	21-22-23-25-26-30	1-7-14-19-24
November	13-17-18-22-23-28	6-19-20-24
December	5-19-20-21-23-24	13-17-22-28

2010 PLANTING GUIDE

	Aboveground Crops	Root Crops
January	18-19-23-24-28	1-6-7-8-9-13-14
February	15-16-20-24	2-3-4-5-9-10
March	19-20-23-24	2-3-4-5-9-10-14-30-31
April	15-16-19-20-26-27	1-5-6-10-11-28
May	17-23-24-25-26	2-3-7-8-13-30-31
June	13-14-19-20-21-22	4-9-10-26-27
July	17-18-19-20-23-24	1-2-6-28-29
August	13-14-15-16-20-21	3-7-8-25-26-30-31
September	9-10-11-12-16-17-21	3-4-26-27
October	7-8-9-13-14-18-19	1-7-24-28
November	10-11-15-16-19-20	3-4-5-24-25-30
December	7-8-12-13-17-18	1-2-3-22-28-29-30-31

	Pruning	Weeds and Pests
January	1-8-9	2-3-4-5-11-12-30-31
February	5-6	1-7-8-12-28
March	4-5-15	6-7-11-12
April	1-10-11-28-29	3-4-8-9-13-30
May	7-8	1-5-6-10-28
June	4	1-2-6-7-11-29-30
July	1-2-28-29	3-4-8-26-27-31
August	7-8-25-26	1-5-9-27-28
September	3-4	1-2-5-6-7-23-24-28-29
October	1-28	3-4-5-26-30-31
November	24-25	1-2-22-23-26-27-28-29
December	3-4-22-30-31	5-24-25-26

MOON'S INFLUENCE OVER PLANTS

Centuries ago it was established that seeds planted when the Moon is in signs and phases called Fruitful will produce more growth than seeds planted when the Moon is in a Barren sign.

Fruitful Signs: Taurus, Cancer, Libra, Scorpio, Capricorn, Pisces
Barren Signs: Aries, Gemini, Leo, Virgo, Sagittarius, Aquarius
Dry Signs: Aries, Gemini, Sagittarius, Aquarius

Activity	Moon In
Mow lawn, trim plants	**Fruitful sign:** 1st & 2nd quarter
Plant flowers	**Fruitful sign:** 2nd quarter; best in Cancer and Libra
Prune	**Fruitful sign:** 3rd & 4th quarter
Destroy pests; spray	**Barren sign:** 4th quarter
Harvest potatoes, root crops	**Dry sign:** 3rd & 4th quarter; Taurus, Leo, and Aquarius

MOON'S INFLUENCE OVER YOUR HEALTH

ARIES	Head, brain, face, upper jaw
TAURUS	Throat, neck, lower jaw
GEMINI	Hands, arms, lungs, shoulders, nervous system
CANCER	Esophagus, stomach, breasts, womb, liver
LEO	Heart, spine
VIRGO	Intestines, liver
LIBRA	Kidneys, lower back
SCORPIO	Sex and eliminative organs
SAGITTARIUS	Hips, thighs, liver
CAPRICORN	Skin, bones, teeth, knees
AQUARIUS	Circulatory system, lower legs
PISCES	Feet, tone of being

Try to avoid work being done on that part of the body when the Moon is in the sign governing that part.

MOON'S INFLUENCE OVER DAILY AFFAIRS

The Moon makes a complete transit of the Zodiac every 27 days 7 hours and 43 minutes. In making this transit the Moon forms different aspects with the planets and consequently has favorable or unfavorable bearings on affairs and events for persons according to the sign of the Zodiac under which they were born.

When the Moon is in conjunction with the Sun it is called a New Moon; when the Moon and Sun are in opposition it is called a Full Moon. From New Moon to Full Moon, first and second quarter—which takes about two weeks—the Moon is increasing or waxing. From Full Moon to New Moon, third and fourth quarter, the Moon is decreasing or waning.

Activity	Moon In
Business: buying and selling new, requiring public support	Sagittarius, Aries, Gemini, Virgo 1st and 2nd quarter
meant to be kept quiet	3rd and 4th quarter
Investigation	3rd and 4th quarter
Signing documents	1st & 2nd quarter, Cancer, Scorpio, Pisces
Advertising	2nd quarter, Sagittarius
Journeys and trips	1st & 2nd quarter, Gemini, Virgo
Renting offices, etc.	Taurus, Leo, Scorpio, Aquarius
Painting of house/apartment	3rd & 4th quarter, Taurus, Scorpio, Aquarius
Decorating	Gemini, Libra, Aquarius
Buying clothes and accessories	Taurus, Virgo
Beauty salon or barber shop visit	1st & 2nd quarter, Taurus, Leo, Libra, Scorpio, Aquarius
Weddings	1st & 2nd quarter

Gemini

GEMINI

Character Analysis

People born under this third sign of the Zodiac are generally known for their versatility, their duality. Quite often they are able to manage several things at the same time. Some of them have two or more sides to their personalities. At one moment they can be happy and fun-loving, the next they can be sullen and morose. For the outsider, this sudden change may be difficult to understand or appreciate.

The Gemini man or woman is interested in all sorts of things and in different ways. Many of the subjects that attract them seem contrary and dissimilar. To Gemini, they're not.

The person born under the sign of the Twins has a mercurial nature. He can fly into a rage one moment, then be absolutely lovable the next. Chances are he won't remember what all the fuss was about after a few moments have passed.

The Gemini man or woman is spiritual in nature. Intellectual challenges whet his appetite. He's a sensitive person. His mind is active, alert. He could even be described as idea-hungry, always on the lookout for new concepts, new ways of doing things. He is always moving along with the times. On the whole, Gemini is very energetic. However, he is apt to bite off more than he can chew at times. He may begin a dozen different projects at once—and never finish any. It's often the doing—starting something—that he finds interesting. As soon as something becomes too familiar or humdrum, he may drop it like a hot coal and begin something else. The cultivated Gemini, however, does not have this problem. He has learned by experience that constancy pays off. He knows how to limit his interests—no matter how great the temptation may be to take on more—and how to finish the work that he has begun. It's a hard lesson for the natural Gemini to learn, but it can be done.

In school, the Twins are quite popular and often at the top of their class. They learn quickly, and when they apply themselves, they can make good use of their powers of concentration. Many do well in languages. They are clever conversationalists; they can keep an audience entranced for hours. Still and all, the depth of their knowledge may be slight. They know how to phrase things well, and this gives the impression of deep learning. They read things too quickly at times and often miss important points. Sometimes they will insist that something is right when in fact it isn't.

Generally, Gemini has a good sense of humor. He knows how to appreciate a good joke, which is apt to make him popular. He seldom fails to see the humorous side of life. In fact, he may irritate others by not acknowledging the serious side of a situation when it is necessary.

All in all, Gemini is open-minded. He is tolerant of others no matter what their views are. He can get along well with various types of people. He's a great mixer. He never has much trouble understanding another's viewpoint.

It is held that the Gemini person is one who prefers to work with concrete things. To him, facts are more important than fantasy. He's practical—or at least attempts to be. He can be quite goal-directed; there is always a reason for what he does. An ambitious person, on the whole, he is never short on projects; there is always something that he has to get done. He could be described as restless; he doesn't like sitting still for long periods of time. He's got to be on the go.

Health

Gemini usually is an active person. He has plenty of energy stored up. Still, he has to be careful at times because he is apt to strain himself emotionally. He gets too wound up and finds it difficult to relax. Troubles, small and large, can turn him into a high-strung person, if he doesn't look out for himself. Weak points of his body are his lungs, arms, and nervous system. During the winter months, some Twins develop one cold after another. Sore throats are sometimes a common Gemini complaint.

On the whole, however, Gemini has a pretty good constitution. He's healthy, but he has to learn how to take care of his health. People often think of Gemini as being weak and sickly, but this isn't so. His physique is often thin and wiry. He may not look like he can endure too much pressure, but his powers for endurance are amazing. He is not delicate, by any stretch of the imagination.

Although the Twins may be bothered by one minor ailment or another, they seldom contract serious illnesses—if they take proper care of themselves. The wise Gemini acknowledges his limits and never tries to exceed them. He will never take on more work than he can comfortably handle. It is important that the Gemini man or woman learns how to relax. Sleep is also an important ingredient for good health. Some Twins feel they have to be constantly on the go; it is as if they were on a treadmill. Of course, they can only keep it up for a short while, then they have to pay the consequences.

The Gemini man or woman is often gifted with handsome looks. Others find them winsome and attractive. Their faces are very lively and expressive, their smiles charming. Most of them tend to be on the slim side. They may seem restless or fidgety from time to time.

Occupation

Geminis are ambitious; they have plenty of drive. They like to keep busy. Most of them do well in jobs that give them a chance to make full use of their intellects. They like to use their minds more than their hands. They are good talkers, generally, and do well in positions where they have to deal directly with the public. They are clever with words and are persuasive in their arguments. Also, they know how to make people feel at ease by making use of their sense of humor. A well-placed joke can work wonders when dealing with the public.

The Twins know how to turn a disadvantage to advantage. They know how to bargain. They are seldom made fools of when it comes to trading. Some of them make excellent salespeople and it is little wonder. Because they can juggle words so well and they have a deep interest in facts, they often become capable journalists. Some of them make good theater or film critics. Writing is one of their chief talents. They generally do well in the arts.

Anything to do with negotiating or bargaining is something in which Gemini is apt to excel. They know how to phrase things, to put them in a favorable light. The Twins fit in almost anywhere in business or profession.

One also finds Geminis in such professions as dentistry, medicine, law, engineering. They excel at logic and reasoning. Some of them have a head for mathematics and make good accountants.

When working with others, they will do what is necessary to make the project successful. However, they do like to go their own way. They do not like someone looking over their shoulder constantly, advising them how something should be done. They like to move around; nothing pleases them more than a job where they are free to come and go as they please. They generally find it difficult to sit at a desk for long stretches at a time. Geminis like movement for its own sake. They are not particularly interested in destinations. It's getting there that absorbs their interest.

They are generally not contented being busy with just one thing. They are apt to try to hold down two jobs at the same time just to be active. Their hobbies are varied; some they manage to develop into side occupations. They abhor dull routine and are creative in their approach to a familiar scheme. They will do what they can to make their work interesting. If they are placed in the wrong position—that is, a position that does not coincide with their interests—they can be grumpy and difficult to get along with.

They like to be attached to a modern, progressive concern that provides a chance to learn new technology. They dislike job situations that are old-fashioned and tiresome.

Geminis aren't money-hungry, generally, but somehow or other they always manage to find jobs that are well-paying. They are not willing to work for nothing. They value their own skills and know how much they are worth.

Money interests the Gemini man or woman because it represents security. The uncultivated Gemini, however, spends his earnings carelessly. He doesn't run out of money, but he mismanages what he has. When he has learned how to economize, he does quite well. He's always looking for a way to better his financial situation. Some Geminis are job hoppers; they are never satisfied with the position they have and they go from one job to another looking for their "proper niche," they think. It is the Gemini who knows how to make the best out of a job situation he already has who wins the day. Job hopping never seems to stop, and in the end the job hopper has nothing to show for all the changing.

People born under this sign usually know how to win the sympathy of influential people. The Twins are often helped, advised, and encouraged by people who hold important positions. People find it easy to believe in Gemini.

The Gemini man or woman is generous with what he has; he does not mind sharing. He can be expansive and doesn't mind paying for others if he can afford it. Once in a while, he may do something unwise with his finances, but, all in all, he manages to keep his financial head above water.

Home and Family

Gemini is adaptable. He is willing to do without if it is necessary. But if he can have his own way, he likes to be surrounded by comfortable and harmonious things. Home is important to him. He likes a house that radiates beauty and calm.

He likes to invite people to his home; he likes entertaining. It is important to Gemini that people feel at home while visiting him. Because he is such a ready host, his house is often full of people—of all description. Although he may be at a loss how he should handle some household matters, he always seems to manage in one way or another. His home is likely to be modern—equipped with the latest conveniences and appliances. He is often amused by gadgets.

Although his home may be important to him, he also likes to pick up and go somewhere whenever the mood strikes. He doesn't like the feeling of being tied down. Home is where he hangs his hat, he likes to think. A Gemini is apt to change his address more than once in his lifetime. This may or may not upset family ties to a certain extent. Still, if they understand him, they will give in to his plans. No one is more difficult to live with than a dissatisfied Gemini. Still, more than likely Gemini has his family conditioned to his moods and there is enough understanding to make life together possible. The culti-vated Gemini learns to stay put and make the most of the home he has.

The Gemini man or woman is a great fixer. He likes to make minor repairs, changing appliances, painting, wallpapering, and so on. He will do many things to make improvements on his home. Sometimes he will go ahead and make changes without consulting those he lives with, which can cause discord.

Outsiders may not think of Gemini as the ideal parent or family man. In fact, they may be open in their criticism. Gemini might resent this strongly because he feels it just isn't true. Children may get on the Gemini man or woman's nerves now and again. They like the kids to be expressive and creative. But the Twins do enjoy moments of peace and quiet. Generally, they know how to get along well with their children. This may be because they do have a youthful streak themselves. They understand the ups and downs of childhood, the trials and tribulations of growing up—also the joys. They may scold once in a while, but children who know them will never pay too much attention to them. The Gemini parent is generally a pushover for the willful child.

Gemini children are usually filled with restless, nervous energy. It comes from their minds, which are like delicately tuned electronic instruments. Mercury, Gemini's planet, is the planet of mind and communication, which bestows the ability to think, speak, write, and observe. So these young sons and daughters of Mercury cannot keep still, mentally or physically. They must be constantly engaged in something that interests them.

Young Gemini is an exceptionally bright child. He or she learns almost instantaneously and has an alert, inquiring mind that demands to know the reason behind anything that catches his or her attention. Parents and teachers of Geminis may find this an exhausting business, mainly because these lovable imps lose inter-est more quickly than most children. When that happens, and no one is around, their capacity for mischief is unbelievable.

Gemini children are sometimes difficult to manage. They usually don't like to be hampered by parental guidance. They like to be allowed to do as they please when they please. They often show signs of artistic ability at a very early age. The perceptive parent knows how to encourage them and to help them develop the characteristics that will help them later on in life.

Social Relationships

Gemini is usually easy to get along with. He likes people and knows how to make them like him. He seldom has serious enemies; he's too friendly for that. Because of his lighthearted ways many people are drawn to him. He is generally sincere in his friendships and expects that sincerity to be reciprocated. A sensitive person, he never forgets or forgives an offense.

The Twins like to be in a crowd—a friendly crowd. They seldom like to be alone for long stretches. They like their friends to be as active and as enthusiastic as they are. Social involvement is important to them. They are apt to throw a party at the drop of a hat. The Gemini man or woman enjoys making others feel good. They are excellent hosts and try to anticipate their guests' needs. Gemini could never be called inhospitable.

Their friends are apt be very different from each other. Gemini gets along well with all types of people. Their social needs may seem contradictory to someone who does not understand the Gemini nature. The cultivated person born under this sign knows how to keep apart those friends who are not likely to get along. He'll avoid social conflict among his friends at all costs.

Meeting new people is important to the man or woman born under the third sign of the Zodiac. He thrives on social activities. He likes exchanging views and ideas.

Gemini does not demand that his friends be his intellectual equal. He can be content discussing trivial matters as well as profound ones. He likes people he can relax with.

Friends may like Gemini but find him hard to understand. The Twins seem to have so many different personas at the same time. They are difficult to pin down.

People are always inviting Geminis to parties; any social affair would seem incomplete without them. Their charm and liveliness are contagious. People enjoy being around them. They can be loose-tongued at social gatherings, and sometimes divulge information about themselves or others that they shouldn't. They can be severe, too, in their criticisms. A Gemini's sharp tongue has cut many a social tie.

Love and Marriage

Gemini longs for affection and understanding. He doesn't always find it, though. Although he's honest in his search, Gemini is apt to be too critical. Once he's won someone, he finds fault with them. The cultivated Gemini learns to take the bitter with the sweet. He realizes that no one is perfect, and he accepts the love of his life for what she is.

It is quite possible for Gemini to have many love relationships before he ever thinks of settling down with one person. He may not be an intense lover. He loves being affectionate, however. Flattery can turn his head.

Gemini does not like to feel that he is tied down. He likes someone who will give him the freedom he needs. He doesn't like to feel imprisoned by love. He is often attracted to someone who is as independent in spirit as he is. He likes a witty and intelligent companion, someone who can discuss things rationally.

It is sometimes difficult for the natural Gemini to give himself to any one person. He does not like being limited in his affections. He flirts just for the pleasure of flirting. He enjoys attention and at times will go to great lengths to get it. He likes variety in romance. The same love diet is apt to bore him after a while.

In spite of his changeability, the intelligent Gemini can settle down to one partner, once he puts his mind to it. The person who wins a Gemini is usually gifted and clever, someone adaptable who knows how to change with his moods. Gemini is not difficult to get along with. He is pleasant and gentle, for the most part. He likes people who are responsive to his moods. If he really loves someone, he sees to it that his demands are not too unreasonable. He's willing to make compromises.

Even after he's married, the average Gemini is given to flirting, but it's nothing for his mate to be concerned about. He'll keep it at a harmless level. He will not risk a love relationship that contains the benefits he appreciates.

Marriage for Gemini is a relationship that should be lively and exciting. He's not the kind of person who accepts a humdrum home life. He wants a family that is as active as he is.

Romance and the Gemini Woman

The Gemini woman has no trouble attracting members of the opposite sex. They find her dazzling and glamorous. Her disposition is almost always gay and fun-loving. She knows how to make her suitors feel appreciated and wanted. However, she is restless and easily changes from one mood to another. This often mystifies and disappoints admirers. Sometimes she seems easy to please, other times not. People who don't understand her think she is difficult and egocentric.

The Gemini woman likes variety in her love relationships. She may go through many romances before she thinks of marrying and settling down. She admires a man who can accept her as an equal, intellectually and emotionally. She is not too fond of domestic duties. After marriage, she wants to pursue her various interests just as she did when she was single.

An intellectual man is apt to appeal to her when she is interested in a serious love relationship. A man who can win her mind can win her heart. Gemini seldom marries someone she considers her inferior intellectually. She wants someone she can respect.

The single Gemini woman can be quite flirtatious. She may even toy with the affections of someone she is not seriously interested in. When she feels a romance has come to an end, she'll say so bluntly and move on. She likes her love relationships to be an adventure—full of amusement and excitement. Men looking for a housekeeper instead of a partner are wasting their time when courting a Gemini woman. She'll never tie herself to the kitchen for the love of a man. She is interested in too many other things.

The considerate Gemini woman, however, will cut down on her interests and confine most of her activities to the home if she feels the love of her man is worth the sacrifice.

The Gemini woman has good taste in decorating a home. She knows how to arrange rooms and how to use color tastefully. She can become a good homemaker once she puts her mind to it. She likes things tidy and neat but is not too fond of domestic chores. If possible, she will see to it that she has some help in carrying out household duties.

Romance and the Gemini Man

The Gemini man is interested in change and adventure in his romantic activities. The woman who desires to keep up with him has to be quick on her feet. His restlessness is apt to puzzle even those who love him. He is quick-witted and fond of challenge. Someone who is likely to drag him into a life of humdrum domesticity will not win him.

In spite of the fact that he may go from romance to romance quite easily, the Gemini man is really in search of a true and lasting love relationship. He is popular with women. They like him because of his charm and intelligence. If he cares for a woman, he can make her feel like the most important person in his life. He is capable of steadfastness in his affections, but there is no guarantee how long this will last.

A girl interested in home and a family—and nothing else—is not one who will appeal to him. He wants someone who is a good companion, someone who can share his interests as well as his moods. He wants someone he can talk with as an equal, someone whose interests go beyond the trivial.

In love, he can be either passionate or mild; it depends on his partner and the circumstances. Some Geminis are easily distracted in romance, and their interests travel from one woman to the other with appalling ease.

When he does meet the ideal mate, Gemini proves himself to be loving and responsible. He does his best to protect the interests of his family and is willing to make the sacrifices necessary to keep his home life in order. He may flirt occasionally after marriage, but it seldom goes beyond that. The woman who marries him must allow him his romantic fantasies. He can become unreasonable if he is reproached for flirting harmlessly.

He will be faithful to the woman who allows him his freedom— the woman who is not suspicious and trusts him.

Life with a Gemini man can be a happy one indeed, but the woman who plans to go through life at his side has to be as adaptable and active as he is.

Woman—Man

GEMINI WOMAN
ARIES MAN

The man born under the sign of Aries is often attracted to the Gemini woman. In you he can find that mixture of intellect and charm that is so often difficult to find in a woman. Like you, he has many interests and is always seeking one adventure after another. He has an insatiable thirst for knowledge of all kinds.

He can do with a woman like you—someone attractive, quick-witted, and intelligent. He'll admire you for your independence. He's not interested in a clinging vine. He wants someone who is there when he needs her; someone who listens and understands what he says; someone who can give advice if he should ever happen to ask for it, which is not likely to be often.

The Aries man wants a woman who is a good companion and a good sport. He is looking for a woman who will look good on his arm without hanging on it too heavily. He is looking for a woman who has both feet on the ground and yet is mysterious and enticing, a modern Helen of Troy whose face or fine speech can launch a thousand business deals, if need be. That woman he is in search of sounds a little like you. If the shoe fits, put it on. You won't be sorry.

The Aries man makes a good husband. He is faithful and attentive. He is an affectionate man. He'll make you feel needed and loved. Love is a serious matter for Aries. He does not believe in flirting or playing the field—especially after he's found the woman of his dreams. He'll expect you to be as constant in your affection as he is in his. Try to curb your bent for harmless flirting if you have your heart set on an Aries. He'll expect you to be a hundred percent his; he won't put up with any nonsense while romancing you.

The Aries man may be progressive and modern about many things, but when it comes to pants wearing, he's downright conventional: it's strictly male attire. The best role you can take in the relationship is a supporting one. He's the boss and that's that. If you can accept it, you'll find the going easy.

The Aries man, with his endless energy and drive, likes to relax in comfort at the end of the day. The Gemini woman who is a good homemaker can be sure of his undying affection. If you see to it that everything in the house is where he expects to find it, you'll have no difficulty keeping the relationship on an even keel.

Aries is generally a good provider. He'll see to it that you never want. Although he is interested in security, he's a man who is not afraid to take risks. Often his gambling pays off.

Aries fathers, while affectionate and playful, sometimes have trouble seeing things through the eyes of a child. Your innate understanding of youth will always come in handy.

GEMINI WOMAN
TAURUS MAN

If your heart is set on a man born under the sign of Taurus, you'll have to learn the art of being patient. Taurus take their time about everything—even love.

The steady and deliberate Taurus is a little slow on the draw; it may take him quite a while before he gets around to popping that question. For the Gemini woman who is adaptable, the waiting and anticipating almost always pays off in the end. Taurus men want to make sure that every step they take is right, especially if the path they're on could lead to the altar.

If you are in the mood for a whirlwind romance, better cast your net in shallower waters. Moreover, most Taurus prefer to do the angling themselves. They are not keen on women taking the lead. Once she does, he may drop her immediately. If the Gemini woman lets herself get caught on his terms, she'll find that her Taurus has fallen for her—hook, line, and sinker.

The Taurus man is fond of a comfortable home life. It is very important to him. If you keep those home fires burning you will have no trouble keeping that flame in the Taurus heart aglow. You have a talent for homemaking. You are an old hand at harmony and color. Your taste in furnishings is excellent. Perhaps, with your moodiness, sense of adventure, and love of change, you could turn out to be a challenging mate for the strong, steady, and protective Bull. Perhaps he could be the anchor for your dreams and plans. He could help you acquire a more balanced outlook and approach to your life. Not one for wild schemes, himself, Taurus can help you to curb your impulsiveness. He's the man who is always there when you need him.

The Taurus man is steady—the kind of man the Gemini woman often needs.

When you tie the knot with a Bull, you can put away fears about creditors pounding on the front door. Taurus is practical about everything including bill paying. When he carries you over the threshold, you can be certain the entire house is paid for.

Married to a Taurus man, you need not worry about having to put aside your many interests for the sake of back-breaking household chores. He'll see to it that you have all the latest time-saving appliances and comforts.

You also can forget about acquiring premature gray hairs due to unruly, ruckus-raising children under your feet. Papa Taurus is a master at keeping youngsters in line. He's crazy about kids but he also knows what's good for them.

GEMINI WOMAN
GEMINI MAN

The Gemini man and the Gemini woman are a couple who understand each other. They are so much alike. Both are intelligent, witty, outgoing, and versatile. The Gemini man could easily turn out to be your better half. One thing that causes a Twin's mind and affection to wander is a bore, and it's highly unlikely that an active Gemini woman would ever allow herself to be accused of that.

The Gemini man who has caught your heart will admire you for your ideas and intellect—perhaps even more than for your good cooking and flawless talent for homemaking. The Gemini woman needn't feel that once she's made her marriage vows she'll have to put her interests and ambition in storage. The Gemini man will admire you for your zeal and liveliness. He's the kind of guy who won't pout and scowl if you let him shift for himself in the kitchen once in a while. In fact, he'll enjoy the challenge of wrestling with pots and pans for a change. Chances are, too, that he might turn out to be a better cook than you—that is, if he isn't already.

The man born under the sign of the Twins is very active. There aren't many women who have enough pep to keep up with him. But this doesn't set a problem for the spry Gemini woman. You are both dreamers, planners, and idealists. The strong Gemini woman can easily fill the role of rudder for her Gemini man's ship-without-a-sail. If you happen to be a cultivated Gemini, he won't mind it too much. The intelligent Twin is often aware of his shortcomings. He doesn't resent it if someone with better bearings gives him a shove in the right direction. The average Gemini does not have serious ego hang-ups and will gracefully accept a well-deserved chewing out from his mate.

When you and your Gemini man team up, you'll probably always have a houseful of people to entertain—interesting people, too. Geminis find it hard to tolerate sluggish minds.

Gemini men are always attractive to the opposite sex. You'll perhaps have to allow him an occasional harmless flirt. It will seldom amount to more than that if you're his proper mate. It will help keep his spirits up. A Twin out of sorts, as you well know, is capable of brewing up a whirlwind of trouble. Better tolerate his flirting—within eyeshot, of course—than lose your cool.

As far as children go, you are both pushovers. One of you will have to learn to fill the role of house disciplinarian, otherwise chaos will reign.

**GEMINI WOMAN
CANCER MAN**

Chances are you won't hit it off too well with the man born under Cancer, but then Cupid has been known to do some pretty unlikely things. Cancer is a very sensitive man, thin-skinned and occasionally moody. You've got to keep on your toes, and not step on his if you're determined to make a go of the relationship.

The Cancer man may be lacking in many of the qualities you seek in a man, but when it comes to being faithful and being a good provider, he's hard to beat.

It is the perceptive Gemini woman who will not mistake the Crab's quietness for sullenness or his thriftiness for penny-pinching. In some respects he can be like the wise old owl out on a limb; he may look like he's dozing but actually he hasn't missed a thing. Moon Children often possess a well of knowledge about human behavior; they can deliver very helpful advice to those in trouble or in need. Cancer certainly can keep you from making unwise investments in time and especially money. He may not say much, but he's always got his wits about him.

The Crab may not be the match or catch for many a Gemini

woman. In fact, he may seem dull to on-the-move Gemini. True to his sign, he can be cranky and crabby when handled the wrong way. He is perhaps more sensitive than he should be.

Geminis are usually as smart as a whip. If you're clever you will never, in any way, convey the idea that you consider your Cancer a little short on brain power. Browbeating is a surefire way of sending the Crab angrily scurrying back to his shell. It's possible all of that lost ground may never be recovered.

The Crab is most comfortable at home. Once settled in for the night or for the weekend, wild horses couldn't drag him away unless those wild horses were dispatched by his mother. The Crab is sometimes a Mama's boy. If his mate does not put her foot down, he will see to it that his mother comes first whenever possible. No self-respecting Gemini would ever allow herself to play second fiddle to her mother-in-law. If she's a tactful Gemini, she may find that slipping into number-one position can be as easy as pie (that legendary apple pie his mother used to make).

If you take enough time to pamper your Cancer man with good cooking and comfort, you'll find that "Mother" turns up less and less—at the front door as well as in conversations.

Cancers make protective, proud, and patient fathers, but they may resent a youngster's bid for freedom.

GEMINI WOMAN
LEO MAN

For the Gemini woman who enjoys being swept off her feet in a romantic whirlwind, Leo is the sign of love. When the Lion puts his mind to romancing, he doesn't stint. It's all wining, dining, and dancing till the wee hours of the morning.

Leo is all heart and knows how to make his woman feel like a woman. The Gemini in constant search of a man she can look up to need go no farther. Leo is ten-feet tall—in spirit if not in stature. He's a man in full control of his faculties, and he also manages to have full control of just about any situation he finds himself in. He's a winner.

The Leo man may not look like Tarzan, but he knows how to roar and beat his chest if he has to. The Gemini woman who has had her fill of weak-kneed men finds in a Leo someone she can at last lean upon. He can support you physically as well as encourage your plans and projects. He's good at giving advice that pays off. Leos are direct. They don't believe in wasting time or effort. They almost never make unwise investments—something a Gemini often does.

Many Leos rise to the top of their profession and through their example prove to be a great inspiration to others.

Although he's a ladies' man, Leo is very particular about his ladies. His standards are high when it comes to love interests. The idealistic and cultivated Gemini should have no trouble keeping her balance on the pedestal the Lion sets her on. Leo believes that romance should be played on a fair give-and-take basis. He won't stand for any monkey business in a love relationship. It's all or nothing.

You'll find him a frank, straight-from-the-shoulder person; he generally says what is on his mind.

The Gemini woman who does decide upon a Leo for a mate must be prepared to stand squarely behind her man. He expects it—and usually deserves it. He's the head of the house and can handle that position without a hitch. He knows how to go about breadwinning and, if he has his way (and most Leos do have their own way), he'll see to it that you'll have all the luxuries you crave and the comforts you need.

It's likely that the romance in your marriage will stay alive. Lions need love like flowers need sunshine. They're ever amorous and generally expect similar attention and affection from their mate. Lions are fond of going out on the town; they love to give parties. You should encounter no difficulties in sharing his interest in this direction.

Leos make strict fathers, generally. You'll have to smooth over your children's roughed-up feelings.

GEMINI WOMAN
VIRGO MAN

The Virgo man is all business—or he may seem so to you. He is usually cool, calm, and collected. He's perhaps too much of a fussbudget to wake up deep romantic interests in a Gemini. Torrid romancing to him is just so much sentimental mush. He can do without it and can make that evident in short order.

He's keen on chastity. If necessary, he can lead a sedentary, sexless life without caring too much about the fun others think he is missing. You may find him a first-class dud. His lack of imagination and dislike for flights of fancy can grate on a Gemini woman's nerves. He is always correct and likes to be handled correctly. Almost everything about him is orderly.

He does have an honest-to-goodness heart, believe it or not. The Gemini who finds herself strangely attracted to his feet-flat-on-the-ground ways will discover that his is a constant heart, not one that goes in for flings or sordid affairs. Virgos take an awfully long time to warm up to someone. A practical man, even in matters of the heart, he wants to know just what kind of a person you are before he takes a chance on love.

The impulsive Gemini had better not make the mistake of kissing her Virgo friend on the street, even if it's only a peck on the cheek. He's not at all demonstrative and hates public displays of affection. Love, according to him, should be kept within the confines of one's home—with the curtains drawn. Once he believes you are on the level with him as far as your love is concerned, you'll see how fast he loses his cool. Virgos are considerate, gentle lovers. He'll spend a long time, though, getting to know you. He'll like you before he loves you.

A Gemini-Virgo romance can be a sometime—or a one-time—thing. If the bottom ever falls out, don't bother to pick up the pieces. Nine times out of ten, he won't care about patching up. He's a once-burnt-twice-shy guy. When he crosses your phone number out of his address book, he's crossing you out of his life—for good.

Neat as a pin, he's thumbs-down on what he considers sloppy housekeeping. An ashtry with just one stubbed-out cigarette in it can be annoying to him, even if it's just two seconds old. Glassware should always sparkle and shine.

If you wind up marrying a Virgo man, keep your kids spic-and-span, at least by the time he gets home from work. Train the children to be kind, respectful, and courteous. He'll expect it.

GEMINI WOMAN
LIBRA MAN

If there's a Libra in your life, you are most likely a very happy woman. Men born under this sign of the Lawgiver have a way with impulsive, intelligent women. You'll always feel at ease in his company; you can always be yourself with him.

Like you, he's given to occasional fits of impulsiveness. His moods can change rapidly. One moment he comes on hard and strong with "I love you", and next moment he's left you like yesterday's mashcd potatoes. He'll come back to you, though; don't worry. Libras are like that. Deep down inside he really knows what he wants even though he may not appear to.

You'll appreciate his admiration of beauty and harmony. If you're dressed to the teeth and never looked better in your life, you'll get a ready compliment—and one that's really deserved. Libras don't indulge in idle flattery. If they don't like something, they are tactful enough to remain silent.

Libras will go to great lengths to preserve peace and harmony—even tell a fat lie if necessary. They don't like showdowns or disagreeable confrontations. But the frank Gemini woman is usually impelled to air grievances and get resentments out into the open, even if it comes out all wrong. To Libra, making a clean breast of everything sometimes seems like sheer folly.

You may lose your patience while waiting for your Libra friend to make up his mind. It takes him ages to make a decision. He weighs both sides carefully before committing himself to anything. You seldom dillydally—at least about small things—and so you will find it difficult to see eye-to-eye with a hesitating Libra when it comes to decision-making methods.

All in all, though, he is a kind, gentle, and fair person. He is interested in the "real" truth. He'll try to balance everything out until he has all the correct answers. It is not difficult for him to see both sides of the story.

Libras don't pose or prance to get attention like a Leo might do. They're not show-offs. Generally, they are well-balanced people. Honest, wholesome, and affectionate, they are serious about every love entanglement they have. If he should find that his date is not really suited to him, he will end the relationship in such a tactful manner that no hard feelings will come about.

He never lets money burn holes in his pockets. You don't have to worry about him throwing his money all over the place, though. Most likely he'll spend it all on you—lavishly.

The Libra father can teach youngsters fairness and tolerance in a gentle, patient way. A peace-loving man, he encourages discussion and debate but frowns on physical fighting. He teaches the children how to play by the rules.

GEMINI WOMAN
SCORPIO MAN

Many find the Scorpio's sting a fate worse than death. The Gemini woman quite often is no exception. When his anger breaks loose, you had better clear out of the vicinity.

The average Scorpio man may strike the Gemini woman as being a brute. He'll stick pins into the balloons of your plans and dreams if they don't line up with what he thinks is right. If you do anything to irritate him—just anything—you'll wish you hadn't. He'll give you a sounding out that would make you pack your bags and vow never to go back.

The Scorpio man hates being tied down to home life—and so do you to a certain extent. Instead of wrestling with pots and pans, you'd rather be out and about, devoting plenty of time to your many interests. The Scorpio man would rather be out on the battlefield of life, belting away at whatever he feels is a just and worthy cause, instead of staying home nestled in a comfortable armchair with the evening paper. If you're a Gemini with a strong homemaking streak, don't keep those home fires burning too brightly too long; you may run out of firewood.

As passionate as he is in business and politics, the Scorpio man has plenty of pep and ginger stored away for lovemaking. Most women are easily attracted to him. The Gemini woman is no exception—at least before she is really aware of what she might be getting into. Those who allow a Scorpio to sweep them off their feet soon find that they're dealing with a pepperpot of seething excitement. The Scorpio man is passionate with a capital P, you can be sure of that.

But even while he is providing so much pleasure to his lover, he can deliver a knockout emotional blow. He can wound on a deep level, and you may not know if he really means it. Scorpio is blunt and can be as cutting as a razor blade. An insult can whiz out even more quickly than a compliment.

If you're a Gemini who can keep a stiff upper lip, take it on the chin, turn a deaf ear because you feel you are still under his love spell in spite of everything—lots of luck.

If you have decided to take the bitter with the sweet, prepare yourself for a lot of ups and downs. Chances are you won't have as much time for your own affairs and interests as you'd like. The Scorpio's love of power may cause you to be at his constant beck and call.

Scorpios like fathering large families, but they seldom give youngsters the attention they need.

GEMINI WOMAN
SAGITTARIUS MAN

The Gemini woman who has set her cap for a man born under the sign of Sagittarius may have to apply a lot of strategy before she can get him to say "Will you marry me?" Although some Archers may be marriage-shy, they're not ones to skitter away from romance. A Gemini woman may find a relationship with a Sagittarius—whether a fling or the real thing—a very enjoyable experience.

As a rule, Sagittarius are bright, happy, and healthy people. They have a strong sense of fair play. Often they're a source of inspirations to others. They're full of ideas and drive.

You'll be taken by the Archer's infectious grin and his light-hearted friendly nature. If you do wind up being the woman in his life, you'll find that he's apt to treat you more like a buddy than the love of his life. It's just his way. Sagittarius is often chummy instead of romantic.

You'll admire his broad-mindedness in most matters—including that of the heart. If, while dating you, he claims that he still wants to play the field, he'll expect you to enjoy the same liberty. Once he's promised to love, honor, and obey, however, he does just that. Marriage for him, once he's taken that big step, is very serious business. The Gemini woman with her keen imagination and love of freedom will not be disappointed if she does tie up with an Archer. The Sagittarius man is quick-witted—but not as quick-witted as you sometimes. Generally, men of this sign have a genuine interest in equality. They hate prejudice and injustice.

If he insists on a night out with the boys once a week, he won't scowl if you decide to let him shift for himself in the kitchen once a week while you go out with the girls.

He's not much of a homebody. Quite often he's occupied with far-away places either in his dreams or in reality. He enjoys—just as you do—being on the go or on the move. He's got ants in his pants and refuses to sit still for long stretches at a time. Humdrum routine—especially at home—bores him. At the drop of a hat, he may ask you to pack your traveling bag for a quick jaunt. He'll take great pride in showing you off to his friends. He'll always be a considerate mate; he will never embarrass or disappoint you intentionally.

His friendly, sunshiny nature is capable of attracting many people. Like you, he's very tolerant when it comes to friends, and you'll most likely spend a great deal of time entertaining.

Sagittarius are all thumbs when it comes to little shavers. He'll develop an interest in youngsters when they get older.

GEMINI WOMAN
CAPRICORN MAN

The with-it Gemini woman is likely to find the average Capricorn man a bit of a drag. The man born under the sign of the Goat is often a closed person and difficult to get to know. Even if you do get to know him, you may not find him very interesting.

In romance, Capricorn men are a little on the rusty side. You'll probably have to make all the passes.

You may find his plodding manner irritating, and his conservative, traditional ways maddening. He's not one to take chances on anything. "If it was good enough for my father, it's good enough for me" may be his motto. He follows a way that is tried and true.

Whenever adventure rears its tantalizing head, the Goat will turn the other way; he's just not interested.

He may be just as ambitious as you are—perhaps even more so. But his ways of accomplishing his aims are more subterranean; at least they seem so. He operates from the background a good deal of the time. At a gathering you may never even notice him, but he's there, taking in everything and sizing up everyone, planning his next careful move.

Although Capricorns may be intellectual, it is generally not the kind of intelligence a Gemini appreciates. He may not be as bright or as quick as you are; it may take ages for him to understand a joke.

The Gemini woman who does take up with a man born under this sign must be pretty good in the cheering up department. The Capricorn man in her love life may act as though he's constantly being followed by a cloud of gloom.

The Capricorn is happiest in the comfort and privacy of his own home. The security possible within four walls can make him a happy man. He'll spend as much time as he can at home. If he is loaded down with extra work, he'll bring it home instead of staying at the office.

You'll most likely find yourself frequently confronted by his relatives. Family is very important to the Capricorn—his family, not yours. They had better take an important place in your life, too, if you want to keep your home a happy one.

Although his caution in most matters may drive you up the wall, you'll find his concerned way with money justified most of the time. He is no squanderer. Everything is planned right down to the last red cent. He'll see to it that you never want.

He can be quite a scold when it comes to disciplining children. You'll have to step in and smooth things over when he goes too far.

GEMINI WOMAN
AQUARIUS MAN

You've never known love unless you've known a man born under the sign of Aquarius. The Gemini woman is likely to find an Aquarius dazzling.

As a rule, Aquarius are extremely friendly and open. Of all the signs, they are perhaps the most tolerant. In the thinking department, they are often miles ahead of others.

The Gemini woman will find her Aquarius man intriguing and interesting. She'll also find the relationship a challenging one. Your high respect for intelligence and imagination may be reason enough for you to settle your heart on a Water Bearer. You can learn a lot from him.

Aquarius love everybody—even their worst enemies, sometimes. Through your relationship with an Aquarius you will run into all sorts of people, ranging from near-genius to downright insane—and they're all friends of his.

In the holding-hands phase of your romance, you may find that your Water Bearer friend has cold feet. Aquarius take quite a bit of warming up before they're ready to come across with that first goodnight kiss. More than likely, he'll just want to be your pal in the beginning. For him, that's an important first step in any relationship—love, included. The poetry and flowers stage—if it ever comes—will come much later. Aquarius is all heart. Still, when it comes to tying himself down to one person and for keeps, he may hesitate. He may even try to get out of it if you breathe down his neck too hard.

The Aquarius man is no Valentino and wouldn't want to be. The Gemini woman is likely to be more impressed by his broadmindedness and high moral standards than by his feeble attempts at romance.

You won't find it difficult to look up to a man born under the sign of the Water Bearer, but you may find the challenge of trying to keep up with him dizzying. He can pierce through the most complicated problem as if it were a matter of simple math. You may find him a little too lofty and high-minded. But don't judge him too harshly if that's the case; he's way ahead of his time—your time, too, most likely.

If you marry this man, he'll stay true to you. He'll certainly admire you for your intelligence and wit. Don't think that, once you're married, he'll keep you chained to the kitchen sink. He'll encourage you to go ahead in your pursuit of knowledge. You'll most likely have a minor tiff with him every now and again but never anything serious.

Kids love him and vice versa. He'll be as tolerant with them as he is with adults.

GEMINI WOMAN
PISCES MAN

The man born under Pisces is a dreamer. Sometimes he's so wrapped up in his dreams that he's difficult to reach. To the average Gemini woman, he may seem a little passive.

He's easygoing most of the time. He seems to take things in his stride. He'll entertain all kinds of views and opinions from just about anyone, nodding or smiling vaguely, giving the impression that he's with them one hundred percent while that may not be the case at all. His attitude may be "why bother" when he is confronted with someone wrong who thinks he's right. The Pisces man will seldom speak his mind if he thinks he'll be rigidly opposed.

The Pisces man is oversensitive at times—he's afraid of getting his feelings hurt. He'll sometimes imagine a personal injury when none's been made. Chances are you'll find this maddening; at times you may feel like giving him a swift kick where it hurts the most. It wouldn't do any good, though. It would just add fuel to the fire of his persecution complex.

One thing you'll admire about Pisces is his concern for people who are sick or troubled. He'll make his shoulder available to anyone in the mood for a good cry. He can listen to one hard-luck story after another without seeming to tire. When his advice is asked, he is capable of coming across with words of wisdom. He often knows what is paining someone before that person is aware of it himself.

It's almost intuitive with Pisces, it seems. Still, at the end of the day, this man will want some peace and quiet. If you've got a problem on your mind when he comes home, don't unload it in his lap. If you do, you may find him short-tempered. He's a good listener, but he can only take so much.

Pisces are not aimless although they may seem so at times. The positive Pisces man is often successful in his profession and is likely to wind up rich and influential. Material gain, however, is not a direct goal for a man born under the sign of the Fishes.

The weaker Pisces are usually content to stay put on the level where they find themselves. They won't complain too much if the roof leaks and the fence is in need of repair. They can evade any responsibility if they feel like it.

Because of their seemingly laissez-faire manner, Pisces are immensely popular with children. For tots the Pisces father plays the double role of confidant and playmate. It will never enter his mind to discipline a child, no matter how spoiled or incorrigible that child becomes.

Man—Woman

GEMINI MAN
ARIES WOMAN

The Aries woman is a charmer. When she tugs at your heart, you'll know it. She's a woman in search of a knight in shining armor. She is a very particular person with very high ideals. She won't accept anyone other than the man of her dreams.

The Aries woman never plays around with passion; she means business when it comes to love.

Don't get the idea that she's dewy-eyed. She isn't. In fact, she can be practical and to the point when she wants to be. She's a gal with plenty of drive and ambition. With an Aries woman behind you, you can go far in life. She knows how to help her man get ahead. She's full of wise advice; you only have to ask. In some cases, Aries women have a keen business sense; many of them become successful career women. There is nothing passive or retiring about her. She is equipped with a good brain and she knows how to use it.

An Aries-Gemini union could be something strong, secure, and romantic. If both of you have your sights fixed in the same direction, there is almost nothing you could not accomplish.

The Gemini man will have to give up flirting if he decides to settle for an Aries partner or wife. The Aries woman is proud, and capable of being quite jealous. While you're with her, never cast your eye in another woman's direction. It could spell disaster for your relationship. The Aries woman won't put up with romantic nonsense even if it's done only in fun.

If the Aries woman backs you up in your business affairs, you can be sure of succeeding. However, if she is only interested in advancing her own career and puts her own interests before yours, she can be sure of rocking the boat. It will put a strain on the relationship. The overambitious Aries woman can be a pain in the neck and make you forget you were once in love with her.

The cultivated Aries woman makes a wonderful wife and mother. She has a natural talent for homemaking. With a pot of paint and some wallpaper she can transform the dreariest domicile into an abode of beauty and snug comfort. The perfect hostess—even when friends just happen by—she knows how to make guests feel at home.

You'll admire your Aries, too, because she knows how to stand on her own two feet. Hers is an independent nature. She won't break down and cry when things go wrong. She'll pick herself up and try to patch things up.

Like you she's social-minded. In the wit department, she can run you a close second. She'll love you as long as she can look forward to a good intellectual challenge.

She makes a fine, affectionate mother and will encourage her children to develop a wide range of talents and skills.

GEMINI MAN
TAURUS WOMAN

The woman born under the sign of Taurus may lack a little of the sparkle and bubble you like. The Taurus woman is generally down to earth and never flighty. It's important to her that she keep both feet flat on the ground. She may fail to appreciate your willingness to run here and there, especially if she's under the impression that there's no profit in it.

On the other hand, if you hit it off with a Taurus woman, you won't be disappointed at all in the romance area. She is all woman, and proud of it, too. She can be very devoted and loving once she decides that her relationship with you is no fly-by-night romance. Basically, she's a passionate person. In sex, she's direct and to the point. If she really loves you, she'll let you know that she's yours—and without reservations. Better not flirt with other women once you've committed yourself to her. She can be jealous and possessive.

She'll stick by you through thick and thin. It's almost certain that if the going ever gets rough, she won't go running home to Mother. She can adjust to hard times just as graciously as she can to good times.

Taurus women are, on the whole, even-tempered. They like to be treated with kindness. Pretty things and soft things make them purr like kittens.

With your quick wit and itchy feet, you may find yourself miles ahead of your Taurus woman. At times you are likely to find this distressing. But if you've developed a talent for patience, you won't mind waiting for her to catch up. Never try grabbing her hand and pulling her along at your normal speed; it won't work. It could lead to a fireworks display that would put Independence Day to shame. The Taurus woman doesn't anger readily but when prodded often enough, she's capable of letting loose with a cyclone of ill will. If you treat her correctly, you'll have no cause for complaint.

Taurus loves doing things for her man. She's a whiz in the kitchen and can whip up feasts fit for a king if she thinks they'll be appreciated. She may not fully understand you, but she'll adore you and be faithful if she feels you're worthy of it.

The woman born under Taurus will make a wonderful mother for your children. She knows how to keep her children loved, cuddled, and warm. She may not be too sympathetic toward them when they reach the teenage stage, however. Their changeability might irk her steadfast ways.

GEMINI MAN
GEMINI WOMAN

Although you and your Gemini woman may be as alike as peas in a pod, there will be certain barriers to overcome in order to make your relationship a smooth-running one. Before settling on anything definite, it would be wise for you both to get to know each other as you really are—without the sparkling veneer, the wit, the irresistible charm that Geminis are so well known for. You're both talkers and if you don't understand each other well enough you can have serious arguments. Get to know each other well; learn what it is that makes you tick. Two Geminis without real knowledge of themselves and their relationship can easily wind up behind the eight ball. But two cultivated, positive Geminis can make a love relationship or marriage work.

You are likely to find a romance with another Twin a many-splendored thing. In her you can find the intellectual companionship you crave and so seldom find. A Gemini woman can appreciate your aims and desires because she travels much the same road as you do, intellectually and emotionally. You'll admire her for her liveliness and mental agility. You'll be attracted by her warmth and grace.

While she's on your arm, you'll probably notice that many male eyes are drawn to her; she may even return a gaze or two, but don't let that worry you. Women born under this sign (the men, too) have nothing against a harmless flirtation; they enjoy the attention. If she feels she's already spoken for, she'll never let it get out of hand.

Although she may not be very handy in the kitchen, you'll never go hungry for a filling and tasty meal. She's in as much a hurry as you are most of the time, and won't feel like she's cheating by breaking out the instant mashed potatoes. She may not feel totally at home at the kitchen range, but she can be clever; with a dash of this and a little bit of that, she can make an uninteresting TV dinner taste like a gourmet meal. Then again, there are some Geminis who find complicated recipes a challenge to their intellect. Every meal they prepare turns out to be a tantalizing and mouth-watering surprise.

The Gemini woman loves people as much as you do—all kinds of people. Together you'll throw some very interesting and successful parties. Geminis do well in organizing social affairs. Everyone invited is bound to have the time of their life.

People may have the impression that your Gemini wife is not the best of mothers. But the children themselves seldom have reason to complain. Gemini women get along with their kids well because they, too, possess a childlike quality.

GEMINI MAN
CANCER WOMAN

If you fall in love with a Cancer woman, be prepared for anything. Moon Children are sometimes difficult to understand when it comes to love. In one hour, she can unravel a range of emotions that will leave you dizzy. She'll keep you guessing for sure.

You may find her a little too uncertain and sensitive for your tastes. You'll spend a lot of time encouraging her—helping her to erase her foolish fears. Tell her she's a living doll a dozen times a day and you'll be well loved in return.

Be careful of the jokes you make when in her company. Don't let them revolve around her, her personal interests, or her family. If you do, you'll most likely reduce her to tears. She can't stand being made fun of. It will take bushels of roses and tons of chocolates to get her to emerge from her shell.

In matters of money managing, she may not easily come around to your way of thinking. Geminis rarely let money burn a hole in their pockets. Cancers are just the opposite. You may get the notion that your Cancer sweetheart or mate is a direct descendent of Scrooge. If she has her way, she'll hang onto that first dollar you earned. She's that way not only with money but with everything from bakery string to jelly jars. She's a saver; she never throws anything away, no matter how trivial.

Once she returns your "I love you," you'll have a very loving, self-sacrificing, and devoted friend. Her love for you will never alter. She'll put you high on a pedestal and will do everything—even if it's against your will—to keep you up there.

Cancer women love home life. For them, marriage is an easy step. They're domestic with a capital D. She'll do her best to make your home comfortable and cozy. She feels more at ease home than anywhere else. She is an excellent hostess.

Cancer women make the best mothers of all the signs of the Zodiac. She'll consider every minor complaint of her child a major catastrophe. She's not the kind of mother who will do anything to get the children off her hands. With her, kids come first. If you are lucky, you'll run a close second. You'll perhaps see her as too devoted to the children; you may have a hard time convincing her to untie her apron strongs. When Junior or Sis is ready for that first date, you have to prevent your Cancer wife from going along.

GEMINI MAN
LEO WOMAN

If you can manage a girl who likes to kick up her heels every now and again, then Leo is for you. You'll have to learn to put away jealous fears when you take up with a Lioness. She makes heads turn and tongues wag. You don't have to believe any of what you hear—it's most likely jealous gossip or wishful thinking.

The Leo woman has more than a fair share of grace and glamour. She knows it, and knows how to put it to good use. Needless to say, other women turn green with envy and will try anything to put her out of the running.

If she's captured your heart and fancy, woo her full force if your intention is to win her. Shower her with expensive gifts and promise her the moon—if you're in a position to go that far—then you'll find her resistance weakening. It's not that she's such a difficult cookie. She'll probably fuss over you once she's decided you're the man for her. But she does enjoy a lot of attention. What's more, she feels she's entitled to it. Her mild arrogance, though, is becoming. The Leo woman knows how to transform the crime of excessive pride into a very charming misdemeanor. It sweeps most men right off their feet. Those who do not succumb to her leonine charm are few and far between.

If you've got an important business deal to clinch and you have doubts as to whether or not it will go over well, bring your Leo partner along to the business luncheon or cocktail party. It will be a cinch that you'll have the contract in your pocket before the meeting is over. She won't have to say or do anything, just be there at your side. The grouchiest oil magnate can be transformed into a gushing, obedient schoolboy if there's a Leo woman in the room.

If you're a rich Gemini, you may have to see to it that your Leo mate doesn't get too heavy-handed with the charge accounts and credit cards. When it comes to spending, Leos tend to overdo. They're even worse than Geminis. If you're a poor Gemini man, you'll have nothing to worry about because a Leo, with her love of luxury, will most likely never give you the time of day, let alone consent to be your wife.

As a mother, she can be both strict and easygoing. She can pal around with her children and still see to it that they know their places. She won't be so apt to spoil them as you will. Still, she'll be a loving and devoted parent.

GEMINI MAN
VIRGO WOMAN

The Virgo woman may be a little too difficult for you to understand at first. Her waters run deep. Even when you think you do know her, don't take any bets on it. She's capable of keeping things hidden in the deep recesses of her womanly soul—things she'll only release when she's sure that you're the man she's been looking for. It may take her some time to come around to this decision. Virgo women are finicky about almost everything; everything has to be letter-perfect before they're satisfied. Many believe that only Virgos can do things correctly.

Nothing offends a Virgo woman more than slovenly dress, sloppy character, or a careless display of affection. Make sure your tie is straight and that your shoes sport a bright shine before you go calling on this lady. Save your off-color jokes for the locker room; she'll have none of that. Take her arm when crossing the street.

Don't rush the romance. Trying to corner her in the back of a cab may be one way of striking out. Never criticize the way she looks. The best policy would be to agree with her as much as possible. Still, you're an impulsive, direct Gemini; all those dos and don'ts you'll have to observe if you want to get to first base with a Virgo may be too much to ask of you. After a few dates, you may come to the conclusion that she just isn't worth all that trouble. However, the Virgo woman is mysterious enough to keep her men running back for more. Chances are you'll be intrigued by her airs and graces.

Lovemaking means a lot to you. You may be disappointed at first in her cool Virgo ways. However, under her glacial facade there lies a hot cauldron of seething excitement. If you're patient and artful in your romantic approach, you'll find that all the caution was well worth the trouble. When Virgos really love, they don't stint. It's all or nothing. Once they're convinced that they love you, they go all the way, tossing all cares to the wind.

One thing a Virgo woman can't stand in love is hypocrisy. They don't give a hoot about what the neighbors might say if their hearts tell them go ahead. They're very concerned with human truths. So if their hearts stumble upon another fancy, they will be true to that new heartthrob and leave you standing in the rain. She's that honest—to her heart, at any rate. But if you are honest about your interest in her, she'll know and she'll respect and reciprocate your interest. Do her wrong once, however, and you can be sure she'll put an end to the relationship for good.

The Virgo mother has high expectations for her children, and she strives to bring out the very best in them. She is both tender and strict, but always devoted. The youngsters sense her unconditional love for them and are quick to respond.

GEMINI MAN
LIBRA WOMAN

Gemini and Libra combine the airy qualities basic to both your zodiacal signs, so there should be an instant rapport between you. A breezy, chatty friendliness could soon lead to love.

You'll find that a woman born under the sign of Libra is worth more than her weight in gold. She's a woman after your own heart.

With her, you'll always come first—make no mistake about that. She'll always support you 100 percent, no matter what you do. When you ask her advice about almost anything, you'll get a very balanced and realistic opinion. She is good at thinking things out and never lets her emotions run away with her when clear logic is called for.

As a homemaker she is hard to beat. She is very concerned with harmony and balance. You can be sure she'll make your house a joy to live in; she'll see to it that the house is tastefully furnished and decorated. A Libra cannot stand filth or disarray—it gives her goose bumps. Anything that does not radiate harmony, in fact, runs against her orderly grain.

She is chock-full of charm and womanly ways. She can sweep just about any man off his feet with one winning smile. When it comes to using her brains, she can outthink almost anyone and, sometimes, with half the effort. She is diplomatic enough, though, never to let this become glaringly apparent. She may even turn the conversation around so that you think you were the one who thought things up. She couldn't care less, really, just as long as you end up doing what is right.

The Libra woman will put you on a high pedestal. You are her man and her idol. She'll leave all the decision making, large or small, up to you. She's not interested in running things and will only offer her assistance if she feels you really need it.

Some find her approach to reason masculine. However, in the areas of love and affection the Libra woman is all woman. She'll shower you with love and kisses during your romance with her. She doesn't believe in holding out. You shouldn't, either, if you want to hang on to her.

She likes to snuggle up to you in front of the fire on chilly autumn nights. She will bring you breakfast in bed Sunday mornings. She'll be very thoughtful about anything that concerns you. If anyone dares suggest you're not the grandest guy in the world, your Libra is bound to defend you. When she makes those marriage vows, she means every word she says.

The Libra woman will be everything you want her to be. As a wife and mother, her mate as well as her children will never lack for anything that could make their lives easier and richer.

The Libra mother is moderate, even-tempered, and balanced. She creates a gracious, refined family life in which the children grow up to be equal partners in terms of responsibility and privilege. The Libra mother knows that youngsters need both guidance and encouragement in an environment that is harmonious.

GEMINI MAN
SCORPIO WOMAN

The Scorpio woman can be a whirlwind of passion—perhaps too much passion to really suit you. When her temper erupts, you'd better lock up the family heirlooms and take cover from flying objects. But when she chooses to be sweet, her magic is sure to put you under the spell of love.

The Scorpio woman can be as hot as a tamale or as cool as a cucumber. But whatever mood she's in, she's in it for real. She does not believe in poses or putting on airs.

The Scorpio woman is often sultry and seductive—her femme fatale charm can pierce the hardest of hearts like a laser ray. She may not look like Mata Hari (quite often Scorpios resemble the tomboy next door) but once she's fixed you with her tantalizing eyes, you're a goner.

Life with the Scorpio woman will not be all smiles and smooth sailing; when prompted, she can unleash a gale of venom. Generally, she'll have the good grace to keep family battles within the walls of your home. When company visits, she's apt to give the impression that married life with you is one great big joyride. It's just one of her ways of expressing her loyalty to you—at least in front of others. She may fight you tooth and nail in the confines of your home. But during an evening out, she'll hang on your arm and have stars in her eyes.

Scorpio woman are good at keeping secrets. She may even keep a few buried from you if she feels like it.

Never cross her up on even the smallest thing. When it comes to revenge, she's an eye-for-eye woman. She's not too keen on forgiveness—especially when she feels she's been wronged. You'd be well-advised not to give her any cause to be jealous, as difficult as that may sound to Gemini ears. When the Scorpio woman sees green, your life will be made far from rosy. Once she's put you in the doghouse, you can be sure you're going to stay there an awfully long time.

You may find life with the Scorpio woman too draining. Although she may be full of spice, she may not be the kind of partner you'd like to spend the rest of your natural life with. You'd prefer someone gentler and not so hot-tempered; someone who can take the highs with the lows and not bellyache; someone who is flexible and understanding. If you've got your sights set on a shapely Scorpion, forget about that angel of your dreams. A woman born under Scorpio can be heavenly, but she can also be the very devil when she chooses.

As a mother, a Scorpio is protective yet encouraging. She will defend her children against any threat or abuse. Although she adores her children, she will not put them on a pedestal. She is devoted to developing their talents. Under her skillful guidance the youngsters learn how to cope with adversity.

GEMINI MAN
SAGITTARIUS WOMAN

In the astrological scheme of things Sagittarius is the true zodiacal mate of Gemini, but also your zodiacal opposite. With your youthful, adventurous streaks the two of you should be able to experience all the variety of life to the full.

You probably have not encountered a more good-natured woman than the one born under the sign of Sagittarius. They're full of bounce and good cheer. Their sunny dispositions seem permanent and can be relied upon even on the rainiest days.

Women Archers are almost never malicious. If ever they seem to be, it is probably due to the fact that they are often a little short on tact. Sagittarius say literally anything that comes into their heads—no matter what the occasion. Sometimes the words that tumble out of their mouths seem downright cutting and cruel. Still, no matter what she says, she means well. The Sagittarius woman is capable of losing some of her friends—and perhaps even some of yours—through a careless slip of the lip.

On the other hand, you appreciate her honesty and good intentions. To you, qualities of this sort play an important part in life. With a little patience and practice, you can probably help cure your Sagittarius of her loose tongue. In most cases, she'll give in to your better judgment and try to follow your advice to the letter.

Chances are, she'll be the outdoors type. Long hikes, fishing trips, and white-water canoeing will appeal to her. She's a busy person; no one could ever call her a slouch. She sets great store in mobility. Like you, she possesses a pair of itchy feet. She won't sit still for a minute if she doesn't have to.

She is great company most of the time and, generally, lots of fun. Even if your buddies drop by for poker and beer, she won't have any trouble fitting in.

On the whole, she is kind and sympathetic. If she feels she's made a mistake, she'll be the first to call your attention to it. She's not afraid to own up to her faults and shortcomings.

You might lose your patience once or twice with her. After she's seen how upset her shortsightedness or tendency to blabber-mouth has made you, she'll do her best to straighten up.

The Sagittarius woman is not the kind who will pry into your business affairs. But she'll always be there, ready to offer advice if you need it. If you come home from a night out with the boys and you tell your Sagittarius wife that the red stains on your collar came from cranberry sauce and not lipstick, she'll believe you. She'll seldom be suspicious; your word will almost always be good enough for her.

The Sagittarius mother is a wonderful and loving friend to her children. She is always a lively playmate and certainly an encouraging guide. She urges youngsters to study and learn, everything from sociology to sports. She wants the children to have a well-rounded education, the best money can buy.

GEMINI MAN
CAPRICORN WOMAN

If you are not a successful business man, or at least on your way to success, it's possible that a Capricorn woman will have no interest in entering your life. Generally, she's a very security-minded female; she'll see to it that she invests her time only in sure things. Men who whittle away their time with one unsuccessful scheme or another seldom attract a Capricorn. Men who are interested in getting somewhere in life and keep their noses close to the grindstone often have a Capricorn woman behind them, helping them to get ahead.

Although the Goat may be a social climber, she is not what you

could call cruel or hard-hearted. Beneath that cool, seemingly calculating exterior there's a warm and desirable woman. She happens
to think it is just as easy to fall in love with a rich or ambitious man
as it is with a poor or lazy one. She's practical.

The Capricorn woman may be interested in rising to the top, but
she'll never be aggressive about it. She'll seldom step on someone's
feet or nudge competitors away with her elbows. She's quiet about
her desires. She sits, waits, and watches. When an opening or opportunity does appear, she'll latch on to it. For an on-the-move Gemini,
an ambitious Capricorn wife or partner can be quite an asset. She
can probably give you some very good advice about business. When
you invite the boss and his wife for dinner, she'll charm them both.

The Capricorn woman is thorough in whatever she does: cooking, cleaning, making a success out of life. Capricorns are excellent
hostesses as well as guests. Generally, they are very well-mannered
and gracious, no matter what their backgrounds are. They have a
built-in sense of what is right. Crude behavior or a careless faux pas
can offend them no end.

If you should marry a Goat you need never worry about her going
on a wild shopping spree. Capricorns are very careful about every
cent that comes into their hands. They understand the value of
money better than most women and have no room in their lives for
careless spending. If you turn over your paycheck to her at the end of
the week, you can be sure that a good part of it will wind up in the
bank.

Capricorn women are generally very fond of family—their own,
that is. With them, family ties run very deep. Don't make jokes about
her relatives—close or distant. She won't stand for it. It would be
good for you to check out her family before you decide to get down
on bended knee. After your marriage, you'll undoubtedly be seeing
lots of them.

The Capricorn mother is very ambitious for her children. She
wants them to have every advantage and to benefit from things
she perhaps lacked as a child. She will teach the youngsters to be
polite and kind, and to honor traditional codes of conduct. A
Capricorn mother can be correct to a fault. But through her loving devotion, the children are so thoroughly taught that they have
an edge when they are out in the world.

GEMINI MAN
AQUARIUS WOMAN
If you've fallen head over heels for a woman born under the sign of
the Water Bearer, you'd better fasten your safety belt. It may take

you quite a while to actually discover what this dame is like—and even then, you may have nothing to go on but a string of vague hunches. Aquarius is like a rainbow, full of bright and shining hues; she is like no other woman you've ever known. There is something elusive about her, something delightfully mysterious. You'll never be able to put your finger on it. It's nothing calculated, either. An Aquarius doesn't believe in phony charm.

There will never be a dull moment in your life with this Water Bearer woman; she seems to radiate adventure and magic. She'll most likely be the most open-minded and tolerant woman you've ever met. She has a strong dislike for injustice and prejudice. Narrow-mindedness runs against her grain.

She is very independent by nature and capable of shifting for herself. She may receive many proposals for marriage from all sorts of people without ever really taking them seriously. Marriage is a very big step for her; she wants to be sure she knows what she's getting into. If she thinks it will seriously curb her independence, she'll return the engagement ring—if indeed she's let the romance get that far.

The line between friendship and romance is a fuzzy one for an Aquarius. It's not difficult for her to remain buddy-buddy with someone with whom she's just broken off. She's tolerant, remember? So if you should ever see her on the arm of an ex-lover, don't jump to any hasty conclusions.

She's not a jealous person herself and doesn't expect you to be, either. You'll find her pretty much of a free spirit most of the time. Just when you think you know her inside out, you'll discover that you don't really know her at all.

She's a very sympathetic and warm person; she can be helpful to people in need of assistance and advice.

The Aquarius woman is like a chameleon in some respects; she can fit in anywhere without looking like she doesn't belong.

She'll seldom be suspicious even if she has every right to be. If the man she loves allows himself a little fling, chances are she'll just turn her head the other way and pretend not to notice that the gleam in his eye is not meant for her. That's pretty understanding! Still, a man married to an Aquarius should never press his luck. Her tolerance does have its limits.

The Aquarius mother is generous and seldom refuses her children anything. Being an air sign like your mate, you both might spoil the children with too much of everything. But the Aquarius mother knows how to prepare the youngsters to get along in life. Her tolerant, open-minded attitude will rub off on the children.

GEMINI MAN
PISCES WOMAN

Many a man dreams of a Pisces lover. You're perhaps no exception. She's alluring and exotic yet capable of total commitment to her man. She's full of imagination and emotion, while at the same time being soft, cuddly, and domestic.

She'll let you be the brains of the family; she's contented to play a behind the scenes role in order to help you achieve your goals. The illusion that you are the master of the household is the kind of magic that the Pisces woman is adept at creating.

She can be very ladylike and proper. Your business associates and friends will be dazzled by her warmth and femininity. Although she's a charmer, there is a lot more to her than just a pretty exterior. There is a brain ticking away behind that soft, womanly facade. You may never become aware of it—that is, until you're married to her. It's no cause for alarm because she'll most likely never use it against you, only to help you and possibly set you on a more successful path.

If she feels you're botching up your married life through careless behavior or if she feels you could be earning more money than you do, she'll tell you about it. But any wife would, really. She will never try to usurp your position as head and breadwinner of the family.

No one had better dare say one uncomplimentary word about you in her presence. It's likely to cause her to break into tears. Pisces women are usually very sensitive beings. Their reaction to adversity, frustration, or anger is just a plain, good, old-fashioned cry. They can weep buckets when inclined.

She can do wonders with a house. She is very fond of dramatic and beautiful things. There will always be plenty of fresh-cut flowers around the house. She will choose charming artwork and antiques, if they are affordable. She'll see to it that the house is decorated in a dazzling yet welcoming style.

She'll have an extra special dinner prepared for you when you come home from an important business meeting. Don't dwell on the boring details of the meeting, though. But if you need that grand vision, the big idea, to seal a contract or make a conquest, your Pisces woman is sure to confide a secret that will guarantee your success. She is canny and shrewd with money, and once you are on her wavelength you can manage the intricacies on your own.

Treat her with tenderness and generosity and your relationship will be an enjoyable one. She's most likely fond of chocolates. A bunch of beautiful flowers will never fail to make her eyes light up. See to it that you never forget her birthday or your anniversary. These things are very important to her. If you let them slip your mind, you'll send her into a crying fit that could last a considerable length of time.

If you are patient and kind, you can keep a Pisces woman happy for a lifetime. She, however, is not without her faults. Her sensitivity may get on your nerves after a while. You may even feel that she uses her tears as a method of getting her own way.

The Pisces mother totally believes in her children, and that faith never wavers. Her unconditional love for them makes her a strong, self-sacrificing mother. That means she can deny herself in order to fulfill their needs. She will teach her youngsters the value of service to the community while not letting them lose their individuality.

GEMINI
LUCKY NUMBERS 2010

Lucky numbers and astrology can be linked through the movements of the Moon. Each phase of the thirteen Moon cycles vibrates with a sequence of numbers for your Sign of the Zodiac over the course of the year. Using your lucky numbers is a fun system that connects you with tradition.

New Moon	First Quarter	Full Moon	Last Quarter
Dec. 15 ('09)	Dec. 24 ('09)	Dec. 31 ('09)	Jan. 7
7 9 4 5	2 4 8 2	2 9 9 7	7 7 3 5
Jan. 15	Jan. 23	Jan. 30	Feb. 5
2 9 8 4	0 5 6 3	9 9 4 7	5 4 2 3
Feb. 13	Feb. 21	Feb. 28	March 7
8 8 1 5	8 9 6 3	7 1 8 0	7 5 6 2
March 15	March 23	March 29	April 6
2 4 4 8	2 8 5 9	3 1 1 7	7 8 4 6
April 14	April 21	April 28	May 5
1 2 8 5	5 2 6 9	7 0 4 5	1 3 7 1
May 13	May 20	May 27	June 4
1 8 5 2	2 6 8 6	0 3 4 9	9 2 6 7
June 12	June 18	June 26	July 4
2 4 0 5	5 8 6 2	1 0 6 8	6 8 3 4
July 11	July 18	July 25	August 3
1 8 7 2	5 3 2 8	8 9 5 7	2 3 9 6
August 9	August 16	August 24	Sept. 1
5 1 4 2	2 0 8 9	5 9 2 6	7 4 0 5
Sept. 8	Sept. 15	Sept. 23	Sept. 30
9 8 6 5	0 3 4 9	9 2 7 8	2 6 9 3
Oct. 7	Oct. 14	Oct. 22	Oct. 30
3 7 0 4	4 5 1 3	3 7 2 8	5 0 3 9
Nov. 6	Nov. 13	Nov. 21	Nov. 28
1 1 7 8	8 4 6 1	1 2 2 8	3 6 4 0
Dec. 5	Dec. 13	Dec. 21	Dec. 27
0 1 2 7	7 7 9 4	5 2 4 8	2 9 8 9

GEMINI
YEARLY FORECAST 2010

*Forecast for 2010 Concerning Business
and Financial Affairs, Job Prospects,
Travel, Health, Romance and Marriage
for Persons Born with the Sun
in the Zodiacal Sign of Gemini.
May 21–June 20*

For those born under the influence of the Sun in the zodiacal sign of Gemini, ruled by Mercury, planet of intellect, logic, and communication, 2010 promises to be a year of grand opportunity, roller-coaster risk, and strategic cooperation. Jump on the chance for exciting career prospects. Year 2010 is one of the best you'll have for your career, which is definitely saying something. During the time benefact planet Jupiter is in Pisces, doors are opening everywhere, all promising success and recognition.

Financial affairs can fluctuate, requiring you to be sensitive to moods and shifts in sentiment as well as capable of seizing the moment. Eclipses are a high-priority event for your money matters. This year kicks off with a peak solar eclipse in mid-January. So you're put on notice to make budgets and earnings a major concern. The trick will be borrowing enough to expand and invest without going too far that you can't pay the debt. By mid-year you will know whether you're on track, so make adjustments as necessary. In December the offer of a partnership with a person who complements your skills and resources should be given serious consideration as an avenue of greater wealth. The best period for accumulating savings and making wise spending decisions occurs from mid-May through July. Manage finances flexibly and responsively while you consider bold moves to enhance your income. June through August can be the time of pouncing on positions that offer wages. There may be fantastic openings in your field for improved earnings, possibly the best opportunities in a decade. Don't be suckered into debt you can't afford just because you've arrived in a higher income bracket. There's no need to impress or outdo friends with flashy purchases and displays of wealth. Families may be a major source of expense, whether it's housing, feeding, clothing, or

129

educating them. Determine the minimum amount you need by the start of September, then work hard until the end of October to earn whatever is required.

Jupiter in Pisces nine months of the year shines bountiful rays on your career. You can rise to the top of your profession or industry, achieving unparalleled recognition and even a dose of fame and celebrity. Believe you deserve it. Believe you are really capable of a position of high esteem. Success will come down to self-belief and self-confidence, especially when you're faced with searching questions at tough interviews, or when you need to handle rough-and-tumble competitors on the way to the top. It won't be all hard work and slogging effort. It could happen effortlessly and swiftly, especially if you're intuitive enough to put yourself in the right place at the right time. Move with speed, seize the moment when it arrives. There will be no prizes for coming in second or procrastinating with uncertainty. In May you could be restrained by responsibilities at home, which may limit the energy and time you have to pursue worldly ambitions. Some Geminis may feel passed over by management for a promotion you deserved, or you've missed the boat in some other way. But the tide turns mid-year. Despite doubts or desperation you harbor at the end of July, by the end of October a big chance or lucky break will arrive. Leading up to this, you could feel stuck in a dead end spinning your wheels, especially in the first quarter of the year. Use this slow period to learn more, to take courses that prepare you for better options. Bide your time through the middle of the year, working around the home and pursuing creative activities that are relaxing and fun. Once autumn arrives, the right job openings become available, and you'll have the drive to make them happen.

As much as Geminis have a reputation for travel and mobility, it's really about a sense of regular motion from day to day, which changes the scene without straying too far from home. So when the mood strikes, take those day trips and short hops you enjoy so much. June and late July though the first half of August are both fine times for this sort of tripping around. You'll be vitalized and rejuvenated by the experience. The periods when your ruling planet Mercury is retrograde are best not scheduled for travel. Mercury retrograde occurs from late 2009 to January 15, April 18 to May 11, August 20 to September 12, and December 10 to 30. If you must journey at these times, be patient for possible delays and mishaps. Overseas trips are seasonally best from late January through February. However, this may not be the best year for such ventures. And that's not because you wouldn't enjoy the journey but because personal responsibilities may keep you tied to home base. Traveling to specific foreign destinations for a dose of high culture and the traditional arts can be an exceptional and memorable experience. Such a trip would be best planned for August and September, while avoiding actual transit during the tricky Mercury retrograde period in the middle.

As the year proceeds, remaining at peak fitness and in good health could be easier said than done. A strong combination of planets in Capricorn signals a heavy mental burden that might narrow your focus and weigh you down with negative expectations. Your usual sense of fun may go missing. The recreational interests that would help to relieve tension and dissipate worry might be put on hold or curtailed altogether. Rather than succumbing to this limited frame of reference, fight hard to sustain a proud sense of surviving and prospering with a smile on your face. Walk, run, or cycle daily to experience a sense of movement and circulation as well as to maintain good breathing practices. Use the motivation of a group experience to involve you in disciplined exercise, whatever form it takes. Active participation in various learning experiences will benefit well-being, stimulate your interest in people, knowledge, and the world around you, and give you a reason to live with a sense of purpose. Meditation is also a great health tool and preventive medicine. Your mind can be a forceful agent for good or ill health. You need clarity and discipline for top functioning. July and August are the months to watch for deteriorating lifestyle and for signs of emergent ailments. Playing hard and burning the candle at both ends can be detrimental. A desire for pure pleasure at the expense of all else will have consequences. If you need to get back on track with a sustainable lifestyle, make that effort late summer to early autumn. Then by late October you should be reaping the benefits.

Single Geminis may find that the first part of the year offers limited opportunities for love and romance. You may be too busy at work. You may have moved to a different location where you just don't know many people. A turn for the better is foreseen in spring. Your social life expands, even explodes through the summer, bringing dynamic and spirited characters into your circle of friends. The workplace is a fertile ground for potential partners, dates, and companions. Sometimes work and love relationships are not a good mix, but this year is an exception to that rule. Let the good times roll might be your motto during July and August. Fun abounds, and there won't be any shortage of playmates. But just when you are getting used to this footloose and fancy-free lifestyle, along comes that special someone. A delightful courtship may rapidly escalate into a full-blown relationship. That may come as a surprise, something you hadn't intended at all.

For partnered Geminis, 2010 could be the year you make a public gesture concerning a long-term relationship that has not yet been formalized. You could finally announce that you're ready to tie the knot and settle down. Celebrate in grand fashion with a fabulous wedding witnessed by everyone you know. Such a commitment is likely in late spring, perhaps closing in on your birthday. Then there's a strong prospect for settling down in relatively conservative security, with a home you can call your own and the desire to raise a family. Gemini women may face the unavoidable choice between having kids or pursuing a career. You can do both, determined to do justice to both so that neither one suffers. Simplify the daily routine so it is sustainable. Share responsibility with a partner so you do not feel cramped as an individual. The dual roles of career maker and home-maker can be managed successfully. Having children is a strong like-lihood for Gemini in 2010 because Saturn is in Libra, your solar house of children, from January to early April and late July into 2012. Saturn in Libra signals a natural period for you to commit to parent-hood.

Ambition and luck play important roles this year, helping Gemini individuals get where you want to go. A combination of self-discipline and opportunism can make the journey safe and lead to a prosperous outcome.

GEMINI DAILY FORECAST

January–December 2010

JANUARY

1. FRIDAY. Lively. As this year begins, intuitive leaps and bright ideas lead to fresh, exciting directions. Opportunities for making money may come your way spontaneously, just waiting for you to pick up the ball and run with it. Rather than getting tied up in other people's issues and agendas, go solo for the day. Let personal urges arise naturally as you follow your Gemini feelings. Make a clear decision to leave the past behind, cutting ties with outworn relationships that have been weighing you down. Repaying debt and lightening the load of unnecessary expenses could be a practical priority. Contact with an old friend can renew a special relationship, which will blossom in the coming months.

2. SATURDAY. Steady. Sticking to the usual routine of weekend recreation will deliver expected satisfaction. There is no need to reinvent the wheel or seek far horizons of adventure and excitement. It's all there at your front door, in ordinary activities you'd normally pursue. Traditional arts and crafts can be especially fulfilling. Counter your tendency for novel twists with a genuine appreciation of time-honored pastimes and their conservative techniques. Steady neighbors and older relatives are a ready source of enjoyable, easygoing company. Your interest in a certain individual may not be reciprocated. Don't waste time pursuing anyone who isn't available or interested.

3. SUNDAY. Hopeful. An imaginative mental journey suits the mood today. Curl up in a warm, cozy space with a novel that transports you into another time and place. Movies, music, and art also offer special doorways to other worlds. You need an influx of ideas and conversations that invoke inspiration, hope, and positive potential, even when it all seems like a pipe dream or a bridge too far. Nothing happens without a concept or vision coming first, followed by the clear intention to follow through. Dream harder and larger, especially where exotic travel or exceptional educational aspirations are in the frame. Political discussion may pose questions about what you truly stand for.

4. MONDAY. Sharing. You are apt to feel like staying home, work or no work, especially if the weather is bleak, chilly, damp, and miserable. At least follow your inclinations and remain indoors as much as possible. Creating a cozy love nest might be a strong inducement to take the day off. Gemini romantics are on a high, with a relationship blossoming as the Sun and Venus hook up in the sky. Listening is a key to better interactions, and there's much to learn from other people. No matter how much you want to interject your opinion and have your say, hold your tongue for a change and hear something from a source other than your own mind. Solving problems may seem tricky but can be accomplished with application and patience.

5. TUESDAY. Settling. You may feel a sudden urge to entertain at home or to invite guests to share your space. This desire to connect with people on your territory is apt to involve business and financial negotiations. Geminis who are in the process of selling property will find plenty of interest from potential buyers. Hosting an open house should help to make a quick sale and seal the deal. Or you could be engaged in purchasing real estate, shopping around for a suitable place and advantageous loan arrangements. Setting up home-based employment can open new avenues for income while saving on travel and other expenses. Be sure you have suitable insurance and a retirement savings plan.

6. WEDNESDAY. Demanding. As much as you'd like to lighten up and have fun, it could be hard to do so. You might receive negative news concerning a partner's finances or your own. Debts can become burdensome, and tax issues need calm, focused attention. This represents an opportunity to make your financial affairs more manageable, getting them under control before it is too late. You may need to consult with creditors, an accountant, or others. Better to act now when you have real choices, rather than letting matters slide and then facing consequences that are out of your hands.

Gemini parents may face tough decisions concerning children and what can and can't be afforded.

7. THURSDAY. Useful. Sticking to your own interests makes good sense, because coordinating and cooperating with anyone else could prove more trouble than it's worth. Trying to develop skill in a sport or hobby with the help of a coach or expert may lead to misunderstandings and even arguments because you and they are not on the same wavelength. However, teaching yourself from a book or from an online source will help you grasp key theoretical concepts. Travel for pleasure is likely to inspire you to further global exploration. Learning a foreign language comes easily now. Enjoying a night of culture at the opera or an exhibit can be shared with the right companion.

8. FRIDAY. Purposeful. If you're feeling out of sorts in any way, make an appointment with your health practitioner. Even if you can't get in to see them today, at least you will have taken appropriate steps. A loved one will appreciate your support, especially with financial or career matters. What they may really need is to communicate their concerns directly and obtain your encouragement. You don't need try to fix their problems, just be a sensitive listener so they feel heard. If you're in the process of hiring an employee or contractor, give them a trial period to prove themselves before signing any binding contract that will lock you in.

9. SATURDAY. Cautious. Take your time with stressful physical tasks, driving, or using tools and machinery. The chance of a mishap is higher than normal, making appropriate care and caution essential. Don't skip safety procedures and checklists in an effort to speed things up. It's easy to blurt out words in a moment of anger or frustration, but you will regret it later. What's said and done can't be taken back or undone, so think twice before letting blind impulse seize control. If you do offend someone, go out of your way to apologize and make amends. They are likely to be forgiving and understanding, at least this time around. Service to loved ones will be much appreciated.

10. SUNDAY. Promising. Spending time with someone on work-related matters is part of today's picture. There may be a special long-term strategy or vision you're tackling together. Collaboration will provide mutual inspiration and levelheaded objectivity as you cross-check and validate each other's input. There could be a dimension of romance in the mix as well, which develops into deeper feelings in the days ahead. Married or partnered Geminis should devote quality time to that special person, lifting their spirits with gestures of affection and care. Single Geminis will have little difficulty finding an almost perfect companion, for the moment, wherever you go or whatever you do.

11. MONDAY. Happy. As the Sun and Venus combine energies, this becomes a potent day for love and all affairs of the heart. However, the relationships that need most effort are those you've already established rather than anything new or unknown. Forestall a tendency to look for greener pastures; focus on what's already in your own backyard. Passion runs hot this evening, so set the scene appropriately, making sure there will be no distractions or interruptions. Financial matters also look fortunate. This is a starred day to meet with an adviser to arrange investments or a loan which will enhance your future wealth. Businesses that involve fashion, health, and the arts are all potential winners.

12. TUESDAY. Bumpy. Just when you think you've got it together, things can fall apart, at least temporarily. Accept changes of plan as they arise, and respond in the moment rather than dwelling on how things should be or what you had expected. Even better results and consequences may emerge from a brief chaotic period that you never anticipated. As a Gemini you are probably an old hand at handling disruption, so make the most of this talent. Your flexible adaptability is a real strength. Expecting other people to be predictable or reliable in the current circumstances would be foolish. Promises and contracts could be hard to keep, so they're better not made at all or left until later.

13. WEDNESDAY. Challenging. Saturn has reached its highwater mark for the first half of this year, which means that certain affairs have gone as far as they currently can. However, that doesn't force you to stop trying or to stop efforts to progress and succeed. It does mean you need to be realistic about your expectations and pragmatic regarding strategies. Allow enough time for projects to become solidly established and to deliver results. Don't be discouraged by pessimism or resistance from other people. There are bound to be obstacles that must be overcome. When the going gets tough, the tough get going with persistence and discipline. Professional advice may not be what you want to hear but is probably worthwhile nonetheless.

14. THURSDAY. Smooth. The New Moon is occurring in a quieter time of the month, allowing for reflection, rest, and regrouping. However, tonight discloses a solar eclipse, heralding a socially active period where older people seem most important for you. Interactions and encounters may be a mix of serious and upbeat. An unexpected job offer might come your way with improved conditions as part of the allure. This offer may also include greater responsibility and longer hours, which will cut into your leisure and family time. An absence can affect your social circle, whether it's a relative, friend, or associate. Yet there can be some unexpected benefit for you as a consequence.

15. FRIDAY. Calm. Love grows stronger in difficult circumstances, which may have been the case recently. The challenge is to keep moving on, remaining open to opportunity and change in order to create the future you truly desire. You will have the undying support and affection of a partner, close friend, or family member who wants the best for you. Trust their genuine feelings and let them help you with any fears, anxieties, or difficulties. No doubt you'll have the chance to return the favor in times to come. If you've been feeling claustrophobic lately, venture out and about into the wider world. A sporting event, cultural happening, or learning experience can be stimulating fun.

16. SATURDAY. Exciting. Sports fans may have a big game to look forward to. Whether you see it live or on television, there will be plenty of excitement and action. For Geminis who prefer more refined entertainment, a movie or show with high drama, tension, and a dangerous edge might be just the ticket. Outdoor enthusiasts will be looking for adventure with an adrenaline buzz. Guard against letting an urge for thrills lead to an accident or harmful incident. Travelers will be eager to get moving, especially if the trip had to be delayed for a while. Nevertheless, it's wise to be thoroughly prepared before departing. Hasty moves might foment trouble you neither want nor need. A rude encounter can be unnerving.

17. SUNDAY. Extraordinary. You are apt to be moved to contemplate the mystery of life and your existence. If you have a committed faith, this is an inspiring spiritual period to immerse yourself in uplifting ritual and devotion. A transcendent experience can occur through reading a captivating novel, seeing a great film, or watching an awesome performance by a gifted artist. This is the sort of day when you intuitively understand there's more to art than mere entertainment. Let yourself be swept away on the magic carpet ride of imagination and fantasy, however it happens. Plan an exotic travel itinerary by surfing relevant websites and checking the travel section of today's newspaper.

18. MONDAY. Variable. The heavens are full of notable events. Saturn and Mercury are bringing extra pressure to bear on Gemini health, family, finances, and studies. Jupiter is doing its yearly change of signs, moving from Aquarius into Pisces. This is less helpful for Geminis, adding excess and confusion to your relationship and career experiences. There may be too many opportunities coming at you all at once, making choice difficult. The options could all look great, but only a few or even just one will prove right for you. This is a test of wisdom, where you need to trust your intuition more than your head. Being greedy or biting off more than you can chew is likely to backfire.

19. TUESDAY. Responsive. Expect an increasingly busy day on the work front, as important people demand personal service and attention from you. A meeting with higher-ups will need you to be organized and ready for anything. Long-term customers may be seeking a face-to-face meeting concerning certain problems, difficulties, or complaints. Or there may be significant negotiations and a deal that need your input and professional expertise. Whatever situation you're handling, cut to the chase for quick satisfaction and speedy results. Once you've dealt with obligations and responsibilities, follow any spontaneous opportunities and suggestions that arise later.

20. WEDNESDAY. Motivating. Friends and associates in high places or faraway lands could get in touch. Information they provide should motivate you to take action with a group endeavor. Representing a political cause can put you in the hot seat, but diplomacy is likely to work better than confrontation. If you can stay calm and cool even under pressure, there will be a happy ending to a potentially tense and stressful situation. The law is on your side, and right prevails over might. An arduous but satisfying journey may get under way now. Putting theory into practice will sort winners from also-rans, so don't be shy about putting your best foot forward and making necessary moves.

21. THURSDAY. Positive. Circumstances lately have been toughening you up to the unavoidable necessity of making direct decisions in difficult situations. When you're feeling between a rock and a hard place, the right support and backup makes all the difference. You have good people behind you, so proceed decisively and with confidence. Talking the talk means you also need to walk the walk, and you can do it. A male neighbor can become a firm friend because of certain shared experiences that create a bond of trust. Turn to a brother or other relative when you need someone to tell you the whole truth. Participating in a community or team activity can involve a quick journey.

22. FRIDAY. Idealistic. Group learning can energize and intrigue you. Vistas of knowledge unfurling in your mind's eye will inspire your career ambitions. Follow up dreams and hunches connected to education or foreign destinations. Travel and study are priorities in this period, and your direction in this regard will become clearer as the days unfold. A friend may prove loyalty to you through a self-less act on your behalf. The old saying that blood is thicker than water may also become very relevant as kinship and family ties take priority in the social sphere of your life. Acting from your highest ideals makes all the difference to a sense of meaning and personal integrity.

23. SATURDAY. Subdued. Time out is called for after this dramatic, active workweek. Private pleasures have been earned and deserved. Enjoy yourself in a place of sanctuary where you will be undisturbed. Certain people might attempt to drag you out with tempting promises of good times and high-spirited adventures. However, you'll be better off with only your own company just now. External events are not only likely to disappoint you but will distract from important inner goals and individual experiences you can only have independently. Sharing your deepest thoughts and concerns with a trusted intimate may be a good way to achieve better understanding of your circumstances. Ignore irrelevant distractions.

24. SUNDAY. Fair. Getting perspective sometimes requires looking calmly from a position in the background and watching the world go by. That is advisable for Geminis today, despite your natural inclination to get involved in all the action. To gain greater understanding of your primary relationships, simply listen carefully to other people and read between the lines. If you allow emotional expression to emerge and arise naturally, you'll learn a lot about yourself and others. Get some extra rest, perhaps even an afternoon snooze or early bedtime. Relaxing by doing what you enjoy most can help slow you down. Take a break for the good of your body and soul. You'll then be fit to tackle the week ahead.

25. MONDAY. Opportune. Your popularity is on the rise and could even become a bit overwhelming. This is a fine time for promoting yourself in your career and in business. Publicize your name and talents with eye-catching, effective advertising. Soon you are apt to have more customers and clients than you can handle, which is surely a good thing. Being lazy is not an option because great opportunities could simply vanish down the drain. Even if you have a lot to handle, disciplined organization and appropriate scheduling can ensure managing the workload effectively. Part of remaining capable and competent depends on taking time out for exercise and recreation to balance your lifestyle.

26. TUESDAY. Focused. Build on the attention and profile you've recently established. Take full advantage of whatever minor celebrity or notoriety has come your way. Rely on visual, graphic, and artistic forms of communication to get ideas across. Attempts at making your point only through words and text could fall on deaf ears because certain people may not be on your wavelength. However, a picture will be worth a thousand words. Travel can be a better experience if you go with a companion or guide who already knows the route, the customs, and the locale. Make a push to get things done as quickly and early as possible, before confusion and chaos descend to upset plans and schedules.

27. WEDNESDAY. Beneficial. The money should flow in despite any negative expectations or anxieties you may be privately harboring. Determine to be optimistic rather than pessimistic and you'll make the most of current opportunities. There's no point worrying that you're not having enough fun, when in fact it's all about working and making a buck. Leave playtime for later and get right down to business. The urge to spend a bonus or extra cash can be strong, but in hindsight you will probably wish you had resisted. Gemini parents can be concerned about the welfare of a child. Youngsters need you to set a good example rather than burden them with arbitrary discipline or disapproval.

28. THURSDAY. Helpful. By taking a progressive approach to finances, you can solve any problems and enhance current opportunities. If you are struggling with existing debt, discuss this situation with lenders and try to renegotiate your obligations. It's not enough to rely on instinct or fly by the seat of your pants where money is concerned. Instead, seek appropriate professional advice so your affairs become well ordered and manageable. Once you take charge, new possibilities will open up. An unusual business suggestion may come your way, maybe even from your boss or top management of your company. Be receptive if given a chance to walk the road less traveled.

29. FRIDAY. Active. Tonight's Full Moon could mark the start of a journey that makes you some real money. Geminis who travel for business are sure to make a success of the current venture and will be well satisfied with the outcome. Good contacts are waiting as you purposefully enlarge your network. This could also be a time when you make a decisive commitment to an educational course designed to improve your earning capacity. Establishing relationships with other people who share your enthusiasm for a particular subject will propel you on a trajectory of exciting learning. A developing attraction for a neighbor or someone you see daily can strike an obstacle. Be patient rather than giving up.

30. SATURDAY. Imaginative. A fascination with exotic foreign countries can be a welcome relief to humdrum reality. It's okay to take a detour from ordinary life and dream yourself into alternative environments and scenarios. You could even determine to book a flight and accommodations for your next vacation. Reading books, magazines, and newspapers won't be as satisfying as real-world meetings and conversations. Meet up for a coffee with neighbors or relatives to catch up on the latest gossip and intrigue. A friend or loved one currently out of town or out of country will appreciate a call or e-mail from you. Live theater, a concert performance, or a dramatic movie offers an escapist outlet.

31. SUNDAY. Encouraging. Being with family members will suit you best. This is the right time for a roundtable discussion of important domestic issues and work-related concerns. A get-together of all household members is important so that everyone stays in touch. Share a meal and listen to one another's stories of the past week. Ideas for renovating or improving your living space can begin to percolate. Go slow with the initial planning stage so there's room for changes and new concepts as the final design takes shape. Visiting parents or in-laws can be a priority, especially if they need your care or assistance. Geminis who are hoping to sell property or find another place to live should make some valuable progress.

FEBRUARY

1. MONDAY. Progressive. Good communication flows between members of the household, making this a fine time for serious discussion of any significant imminent decisions. Parents may need to have a serious talk with children, even if they're already quite mature. Certain facts of life need to be laid bare for them so they can continue to grow into responsible adults. Inquiries into getting a loan for a real estate purchase or renegotiating a current mortgage should be satisfying, saving you money and offering greater personal security. Listing a home for sale should produce ready buyers willing to pay a reasonable price. There's good news regarding a loved one's salary and career, bringing greater abundance to be shared.

2. TUESDAY. Challenging. Anticipate a much tougher day than yesterday, one which won't be for the fainthearted. Prepare for the challenges that lay ahead as you walk out the door this morning. The burden of other people's problems can seem to fall on you, whether you think that's fair or not. In truth you probably want to help, but be realistic about how much you can actually do. Some folk will just want you to listen briefly to their tale of woe. However, there will be those you must refuse to help further because they want you to do all the fixing for them. Immediately tackle the hardest tasks without delay. You'll then be glad that's done, and more pleasant activities and experiences lay in store.

3. WEDNESDAY. Happy. There's opportunity for good times if you focus your attention positively. The potential exists to debate with those who think they know better or have more experience. You're never going to persuade them otherwise, so don't even bother. Materialistic considerations can weigh you down. Certain individuals only can think in terms of the bottom line. As an antidote, expand your horizons with a new enjoyable pastime. Learn more about what interests you most. Go to an exhibit, museum, or concert. Love and joy awaits in the wider world beyond the confines of office, workplace, and domestic necessity. The world will prove to be a wonderful place if you take the time to explore.

4. THURSDAY. Upbeat. It's your lucky day, but it happens in the most ordinary of circumstances. The right attitude to your daily routine should produce better results than hoped for. Magical opportunities may develop while you are just doing your job, whether at the office or at home. Gemini job seekers should make an extra effort because prospects for finding a satisfying position are good. Employers will easily attract great potential employees, ready and willing to help build greater success in your enterprise. Any health problem can be overcome with appropriate remedies and won't be serious. Doing the right thing at work brings deserved rewards. If this effort makes you tense or stressed, don't take it out on anyone else this evening.

5. FRIDAY. Frustrating. Practical tasks could produce a high level of frustration. Do-it-yourself fixes and maintenance that initially looked simple may need the assistance of a professional. If a neighbor or relative offers a helping hand, it might be better to politely refuse; good intentions won't prevent problems from happening if neither of you actually know what you're doing. Putting knowledge into practice is often harder than it looks, so be patient with the process. Be wary of losing your temper or impulsively breaking something. Deal with the small stuff and let the bigger picture take care of itself. Religion and politics in the workplace won't be a good brew.

6. SATURDAY. Slow. Take it easy and don't schedule anything complex for today. You could benefit from extra rest, even if there's work you feel you must do. This is the wrong time to let guilt or a false sense of duty drive the agenda. If you keep hammering away at the to-do list, it may actually grow longer due to mistakes being made. Leave well enough alone for the moment and enjoy some time out. Order food to be delivered rather than cooking. If you must go out this evening, have a nap beforehand. Also make sure directions and timing are clear. Hearing the concerns of someone close may arouse doubt or anxiety, but this could simply be a misunderstanding of their situation.

7. SUNDAY. Interactive. Expect a few lively personal encounters, and positive ones at that. Any recent differences with a relative or neighbor can be smoothed over and resolved. A deal with a contractor for routine repairs and maintenance can be arranged swiftly and effectively, freeing up time for more enjoyable activities. You'll benefit from being coached and tutored in a subject or skill where you want learning to progress quickly. Take a trip with your mate, partner, or another companion to explore locally, appreciating quality time together. If you don't want to go too far, just take a stroll or bicycle ride around the neighborhood. Singles can meet a potential date while out cruising.

8. MONDAY. Erratic. This is the sort of day that makes you think some people are just plain crazy. It's going to be hard to depend on anyone, as topsy-turvy incidents put everything in a spin. Try to accommodate changes which seem to be everywhere. Meetings and appointments are likely to be rescheduled at the last minute. Deals and agreements may descend into unresolved renegotiation, making it difficult to know where you stand at the moment. A family member could maddeningly change their mind more than once. Fortunately you, as a Gemini, are flexible, making it easier to adapt. It's important to maintain your good reputation by informing other involved people of any delays or problems as they arise.

9. TUESDAY. Pressured. Experiences may be somewhat mixed, with career and professional matters making steady progress while personal issues become decidedly problematic. If someone has disputes with you, they're likely to confront you. Debts or overdue payments can't be put off forever, and time's running out for extending them. Pressure is being applied all the way down the line, providing little allowance for extenuating circumstances. School fees, alimony payments, or other expenses involving children can be a significant burden. However, prospects at work give hope of being better paid in the period ahead. Your mate or partner's family may be helpful and supportive financially.

10. WEDNESDAY. Supportive. This is an important time for Gemini parents to bond with kids. Youngsters want approval and quality attention, as well as the benefit of your experience. Special relationships can be forged with those who share your favorite hobbies and sports. Better cooperation and deeper trust can be built within work groups by scheduling recreational experiences together. Artists and creative types are in a great position to negotiate the sale of their work at fair prices. If you are seeking company you will find it readily. However, the more specialized your interests, the fewer people there will be who fill the bill. Let newcomers prove themselves before you jump to any conclusions or judge them.

11. THURSDAY. Helpful. The early part of the day will be most exciting and eventful. Get out and about first thing to catch all the action and opportunities being offered. This is especially important for job seekers and house hunters. Be ready for a spontaneous interview regarding a position or property. Events are apt to unfold much faster than you ever expected. There may be a need to help a parent or other older person with their financial affairs. Be patient, allowing them enough time to get organized and to understand what you want them to do. Respect goes a long way in creating and maintaining good relationships, so be aware of the standards of behavior that are expected in every situation.

12. FRIDAY. Active. Communications are firing on all cylinders, and you'll be in your element handling calls and fielding inquiries. Keep conversations short, sharp, and to the point. No one will be in the mood for wasting time in idle chat and gossip. Official correspondence can be dealt with effectively and to the satisfaction of all. If you need to launch a legal matter or connect with bureaucrats, this is a perfect time to do so. Some Geminis may be traveling with a focused purpose to fulfill a long-held plan or strategy. Whether a journey is short or long, it should be useful and rewarding. Pay close attention and take extra care when driving or using power tools.

13. SATURDAY. Expansive. Not only is the approaching New Moon in Aquarius, a fellow air sign, but both Mercury and Venus have changed signs. So this marks a period of fresh energy and different styles. The Chinese New Year kicks in, making this a good day for reflecting on the goals and objectives you want to achieve in the months ahead. Plans could center on travel, education, politics, and religious experience. It's also worth creating a long-term perspective for any business or enterprise with which you're associated, especially one that is all your own. Get a good night's sleep. There's every chance that a significant and revealing dream will point the way to achieving future success.

14. SUNDAY. Lovely. It's a perfect romantic day for lovers and sweethearts, as the Moon joins Venus and Jupiter in gentle Pisces. All of these planets are strong in Pisces, offering their very best qualities for happiness, joy, and good fortune. The challenge for mercurial Geminis is to step out of your heads, stop thinking so much, and to let feelings and emotion flow freely. Special touches of affection and gifts of appreciation will speak volumes about the truth of your heart. Relations with your partner's family can be especially good now, so enjoy spending time with relatives and in-laws. Although it is the weekend, a great job opportunity could land at your door.

15. MONDAY. Lucky. Positive energy and good vibes keep flowing from yesterday, infecting the workplace with happy attitudes and good humor. It's as if everyone is in tune with life and each other, making this a very pleasant day to be on the job. This is the best possible time to approach the boss for a raise, bonus, promotion, or better working conditions. It's also an excellent period for promoting a venture by advertising goods and services in the grandest manner affordable. Launching an enterprise now should lead to very favorable outcomes. Your current peak of ambition and confidence can transport you to the next level of success. Aim high, and settle for nothing less than your best effort.

16. TUESDAY. Stimulating. On this surprise day you should expect the unexpected. Don't imagine it will be difficult or anxious. Rather, the experiences should be good, putting a new spin on your potential, especially regarding your career. Starting a different job or in a new field can be refreshing, exciting, and invigorating. Challenges and roles you've never experienced before lend a buzz and provide a much needed antidote for creeping boredom and the dull predictability that existed in a previous situation. A sudden windfall could fatten your wallet, perhaps because you're simply in the right place at the right time. Get the most out of the day, but make it an early night.

17. WEDNESDAY. Testy. A loose comment or smart wisecrack could land you in hot water. Avoid the temptation to answer back or give someone lip. Be wary of biting off more than you can chew. Even friendly jibes and joking around can make trouble for you, so stay on the side of polite diplomacy. It can be hard to take direction from a bossy control freak, especially if you don't like or respect that person. However, you'll need to bend to the one who holds the reins of power, like it or not. With the right attitude, it's actually possible to learn something important, although the style of delivery may be intentionally confrontational. Be open to new knowledge; you don't know it all already.

18. THURSDAY. Sociable. Try as you may, it isn't possible to get along with everybody. It's unrealistic to expect that all people you encounter will like you or approve of you. Nevertheless, it's important to distinguish those people you need to accommodate because of their status, position, authority, or influence. Being an outsider and a rebel in the group might be okay for dramatic effect, but it can wear thin when you don't have community support. Getting ahead in life requires adopting and upholding social skills. Loners and misfits will have a hard time. Your current challenge is to get the balance right between strong individuality and sensible cooperation.

19. FRIDAY. Reflective. It would be easy to become paranoid imagining someone in a group or team is working against you behind your back. If you're harboring any suspicions, a direct talk might clear up the situation. You'll probably discover you're both on the same side despite earlier appearances to the contrary. Don't waste time rushing around on petty errands or handling minor issues. Sweating the small stuff will only use up your limited energy pointlessly. Calm down, stay still in one place, and do some deep thinking. Mull over recent events and put everything that has occurred into a larger perspective. A close confidante can be a supportive sounding board for your thoughts and proposals.

20. SATURDAY. Cloistered. Curl up in a snug, comfortable place and retreat for the day. There is nowhere you currently need to go that will make a positive difference to your life, so politely refuse invitations and close down to the world. This is an ideal time to share intimacy with that special person in your life. A close friend can become even closer, especially when there's no one else around to judge the relationship or reveal it to outsiders. If you're not paired, this is a golden opportunity to put into practice all that theory about yoga, meditation, prayer, and devotion. Disengage from your fears and anxiety, and come into a more direct experience of soulful existence.

21. SUNDAY. Positive. There could be a few surprise calls from friends trying to get you to go out and spend time in their company. Depending on your mood, you may or may not want to be social, so consider each offer independently. If you do decide to spend time with friends, schedule a get-together for later in the day when you'll be more on the ball and more self-confident. If you feel you're wasting time with the wrong crowd, choose to do your own thing in purposeful solitary fashion. Be your own best friend for now, strengthening your individuality. This is a time to learn more about yourself rather than getting caught up in the agendas and reflections of other people.

22. MONDAY. Bright. You can enjoy a fast start to the workweek if you stay focused, clear-headed, and uninfluenced by the emotions of those around you. Calm rationality and incisive intelligence prevail over intuitive indecision and vulnerable weakness. It's up to you to tell it like it is. Be fearless in expressing the facts of any matter and the truth of the situation as you see it. People will listen to what you have to say even if they don't agree at first. Social temptations need to take a backseat when you have places to go and official affairs to deal with. Lazy or indulgent friends might try to steer you off course by proposing one detour or another, but stick to what's really important.

23. TUESDAY. Variable. Mixed up and confused could be part of today, but you can take it all in stride. If you're directing activities in the workplace, be clear as crystal and straight as an arrow about what you want done and what you expect to happen. Otherwise developments may get twisted beyond recognition as imaginative distortions get a grip. Check all details of any instructions and communications you receive to prevent future problems and anxiety. This is a starred time for creative inspiration. Filter out the noise and distraction around you, then let your thoughts take flight. Artistic and spiritual studies will be especially rewarding. Focus on what is not yet clear to you.

24. WEDNESDAY. Fortunate. A prosperous day awaits you if you are prepared to get out and make it happen. Shrug off any sense of discouragement and personal blocks as you prepare to enhance your earnings and cash flow. Nobody can ever make enough money, so don't limit your expectations or capacity. The sky's the limit, and you can be very lucky. The most likely source of this will be your profession or job, thanks to establishing a great reputation with happy customers and pleased bosses. A well-deserved bonus or raise is likely to come your way. Selling and creating will be easy now, so make an effort to break all prior records. The only potential financial problem is the desire to spend too much.

25. THURSDAY. Purposeful. The early part of the day should flow effortlessly, especially where work and finances are concerned. Follow up on yesterday's positive momentum and keep the good times rolling. Fortune favors the brave, and now's the time to show what you're made of. When the Moon collides with Mars later on, it will be showtime. You'll then be able to put rehearsed moves to excellent use. If your daily activities tend to be physically challenging, you'll benefit from current planetary energies. Don't hold back, just go for it. Driving can be very satisfying, along with using dynamic machinery and power tools. Martial arts can hold real appeal, combining discipline with explosive moves.

26. FRIDAY. Disenchanting. You could experience a sense of disconnection from the group or team, as if you're not on their wavelength. This might even make you feel like the proverbial square peg in a round hole. Making too much of such feelings is a mistake, as it is likely to pass soon. Don't bother trying so hard to communicate with friends and associates. You are not likely to be heard or understood; in fact, you may just be ignored. Sometimes people have agendas and interests that don't involve you, and you need to accept that without becoming angry or resentful. A neighbor or relative could be a better companion. Or just go out on your own and cruise the sights and sounds of the social scene.

27. SATURDAY. Chancy. A certain person you're interested in or want to contact is apt to be busy with other people or involved with them. Chasing after them or trying to track them down appears a futile exercise, especially if you don't know their whereabouts or they are preoccupied. Instead, you can lose yourself in a good book or movie, at least for the time being. You'll be amply rewarded by undertaking such a mental journey, ideally one that immerses you in another space and time entirely. Get in touch with a family member who is far away. With the wonders of modern technology you can almost imagine you're in the same room as you swap the latest news and catch up on all that has been happening.

28. SUNDAY. Diverse. Family and career are in the spotlight with the Full Moon in Virgo. This time of year tends to get a little tense and stressful for Geminis. It becomes clear that someone you love and care for may think differently and does not easily appreciate your views. Added to that is an overwhelming of emotion which may seem downright irrational to you. Make more of an effort to appreciate styles and approaches that are completely different from yours, no matter how critical you are or how uncomfortable you feel. Your mate or partner's family may decide to visit, making it necessary to improvise for the occasion and also to be on your best behavior. Recent career success could allow you to buy your own home.

MARCH

1. MONDAY. Innovative. Use lateral thinking to solve any worries. Instead of doing what you think you should, try something different. The old saying indicates that necessity is the mother of invention, and for you the result may be startling. New doors are opening, offering opportunities to move into uncharted territory. Although this might threaten your sense of security, nothing ventured, nothing gained is the best approach to take. Be brave and you will discover renewed faith in your own abilities as well as rewards for your efforts. Whatever you are into, your horizons are broadening, with exciting new directions to energize your mind and fatten your purse. A love interest might keep you out late tonight.

2. TUESDAY. Cautious. Important matters may move a little too fast for you. Someone may be trying to push you in a direction you feel unsure about. The best approach is to put off making any important decisions, giving you at least this evening to digest all the information you have received. Beware the urge to gamble, and don't listen to anyone selling an investment with promises to double your money. Chances are your money will double theirs! Romance can take an unpleasant twist, and the best action is to withdraw and do some soul-searching on your own. As a Gemini you are easily sidetracked by other people, but a period of isolation will put you in touch with your own true feelings.

3. WEDNESDAY. Problematic. Be on guard at work. Someone is not being honest and may steal your ideas, claiming them as their own and receiving recognition for themselves. Exciting offers can fall flat and leave you floundering. Improvise where you can; your own creativity might win the day for you. If you are going to be out and about, take extra care to avoid an incident or an accident. Be mindful not to rush. Gemini parents should ensure children's safety and should know where they are and who they are with at any given time. A visit to their school can sort out any difficulty they may be having with bullying or other behavior problems.

4. THURSDAY. Refreshing. Apart from minor hiccups you should be able to get a lot done today. Write down a list of everything you need to attend to so that you don't miss anything. You will impress the boss with your methodical, effective approach to your assignments, and you could receive a promotion or cash bonus for going above and beyond. A romance can move into the next stage of greater commitment, sparking much discussion about your future together. Be honest with yourself when it comes to promises and plans. Make sure it is really what you want to do, not just talking, otherwise you might not be so satisfied later on.

5. FRIDAY. Fragmented. You may feel like just laying low and taking the day off. However, if you throw yourself into your work this morning you will be able to achieve plenty. Rumors at work could make you suspicious. Geminis who have just started a new job might feel unnerved by office politics. If you take no notice, you can rise above the gossip and end up getting along with everybody. The travel bug may bite you. This is a good time to book a cruise or a tour of some far-distant land. Or you could be attracted by an enchanting foreigner. Life after dark promises to heat up. Take your camera when you go out so that you can capture a once-in-a-lifetime glimpse of a famous person.

6. SATURDAY. Arousing. An inner need for freedom may goad you to experiment within your relationships. Whether you are discussing business or romance, you are likely to be more daring, ready to try an approach that is foreign to you just to see what happens. Emotions will be high. To avoid any hot issues, be kind and thoughtful but not overly accommodating. In this way you will stay in control. Your creativity is flowing, and Gemini artists of all kinds should enjoy the creative burst of energy that is readily available. Let your imagination take flight, conjuring up ideas that are definitely first-class. A neighbor can give you a tip that steers you in the right direction.

7. SUNDAY. Enjoyable. Venus, the planet of love and personal values, moves into Aries and your solar sector of social contacts and connections. This will make for some great socializing over the next month, with new introductions that will be valuable to your social network. Get out and mix, visit neighbors, or ask friends and neighbors to come by for food, drink, and good conversation. Don't let partnership difficulties bring you down. Making some concessions to your mate or partner's own nature by accepting that they are different from you can lead to forging a heightened commitment between you, adding new levels of joy. No pain, no gain; you have a lot to gain by today's decisions.

8. MONDAY. Disruptive. A few upsets could spoil even your well-laid plans and expectations. Don't leave the house without checking that you have all that you might need or want. A business deal could be called off or an offer refused as the stress factor leads to frayed tempers and disagreements. Paperwork is very important. It will pay you to personally go over all details to be sure you have dotted all the i's and crossed all the t's. Traffic congestion or a transportation breakdown could add to the day's annoyances. End the day with a candlelit dinner for two, enjoying the romance and relaxation of being with that special person in your life.

9. TUESDAY. Optimistic. A variety of plans will surface today as you mix and mingle with business associates, friends, and social connections. Don't stay in the background. Speak out. Accept a good offer when it is proposed because it might not come again. Younger Geminis might be considering an affair with someone older. This won't be an easily accepted relationship, and there will be much social judgment and disapproval if you become involved romantically. Gemini parents may be juggling work and home commitments, needing some extra family support. A brother or sister may be happy to do some babysitting or yardwork for you while you get established financially. Remember not to try to do too much too soon.

10. WEDNESDAY. Supportive. Unexpected gains can come your way thanks to help from associates or friends. Your popularity might push you into a leadership position that you quite frankly hadn't seen coming, but don't let doubts hold you back. You will get all the support you need to do a good job and be able to impress the right people. Dealing directly with the public is also foreseen. Your quick intellect and wit will come to your aid if you have to make an impromptu speech. Some of you might have had a bereavement in the family and should expect a bit of family infighting over a will or if an older relative is downsizing personal belongings. Stay out of petty bickering; everything will get sorted out in good time.

11. THURSDAY. Smooth. Apart from a few minor hassles early in the morning, this day should be a corker! Contacts with foreign people or agencies are indicated. Even though communication may be difficult due to a language barrier, you should be able to come up with inventive ways around the problem. New customs may be introduced to you which change your perspective of the world. An invitation to an important social function can lead to shopping for the right outfit to impress. You want to see and be seen. Gemini grandparents might be treating the youngsters to an interesting educational outing and will enjoy looking at life through the eyes of a child once again.

12. FRIDAY. Disconcerting. A trivial misundertstanding with a family member or neighbor can conjure up hurts from the past and cause you to lose your cool. Take a deep breath and keep these feelings to yourself. Later on you can examine them when you are alone and learn a bit more of what makes you tick. The past can lie dormant in your subconscious, influencing many of your thoughts, feelings, and expectations. Any chance to exhume them and free yourself from them through forgiveness is valuable. A promotion or pay raise is possible, as is a change of job into a more stimulating and satisfying position. You may want to consider night school in order to give your career a boost.

13. SATURDAY. Sensitive. Expect to encounter a few touchy people. Avoid putting your foot in your mouth or upsetting somebody inadvertently. There is a psychic feel in the air, and you might decide to have your fortune told or visit an astrologer for an in-depth analysis. When mixing with other people be careful that you don't pick up a virus or an infection of some sort. Be sure to wash your hands more frequently than usual. Politics is also indicated. If you are involved with a group, don't be surprised if there is a factional split and you are forced to choose a side. With your popularity, you might be asked to take over a recently vacated position.

14. SUNDAY. Active. Put all sorts of social activities, especially sports, on your to-do list today. Gemini parents may take over a coaching or fund-raising role for a child's team in order to better help them achieve a personal best. You or someone close to you may receive an award or other honor amidst fanfare, pomp, and ceremony. You might have to work on a speech for the occasion. If planning a quiet day at home, think twice; friends are bound to drop by unannounced, so stock up your refrigerator in advance and don't make elaborate personal plans. The intensity of a romantic affair could start to fade and leave you feeling like getting out altogether. Be honest for both your sakes.

15. MONDAY. Opportune. The New Moon in Pisces is highlighting your career. This is a good time to begin something new, whether it is finding another job, starting a new project, or applying for a higher position with your present employer. Think about your plan of action before taking the first step, because you will probably succeed in all that you attempt. Your mind is quick and inventive, and you can keep associates interested with your antics and fun conversation. Apply the same talent to a problem and the solution won't elude you. A female friend may be in financial need and ask for a loan. Only provide what you can do without, because it may be a long time before you are repaid.

16. TUESDAY. Harmonious. Your energy level is high, allowing you to enjoy whatever you have to do. Shopping will be fun, and you should run into people you haven't seen for ages. The neighbor next door might pass on some juicy gossip, and you will have a good laugh together. A new romance may be gaining momentum. Try not to spend all day on the phone when you should be doing your work. An important meeting that has had everybody on edge for weeks of preparation can be a surprise when it turns out to be a simple matter of total consensus. A concert or show this evening may get canceled. Stay local instead and enjoy all that your own neighborhood has to offer.

17. WEDNESDAY. Diverse. Expect the unexpected and you won't be disappointed. The Sun is side by side with Uranus, the planet of the unexpected, eccentricity, and electricity. This alignment also suggests the need to be careful when driving, operating machinery, or using electricity. You are apt to be more impulsive than usual. However, because your intuition should be working well, you will probably make the right decisions. You are also likely to meet some interesting new people whose background is different than yours, giving you fresh ideas. You will not be happy with the ordinary aspects of life, so paperwork and housework may pile up. Don't worry, tomorrow is another day.

18. THURSDAY. Interesting. A slow start will give you a chance to get your thoughts in order. After yesterday's influences you are likely to have a lot of ideas swirling around in your head. You might even be nervous or worried about making a new move. Take the day off work if you need to; your health must be looked after, and your vitality could be down a bit. A newfound interest in the occult could lead to reading and exploring your own interests without any outside interruptions. Whatever you do today, you are bound to experience some profound insights that give you plenty of food for thought and help you understand more about yourself and your world.

19. FRIDAY. Beneficial. Contact with government officials or the judiciary is possible. Whatever the circumstances, you are likely to be well satisfied with the results. You may sense an aura of protection around you which will help you achieve whatever you set out to do. Gemini students should spend the day at the library or on the Internet and get some valuable research and some studying done. What you learn today will stick with you, broadening your knowledge and understanding of the subject. If you're planning to invest a large sum in the stock market, get expert advice regarding which companies or funds to buy. There is an aspect of wastefulness to the day which you must avoid at all costs.

20. SATURDAY. Relaxed. Sleep late this morning to give your body, mind, and soul a break from your hectic schedule. You may especially benefit from meditation or tai chi and from the development of your spiritual life. A local forum or class on these topics would be beneficial for you. Take a walk around town and enjoy the local sights, sounds, and smells, feeling the ground under your feet and the wind in your hair. You may have extra work to do, but ignore it for now. Make this a day of rest and nothing more. If you have to work, head straight home afterward. Leave the partying for next week.

21. SUNDAY. Excellent. The Moon entering your own sign of Gemini puts the focus on your appearance and personal desires. The urge to change your hairstyle, purchase some new clothes, and update your image may be irresistible. There is a chance you could splurge more than you can afford, so leave your credit cards behind and only take to the mall the sum you can comfortably spend. With the Sun just moved into Aries and your social sector, you are sure to get some special invitations to important events. These will give you a chance to be seen in the scene. All aspects look promising for a great day. Before you leave home look in the mirror and tell yourself that you deserve all the good that is coming your way.

22. MONDAY. Uneven. There could be a lot of stress around you now. If you can manage it, take an hour out of your day to get a massage that will clear your mind and relax your body. The feeling that you have forgotten something could nag at you and make everything that bit harder. Instead of rushing to beat the clock, proceed with your work in order. If you are late, don't worry about it; you will be calm, cool, and collected, and ready to impress. An artistic interest should be followed. You might be able to sign up for a beginner's class to get started. Such an interest can give hours of relaxation and act like a meditation to ease times of stress.

23. TUESDAY. Intense. If money matters are on your mind, work out a comprehensive budget that is moderate and sensible. Don't deny yourself some money for fun or the budget may be too hard to stick to. If you feel you are in over your head financially see an adviser for professional help. If you are worried about your partner's fidelity and finding it hard to trust, don't resort to checking e-mails or listening in on phone calls. Instead, explain how and why you feel as you do. It is likely your mind will be put at ease by a logical explanation. A child may be having problems with low self-esteem. Find out what they are good at and help them to develop those skills and talents.

24. WEDNESDAY. Busy. Your social calendar is apt to be packed, and you might have to resort to picking and choosing as you simply can't accept all invitations. You are likely to meet someone very special during the course of day and feel that you have a spiritual link with this person. Or you may say goodbye to somebody and realize that this parting will leave a big hole in your life. You and your mate or partner might decide to tie the knot or repeat your vows, and start planning what type of ceremony you will have. Expect a few minor disagreements when it comes to compiling a guest list. Internet bloggers can have fun with a public issue and could win accolades for research and insight.

25. THURSDAY. Unsettling. Expect to be out and about a lot, caught in traffic or stuck on public transportation. If you recently moved you may be finding the traveling tedious. This is not a good time to apply for a driver's license. But if you are in that process, be extra careful and expect the unexpected. Phone calls may not be returned and your computer may cause delays. If you want to stay in top shape, don't drink too much caffeine; it will only hype you up more and turn up the stress factor. Fresh water will help you relax. Enjoy a long lunch with associates; the work will all be there when you get back. For Gemini singles, a romantic date might be more trouble than it's worth.

26. FRIDAY. Receptive. Listening to other people can give you ideas regarding how to better yourself and improve your career potential. You might get some hints at a meeting or seminar. Gemini students will benefit from forming a study group. Hook up on the Internet and benefit from the wide range of perspectives available on your subject. You are likely to have a flair for writing; write a few letters or cards to send to friends or loved ones who live at a distance or are traveling. You may even try your hand at a short story to send to a magazine. Avoid personal phone calls while on the job; the boss could be watching or listening in. Also be wary of giving out any personal information.

27. SATURDAY. Satisfactory. Working around the house will be rewarding, maybe painting a room, redecorating, or cleaning. At the end of the day you will enjoy what you have achieved. Part-nered Geminis can renew romance. Shut the door, turn off the lights, and avoid visitors or socializing while planning your future and enjoying the intimacy. Single Geminis are likely to meet someone alluring who arouses feelings you least expected, turning the day into something far better than anticipated. Your family is particularly important now. You may need to visit your parents or older siblings and talk over your week, gaining insight from their wisdom, understanding, and experience.

28. SUNDAY. Lucky. A political rally or cultural festival in your local area will be enjoyed for its intellectual stimulation and interesting perspectives on the world and the human race. This could lead to a whole new era in your life as you make new associations and take on a responsible public role. If you are thinking about buying a new home, obtain a list of places to inspect from a real estate agent or from postings of open houses. Take your time and be ready to bargain. A drive in the country might spark an interest in rural land. You can spend hours on the Internet looking for cheap property in out-of-the-way locales.

29. MONDAY. Pleasant. Today's Full Moon in Libra shines its light on your sector of fun, lovers, and children. All of this could give you a dose of Monday blues, but don't do anything stupid or you could lose your job. Romance is high on today's agenda. Practicalities may fly out the window at this time, but you would be wise to take your time. A new hobby might take over your life and consume all your spare time, leaving lovers and friends out in the cold. Find time to get together with loved ones for an impromptu party, eating, drinking, as you enjoy each other's company. Gemini parents might take the kids out for dinner or have a pizza delivered.

30. TUESDAY. Tense. Tension levels are likely to be high. For no apparent reason somebody could snap at you and get you angry.

Try to remain calm if possible. It probably isn't personal. Breathe deeply and pause, which will act as a stress release. If you are having problems in your personal life, there are many self-help groups that you might benefit from. These will allow you to make friends and avoid large bills at the same time. Start an exercise regime or play a sport as a way to keep fit, release pent-up energy, and meet new people; you will be surprised how much better you feel in a few weeks. You may be asked to teach a favorite hobby and pass on all that you've learned.

31. WEDNESDAY. Industrious. This is a great day for spring-cleaning. It's out with the old and in with the new. If you have the time, go through all of your closets. Dispose of what you haven't used in the last year, or donate items to charity. Do the same with your body by starting a diet to give your system a fresh start; you'll be amazed by how good this makes you feel. If preparing for an overseas trip be sure to get necessary inoculations. Prepare a nutritious dinner, and drink plenty of water during the day. A coworker could call for your support. If workplace bullying is the problem, help them lodge a complaint through the right channels.

APRIL

1. THURSDAY. Smooth. Work is on a roll, so don't become distracted with social prospects and invitations to hang out with pals. Certain characters may want to lead you astray and are possibly up to no good. Instead, give maximum attention and energy to getting the job done. Then you'll be satisfied, the boss will be satisfied, and customers will be satisfied. That makes it a winning combination. Geminis looking for employment are in luck today. And if you're seeking an employee for your business, the right person could walk through the door. Hiring contractors for home maintenance, gardening, or landscaping is timely. It's also worthwhile having your car serviced or repaired.

2. FRIDAY. Revealing. Sharing an award or honor with your partner is indicated, especially if they've been particularly supportive and played a large part in helping you succeed. Geminis in long-term relationships might be celebrating an anniversary. If you haven't tied the knot or made a decisive commitment, this could be the time to announce your intentions. Singles may be playing the field with a few people. Make sure they don't find out about one another or see you with someone else. A secret affair could become stressful if you're tempted to keep pursuing it. Life will be a lot more relaxed and open if you choose one person as your steady companion and lover.

3. SATURDAY. Sociable. Work issues might still be on your mind and agenda. There may be a need to meet with clients or coworkers to discuss upcoming plans and projects for the period ahead. Or there may be ongoing jobs that continue to need your personal attention and input. However, don't become overly consumed with business matters. There are sure to be a range of social events and invitations. Friends may want you to join them for the weekend, perhaps to go on an outdoor adventure or to drive out of town. Your partner's family can be a priority; keep everyone happy by being a willing part of the action. Singles will find good company with friends and workmates.

4. SUNDAY. Muddled. You could be led on a merry chase if you get caught up in the roundabout of other people's plans and agendas. A partner or companion may change their mind more than once about what they want to do. You may even wonder whether it's really worth all the hassle to be in a relationship. However, this is not the time for a confrontational encounter. Stay focused on what's happening in the wider world, and try to enjoy today's round of activities. Don't rely on anyone else for your kicks or decisions. People may come and go quickly in your life, making it wise not to get too attached or involved. Singles may start the evening with one person and wind up with someone else.

5. MONDAY. Intense. Events and experiences should be a lot clearer today than yesterday. A certain relationship has come into sharp focus, and there's no beating around the bush now. Being decisive and strong-willed is a positive Gemini attribute, especially when handling an individual who is determined. A partnership may have reached a terminal juncture, making it necessary to call things off. You may even have a successor waiting in the wings. A secret affair could become serious, as the two of you edge into deeper intimacy. There may be no going back if that is what you both truly want. However, the liaison is best kept private and under wraps while it's still germinating and developing strength and commitment.

6. TUESDAY. Eventful. This is an active social period, with a range of significant encounters consuming your day. Despite all that you need to take care of, make children a priority. If there's a difficult family situation to deal with, loved ones will be looking to you for security and reassurance. Handling accounting and tax issues might cause anxiety, but these matters can be resolved more swiftly and smoothly than you anticipate. Help and support are available for problems that don't seem to be going away. It's better to face them with the aid of someone who has the necessary experience and training. Don't bury your head in the sand and wish for a miracle.

7. WEDNESDAY. Active. With Saturn slipping back into Virgo until July, this is a timely period to tie up affairs of the past couple of years so you can move forward in life. If legal issues are part of that unfinished business, take the necessary action to have them resolved once and for all. Even though doing so may take time, at least make a start. A journey you've been wanting to go on for a while could get under way now. Although it may not be easy to go, the trip probably can't be delayed any longer. You may feel the urge to improve or update your educational qualifications in order to enhance your career prospects. Geminis already in a learning program should review material and prepare for an upcoming exam.

8. THURSDAY. Integrating. You'll benefit in many ways from group involvements and interactions. Whether it's a team of coworkers collaborating on a project, a collective of students sharing knowledge, or a community of people devoted to a common interest, many heads are better than one. However, take care to be discriminating about the company you keep. A situation where the blind are leading the blind won't get anyone very far. Either respect those you choose to associate with or don't stay involved with them. There's too much real opportunity to waste time on people who are going nowhere. Loyalty is one thing, but not blind adherence.

9. FRIDAY. Inspiring. It may seem difficult to mesh idealism with practicality. An older relative could be a good sounding board for your more extreme goals. While it's fine to shoot for the stars and aim for the highest possible accomplishments, you need to keep your feet on the ground and be prepared for obstacles and tough challenges along the way. Successful people see failures as learning experiences rather than the end of the line. Persevering endurance and steady discipline will be needed to turn your dreams into reality. Your attraction and desire for a special someone could have you gliding on cloud nine, entranced by a romantic vision of future happiness.

10. SATURDAY. Opportune. Inside information works to Gemini career advantage, especially in buying and selling activities. Market players might get certain news that influences your position, especially when the source is someone who knows the game and is close to the action. Gamblers who speculate on sports may receive a hot tip that offers a big win. Perhaps an outsider will come in at long odds. Success in these endeavors will be a matter of knowledge rather than luck. A powerful contact could put in a good word for you in a job selection process, which will seal the deal in your favor. Entrepreneurs can make money securing a valuable item cheaply and finding a guaranteed buyer ready to pay much more.

11. SUNDAY. Lucky. If yesterday was about being clever, today's about good fortune. An older relative might generously include you in their will, assuring a handsome inheritance to come. While you can't take it to the bank yet, it's sure to make your financial future rosier. Work for today will be more interesting and eventful than usual, making the time fly. Geminis who are searching for new employment opportunities should make a greater effort now. What you're looking for is out there, and prospects are positive. Your application is sure to be well received. Getting serious about an evolving relationship may mean meeting your lover's family. This is a perfect day to be introduced and to make a great impression.

12. MONDAY. Dynamic. Get a bright and early start to the day. The action will be fast and furious from the get-go. Higher-ups will be pleased to see you arriving as soon as the office or store opens. This is a time to go above and beyond the call of duty. You'll be able to perform high-wire acts and tricky moves at work if you're thoroughly organized. You can afford to take a few calculated risks in your career, keeping you from getting stale and bored. Meanwhile, keep your personal life steady, erring on the side of conservatism and caution. Travel is best late in the day, when you can expect a fast transit to your destination.

13. TUESDAY. Fair. Making friends might not be your strong suit, so there's no need to try too hard. It's impossible to pretend that you like someone you actually have no time for, so don't feign interest or familiarity. People will respect your upfront honesty rather than any fake niceness. A group or team could fall into disarray without a firm hand and strong leadership. If you're the person in charge, lay down the law. Even if you are actually bluffing anger, everyone won't necessarily know that, and your points will be made loud and clear. As the New Moon closes in overnight, make sure that schedules are in good order and assigned tasks have been completed.

14. WEDNESDAY. Rewarding. Hopefully you can engineer some free time and extra space despite today's busy agenda. Open your mind to possibilities stretching ahead for the rest of this year. The

New Moon in Aries marks a visionary seeding point in your personal astrological cycle. Dream more, and be open up to the highest potentials you want for your life. Grace and inspiration are available in a special way, which will renew energy and hope for the days to come. It can be good to have nothing solid planned so that fresh possibilities can flow and unfold into this space. Once a clear strategy has been consolidated, it will simply be a matter of putting it into action.

15. THURSDAY. Satisfactory. Best results can be achieved behind closed doors. Private discussions and confidential encounters will be fruitful, allowing those involved to engage in full and frank communication without fear of negative consequences. Trust is essential in these circumstances, and you must keep whatever information is revealed to you totally secret. Your mate or partner's work may be so fulfilling and consuming at present that you're left out of the loop and are missing their consistent company. Spend some time creating a comfortable sanctuary as a personal retreat. An older relative who is hospitalized or confined at home would greatly appreciate a visit or call to cheer them up.

16. FRIDAY. Volatile. Appearances may be deceptive, so dig deeper to get to the real substance of what's going on. Judging a book by its cover is a lazy approach, which will lead you astray and cause errors. If you're impressed by style without substance, you deserve the consequences. By being thoughtful and thorough you'll find the truth, which will then let you stand confidently on solid ground. Mull over knowledge and opinions that are proposed but come to your own conclusions. You'll do your job best by keeping to yourself, effectively managing and completing your own workload, then disappearing as early as possible. This is the wrong night to stay out late or to indulge yourself.

17. SATURDAY. Motivating. Make this a physically active day, focusing on your body and pushing yourself to get the blood pumping. As a Gemini you have a reputation for living too much in your head, so make a conscious, disciplined effort to exercise and stay fit. Walking, running, hiking, and cycling are pleasant ways to do this, with the added benefit of stress release while calming and clearing your mind. Or you may prefer a skill-based sport that requires adept hand-eye coordination, such as tennis, golf, or baseball. Taking a stroll around town will satisfy curiosity about what's happening in the local scene, with lively encounters to pique your interest along the way.

18. SUNDAY. Reflective. Being multifaceted and multidimensional has both advantages and drawbacks. Too much choice can be a problem, as is boredom. Today you have two options, but before doing anything you should take time to quietly reflect on your existence. This could mean ritual faith-based devotion, personal meditation, and contemplation. Or you might just sit quietly and get in touch with the state of the world by reading the newspaper and listening to talk TV. Then it's a matter of going the positive high road of hope and inspiration, or traveling the low road of anxiety and worry. Both approaches have relevance, but only one of them will really help you to be happy, fulfilled, and successful.

19. MONDAY. Demanding. The last day of the Sun in Aries is a good time to get back on track with certain people through direct communication. Spell out with crystal clarity what you want them to hear and understand completely. Then move on. This is a period to get down to business in more ways than one, but money is the current priority. Someone or some organization may be pressuring you to pay a debt. Or you may be steamrolled and manipulated into a purchase you neither want nor need. Give as good as you get, and tell pushy characters to back off while you manage essential financial tasks. By paying attention to earning strategies you will be able to afford your life.

20. TUESDAY. Resourceful. Old contacts in business can be a source of the best opportunities as well as offering optimal income and profits. As much as you seek fresh fields and greener pastures, don't neglect familiar faces and timeworn paths. A network based on family ties, school alumni, and former coworkers is a fertile arena for getting ahead. If you're seeking further financing to launch or grow an enterprise, a parent or relative is a likely person to guarantee a loan. There's also the option of taking out a second mortgage on real estate you own. An inheritance could provide you with needed resources to secure your domestic and economic circumstances.

21. WEDNESDAY. Stressful. You may reach a point when you really feel the stress and strain of existence. It might even be enough to make you want to give up, throwing it all away in a fit of disgust and frustration. Don't do it. Realize that these feelings could simply indicate that you need to calm down and relax. That means a real vacation, not just a few hours chilling out or a couple of days off work. If you don't read the signs and take a break, you're heading for a breakdown or some type of illness which will stop you in your tracks. Traffic can be a major headache in peak hours, but if you must navigate the gridlock prepare to grin and bear it.

22. THURSDAY. Grating. You may be consumed by thoughts of wanting to get away from it all one way or another. The very least you can do is to take a long drive, leaving the familiar everyday environment behind you temporarily. If even that's too much to ask, there's always a walk in the park away from the workplace. Arguments, debates, and disputes will erupt all too easily. Don't even go there, even when talk starts out in the guise of a discussion. Matters can quickly deteriorate from a civilized plane to the caveman level before you realize what's happening. The best strategy to keep your blood pressure down is to avoid troublesome people, places, and activities.

23. FRIDAY. Uneven. Fantasies of being with a lover might have to be put on hold. Don't be disappointed if high hopes for love and affection are not reciprocated or fulfilled. Just because it's not happening now doesn't mean it never will. While you can't always get what you want, it's likely you'll get what you need. As the saying goes, if you can't be with the one you love, love the one you're with. You may be suffering from shyness, not revealing an attraction to the object of your desire. This person won't guess what's on your mind or in your heart, so speak up and see what happens. If expectations of a big night out on the town do not eventuate, you'll be wise to go home early.

24. SATURDAY. Encouraging. There will be an improved quality to this day if you tune in and take advantage of what is being offered. Basing yourself at home for the weekend makes good sense. If you feel like company, stick to immediate family members and close friends so you can relax and be yourself without fuss and bother. You will benefit from time alone to think, ponder, and reflect on the year that's been and what may come. Keeping a journal can be helpful and even therapeutic for getting in touch with deeper emotions. Physical practices such as yoga and tai chi may prove beneficial, creating a calm center. Do-it-yourself carpentry, home maintenance, or landscaping and gardening will be useful.

25. SUNDAY. Interesting. This intriguing day is infused with the energy of three major planets: Jupiter, Saturn, and Uranus. There is apt to be a collision of choice between the old ways of tradition and conservatism and the new ways of experimentation and invention. Rather than seeing these options as opposed, try to think of ways in which you can have the best of both worlds. Sticking to your roots and securing your home and family makes sense. At the same time, explore more risky options and clever angles in your career, trade, or profession. A job change may be what you need, but not one where you have to leave town or uproot your loved ones.

26. MONDAY. Bright. Treat yourself to what feels good. It doesn't matter what anyone thinks, it's about what you like and want. A day off from work might be needed or deserved, allowing you to extend the weekend break and enjoy yourself with further recreational free time. Beauty treatments and personal care feature today, with the hairdresser and masseuse worthy of a visit. Dress to enhance your image and well-being. If your wardrobe needs a lift, go out and buy a stylish new outfit that really suits you. You're looking good at the moment and will readily attract an enthusiastic admirer or two. Take advantage of the positive profile and go out tonight.

27. TUESDAY. Mixed. The first part of the day can be spent prolonging and extending feel-good experiences. The more you get to play and goof off, the better you will like it. You may enjoy reading a novel or watching a movie, dreaming as a way to take a break from everyday routine. Personal fun must come to an end later in the day, when the demands of your job or household chores call you to take care of business. At least you'll be fresher and more efficient due to the recent break. Back at work you're apt to be thrown into the deep end, possibly having to tackle a tough assignment or get involved with a colleague or customer who expects a professional performance and committed attention from you.

28. WEDNESDAY. Confrontational. The Scorpio Full Moon is a signal for Geminis to take extra care of your health. Schedule a thorough checkup and physical examination as a preventive measure. Although you may be resistant or anxious about medical procedures and environments, they are for your own benefit in the long term. If acute symptoms or conditions arise, it's essential to treat them immediately. Even if you feel totally fit, it will be worth making an effort to investigate lifestyle options such as nutrition and exercise which promote ongoing and sustainable wellness. There may be a sharp confrontation with a person you discover has been undermining or even betraying you.

29. THURSDAY. Sensitive. Your stamina and vitality are not at a peak, so don't push yourself too hard. If you're experienced at your job, you'll know the shortcuts and easy paths that can make your day as relaxed and stress-free as possible. In addition, try to invent better ways of getting things done. Work on more effective procedures to accomplish the same old tasks with less effort and energy. A cloud of anxiety could hang over you about an application for another job or a promotion. There may even be a degree of confusion about the outcome. Good news is likely at the last minute, and there can be a surprise result which favors and benefits you.

30. FRIDAY. Tense. There may be disagreement between you and your mate or partner about what you both want. As much as you'd love to please and satisfy their desires, you also want to have your own needs acknowledged and fulfilled. Every relationship requires give-and-take in order to negotiate the path of life together. This is one of those times when each of you should bend a little to accommodate the other person, a winning combination for both. If you feel you're doing all the giving and making too many personal sacrifices, speak up. Let the other person know how you feel so they can understand the situation better and treat you differently. Bottling up emotions won't resolve anything.

MAY

1. SATURDAY. Challenging. There are difficult choices to be made as alternate interests and demands compete for your available time. Family duties look dull and tedious but may be unavoidable, especially if you feel responsible to honoring promises and commitments you've already made. Certain relatives will be disappointed if you don't make an appearance. Exciting career prospects are also in the mix, which seem both opportune and intriguing. Their interesting and unknown qualities will surely tempt you away from other activities. And your partner or lover may expect to spend some quality time with you. Make the best attempt at covering all bases.

2. SUNDAY. Intriguing. There's no need to spread yourself thin today. A significant person has your total attention for a change, and the time you devote to them will be rewarded. A parent or other older relative might reveal secrets of the clan, which deepens an understanding of your ancestors and enlightens you about your roots. There may be an intrigue over property or an inheritance, which gives you privileged information and an upper hand. Your partner or a close pal could seek your intelligent input concerning practical issues about their job and finances. Such trust placed in you is both an honor and a burden. Keep the strictest confidence on whatever is shared in private.

3. MONDAY. Insightful. Despite a tendency to want to keep to yourself, there will be necessary meetings and encounters that are very worthwhile. Seeking professional advice should provide the support and clarity to help you understand and appreciate certain circumstances with much greater awareness and certainty. Inner confidence and self-assurance might stem from wise, experienced counsel by the right parties. Whether it's a legal, financial, or medical opinion, it should prove trustworthy, so give it the attention it deserves. Negotiations concerning real estate or some other major issue can make satisfying progress even though the deal won't be finalized just yet.

4. TUESDAY. Opportune. Now that you're armed with solid information and reliable advice, the time for significant decision is drawing closer. What's important at this point is to create a watertight game plan you'll be able to stick with despite temporary setbacks or disappointments along the way. A well-thought-out strategy is the antidote to fickle responses and knee-jerk reactions. Rather than changing like the weather, you need to be as solid as a rock. Before making an ultimate commitment, double-check all details, from equipment and transport to personnel and finances. If it's a more personal and intimate matter, run it by relevant others one more time.

5. WEDNESDAY. Tense. A heated family debate might erupt that you would rather not be part of. If you sense trouble brewing as an issue comes to a head between certain individuals, you could disappear from the scene to avoid unpleasantness. However, you may be dragged into it simply by being in the wrong place at the wrong time. Even worse, one or both antagonists may single you out as a scapegoat for their troubles and concerns. If you can be as obliging and diplomatic as possible in the circumstances, the trouble should blow over. Travel may look appealing at the moment, but once you step out the door you could encounter one annoying delay after another. Try to make the most of the trip, even if it takes longer than anticipated.

6. THURSDAY. Beneficial. A dose of escapism would do wonders for your spirits, providing some respite from recent hassles. Whatever helps to turn your attention away from worries and anxieties will do the trick. A trip to the movies where you can lose yourself in the big screen and in surround sound will whisk you away to another world at least for a few hours. The quiet tranquility of a lunchtime visit to an art gallery or museum is another option to consider. Planning a family vacation might be relaxing as well, offering a getaway to look forward to. Browse available options for travel and accommodations online, and let your imagination run away with the potential delights being offered.

7. FRIDAY. Strategic. Thorough research and background investigation will benefit your job performance and career potential. While other people are making up responses and action as they go along, you'll be strutting your stuff with solid confidence. If you are in the running for a promotion or a job you applied for lately, you could find yourself on the short list. The depth of your knowledge, the degree of your preparation, and your convincing self-assurance will distinguish you from other candidates. Self-promotion for business purposes comes easily; you're looking good and presenting a positive image. Get down to personal correspondence you've been putting off for too long.

8. SATURDAY. Mixed. You can attend to professional and business concerns even when you're not actually at work. Be available to take calls and reply to messages about ongoing projects and situations, responding as necessary in a timely fashion. Staying on top of things means less effort and fewer problems next week, helping to ensure eventual success. Pay attention to social contexts and expectations or you may find yourself dressed inappropriately for an occasion and completely unprepared for what is going on. Your sense of style may be at odds with current fashion trends, making this a poor time to buy clothes or fashion accessories. A personal makeover may not produce the results you hoped for.

9. SUNDAY. Stimulating. Don't let fear or caution inhibit your approach to life. Behaving like your parents or doing what the family expects won't lead to the ultimate prize of success and fulfillment. Playing it safe will deliver the expected security and limited outcomes that accompany such an approach. On the other hand, taking a risk with the unknown and taking your chances is more likely to put you on top of the world. Luck and good fortune flow from innovation and from acting independently with a unique personal style. Trekking the path less traveled opens up vistas of opportunity you never expected. In addition, you won't be bored. Feeling restless might be the signal that change is required.

10. MONDAY. Active. With the Moon in the domain of a fiery Mars, go directly for what you want. Nobody's in the mood for subtlety or politeness. Instead, it's a period for straight shooting as you talk the talk and then walk the walk. An attractive coworker may be impossible to ignore on the job and in a team situation. Being part of community activities will lead to positive social connections. Married Geminis should be wary of obvious flirtation and indiscreet public temptation. Singles, on the other hand, are well served by current energies, with desirability a bonus in the right company. Friendship can grow into closer, more intimate bonds, especially with someone living nearby.

11. TUESDAY. Positive. This is another Mars day when spirits are high and energies motivated. Keeping company with active individuals who make things happen is sure to rub off on you. As a Gemini you are likely to be highly regarded and a valued member of a team which is achieving all its goals and aims, and then some. A certain project may be proceeding so successfully that it is now appropriate to reassess the timeline and the scope of its objectives. Hanging out with workmates or friends after work would be a pleasant end to a satisfying day. Before going to bed make a call to someone who is currently living or traveling in a far-off time zone.

12. WEDNESDAY. Reflective. Use today's quieter mood to reflect on yourself and the course of your life. It's worthwhile keeping a journal or diary to remind yourself of recent history, with its variety of characters, events, and impressions. Give yourself time to think carefully and methodically about your own needs. Caring for your inner self is just as important to your well-being as taking care of business in the external world. Matters needing attention could include health and appearance, finances, family and domestic affairs, real estate, and creative and spiritual aspirations. The potential scope is large, but focus primarily on those specific issues with the most immediate relevance to you.

13. THURSDAY. Renewing. Take it easy as the Moon finishes one cycle and starts a fresh round. This is the best chance you'll get all year to recuperate body, mind, and spirit. It's important to make time for renewal and regeneration. Physical healing and relaxation should be at the top of your list. There's a sense of throwing out old items and attitudes from the past year, regrouping with a different style which reflects the new you. Treat yourself to pampering and a make-over, as well as to the height of this season's fashion. While you may feel somewhat needy and vulnerable, as if you want someone to look after you, the truth is you can care for yourself perfectly well.

14. FRIDAY. Vital. With the Moon in your sign you might feel a new surge of energy and vitality. If it seems that events and projects have slowed to a crawl, take heart; they will slowly but surely get back on the move once more. Rather than focusing on what's not happening, turn your attention forward to the future and to all that is in store. Anyone you feel has been undermining your interests or behaving dishonestly toward you can be cut out of your life altogether without a second thought. Wanting to concern yourself with people who are far less fortunate than you is a generous instinct and a worthy endeavor. Spend time or money supporting humane causes that you know are making a difference.

15. SATURDAY. Bright. Suiting yourself this weekend might be the optimum choice. As much as you'd like to keep everyone else happy by paying attention to their needs, it's essential to look after number one. You're unlikely to be in the mood for any compromise or negotiation, preferring your own company. The only exceptions might be people you can't avoid, such as close neighbors or an insistent sibling. If you leave on a solo venture, whatever the means of transportation, you'll encounter enough engaging companionship to keep you happy, and all without ties or commitment. Running or cycling would be great exercise; get the wind in your hair and enjoy the delightful sense of movement.

16. SUNDAY. Demanding. There's plenty of stress building early, with too many decisions for any one person to make. You're either going to spin out or opt out. A love relationship or romantic entanglement will become especially intense. You may not be sure whether you want to be with a certain someone. The old freedom and closeness dilemma raises its head as you realize you don't want to be alone but also don't want to be restricted. Rather than responding immediately, weigh the situation carefully on its own unique merits. It may seem familiar or repetitive, but it's probably something you've never experienced before. By the end of the day you will come to know your own mind.

17. MONDAY. Focused. The first thing to do at the start of this workweek is pay attention to money matters. There are two aspects to this: how much you make and how much you spend. A penny saved is indeed a penny earned, so look into your savings goal and see if it meets the requirements to give you the life you want. Another dimension that warrants consideration is how much you owe and how much you're owed. If your debts are unsustainable in the long term, consolidate and pay them off as soon as possible. If anyone hasn't paid you for services or repaid a loan you made to them, now's the time to collect what's due, purely as a necessary matter of self-interest. Don't mix emotion with business.

18. TUESDAY. Fortunate. Income from an exceptional opportunity should help fill the coffers with ready cash. You're likely to be so busy raking it in that there's no time to think about spending it. For long-term investors with an astute eye for a bargain, real estate is likely to represent great potential, especially if expected profits are realistic. Geminis who are in the market for a family home could trade up to a quality property that offers class and security. An exciting new venture that is in the final phase of preparation before its launch is likely to make money and last the distance. A silent backer for an enterprise can make all the difference to ultimate success.

19. WEDNESDAY. Frustrating. If you feel you're not being heard or listened to, you could become frustrated and even infuriated. Try not to get angry if you feel your words and ideas are falling on deaf ears. Sometimes even the best suggestions turn out to be rejected. There's not much that can be done if other people choose to be close-minded. If what you have to say is worth communicating, you will need to patient and persistent in getting the message across. If it's important, write it down for posterity so it won't be lost or cast aside. Actions speak louder than words, and a decisive move is needed presently. Check that you're not unconsciously looking for trouble.

20. THURSDAY. Testing. Determining whether you want to make practical moves in the real world or idle time away in fantasyland might be a tough call to make. If the wind is out of your sails due to a recent disappointment or dashed hope, giving up on reaching your goal seems an option. It's easier to dwell on what might have been, or to tell tall stories about the one that got away, than make your dreams a reality. Clashing with a stubborn, willful neighbor is sure to get your back up. Legal options or appeals to authorities may seem fruitless in resolving a territorial or personal dispute. You'll probably need to stand your ground and take matters into your own hands.

21. FRIDAY. Uplifting. The first day of the Sun in Gemini is a point of renewed self-confidence and personal strength. However, nothing will simply bend to your will, and the world won't immediately fall at your feet. For best effect you need to compromise, accommodating circumstances as you find them. Simple direct thinking along with planning practical matters should work wonders for you. If you need inspiration or guidance, turn to the world of nature. In personal affairs and human encounters, emotional intelligence counts for more than mental cleverness and educated smarts. Most of all you need your family on your side and in your corner, which may be a greater balancing act than you expect.

22. SATURDAY. Variable. Dealing with parents or other older relatives is a priority. You may not be the center of attention you'd ideally like to be. Perhaps a family member is ill or needs support. At the same time another relative may hit a peak of success and want to celebrate. Good and bad events occur simultaneously, making it hard to fully participate in any of them. Births and deaths as well as weddings and funerals could come in pairs. In a less dramatic sense, there may be a need to move due to a tempting job opportunity that you can't turn down because it's a career promotion. Nonetheless, everyone won't be happy about household changes even if they are for a limited time.

23. SUNDAY. Enjoyable. This should be a fun day, when you appreciate an opportunity to do what you love. Spending extravagantly to have a good time might drain the bank account, but you only live once. Gemini parents can enjoy playful activities with kids, although this is apt to be expensive. You may feel generous toward a special person, arranging a gift that is lavish and impressive. Be sure to pick out an item that suits their tastes and preferences rather than just focusing on the cost or value. An easygoing attitude is the best response to a partner who seems intent on attempting to control you. Above all, don't feel guilty about having fun and doing what you want.

24. MONDAY. Upbeat. Good feelings and happy times flow from the weekend, which means you'll turn up for work with a smile on your face and in an upbeat mood. Tackle tasks and activities that require a creative touch. Design, advertising, and promotion will all benefit from your special attention, and you're likely to do a very fine job. Gemini artists will appreciate the inspiration and vision of this period. You should feel confident to display your works to the public. Presentations, lectures, and teaching that allow you to share knowledge in a positive way will be well received by a wide audience. If you are planning a vacation, consider all the wonderful worldwide possibilities.

25. TUESDAY. Satisfying. A working bee around the house or office could raise enthusiasm and productivity. Call on the assistance of a neighbor or coworker to assist with any arduous tasks. This is one of those days when many hands make lighter work all around. You're definitely in the mood to make things happen, so the more active you are the better you'll feel. Make it a priority to tackle anything you previously assigned to the too-hard basket or which you've been procrastinating about for too long. Once they're done and cleared away, you'll feel much lighter and capable of taking on even more. Earnings and profits should prosperous. There's even the prospect of romance in the workplace.

26. WEDNESDAY. Tiring. Expect a degree of stress and strain as you attempt to complete a heavy workload. Be wary of pushing yourself so hard that you snap or break down, in which case all activity will come to a halt. Pace yourself with a measured routine, although that may be easier said than done. Hasty, impulsive moves will likely prove to be counterproductive, sapping more energy in the long run. Get beyond an immediate sense of urgency and keep everything in perspective. The pressure other people put on you to take an active role in community affairs or certain group activities might be contrary to your own well-being. Family and career commitments should take precedence over social demands.

27. THURSDAY. Encouraging. Interpersonal relationships are in the spotlight at this Full Moon. For all Geminis this is a high point of the birthday period, where celebration and notoriety are part of the scene. Expect your partner or lover to shower you with special attention, even organizing a surprise party to show appreciation for your presence in their life. Singles have a clear opportunity for meaningful connection with another person, which might lead to a growing emotional involvement. Even if you're not interested in serious intimacy, you can enjoy fine companionship and worthwhile shared experiences. Being with another person who is totally your opposite will let you understand yourself better.

28. FRIDAY. Interactive. You'll still be in the mood for good company today. Make yourself available to people rather than drifting away into your own private world. Work-related meetings and negotiations might be scheduled one after another, presenting a passing parade of different characters. This variety should be entertaining and amusing, even if it takes you away from your own concerns temporarily. Geminis in sales, consulting, or coaching will be in high demand and can be notably successful through effective communication, persuasive charm, and a convincing manner. Seeking professional advice on your own behalf might be relevant, so schedule whatever appointment needs to be made.

29. SATURDAY. Distracting. Events could be in a state of confusion early, with plans and scheduled activities going through a series of inconvenient changes. A rendezvous may be canceled as circumstances shift completely. A previously arranged family or domestic event can also suffer a setback and may not happen. A crisis or sudden demand from work might mean having to put in some overtime or extra effort right now, disrupting your recreational and social commitments. However, these surprise demands may prove to be for the best because later in the day a successful agreement may be reached or an important relationship consolidated and deepened. Contacts with movers and shakers are advantageous.

30. SUNDAY. Harmonious. Deep, meaningful conversations are the order of the day. You're likely to find yourself in the unaccustomed role of quietly attentive listener, as your partner or a close friend pours out their heart. There's no need to analyze, judge, or even respond. More likely the other person just wants to be witnessed and really heard. It's imperative to keep any private revelations entirely confidential, even if you would like to share them with someone who is intimately involved in some way. Approach a relative or parent for a loan, but only if it's for something essential. Love and money become strangely intertwined, and you'll find that blood is thicker than water, especially in financial dealings.

31. MONDAY. Steady. Try to keep your mind on work and domestic duties. There may be compelling distractions and temptations nearby. However, they're actually void of real worth or meaning and are irrelevant, at least for today. Don't be fooled by the exaggerations of advertising and by promises that are too good to be true. Hang on to what you've got, and appreciate what you've established. Maintain the status quo, and keep your daily routine chugging along without a hitch. Security in your personal and career life is important to sustain. Your family is sure to be thankful for a dependable environment and lifestyle. Support and help are available from loved ones if you need assistance.

JUNE

1. TUESDAY. Stimulating. Associating or becoming friendly with an exciting person from a foreign culture can add a very different dimension to your life. Their background and upbringing could contrast sharply with your own, which should be a delight and a breath of fresh air. Expanding your network of acquaintances and contacts can be accomplished by using the Internet as a potential source of new connections. Develop your social networking presence on various specialized sites that pertain to your interests and are publicly available. Through stimulating and challenging group interaction, you can discover a fresh perspective on traditional subjects. Don't presume you already know it all.

2. WEDNESDAY. Mixed. To develop your understanding of certain subjects you need to work hard and be patient; results will soon show up. It would be all too easy to become frustrated and blocked in efforts to gain knowledge and expertise. Such accomplishments take time, no matter how clever you are. Current travel could prove tedious, with transportation delays and generally slow progress. Dealing with officials can reveal a hidden agenda, making you feel your privacy is being compromised for the sake of bureaucratic processes. Keep a confidential record of all such dealings and transactions because the evidence might prove useful in the future.

3. THURSDAY. Spirited. A journey can be arduous and uncomfortable again today, especially first thing this morning. Only go places if there are emergencies or crises that need you to be there no matter what. A better option is to take a mental trip via your imagination. Books, movies, and live shows are all great sources of escape and entertainment, helping you unwind from present stress. Political idealism might have you in its grip, motivating you to get involved in a public cause with humanitarian aims and goals. Later in the day the mood can mellow, softening hard edges and tense situations. Among everything else, make sure to get your job done to the satisfaction of customers and management.

4. FRIDAY. Successful. Powerful allies and backers in the workplace can give your career a boost in the right direction. Who you know will feature significantly in getting ahead. Your negotiating skills are strong and your people instinct is keen, making encounters and meetings doubly effective. The evening should be both pleasurable and romantic. However, in your effort to impress you could carelessly spend extravagantly, only to wake up with an over-the-top budget and a financial hangover. Treat your mate or partner to a lavish night out on the town, but only what you can genuinely afford. Loving your work or loving someone at work is a current theme. Love and money will mix well, at least for now.

5. SATURDAY. Opportune. Growing a business to a larger scale or blasting a career into a stratospheric trajectory takes planning and a steady building process. It may look as if success and recognition just happened overnight, out of the blue. However, what usually underlies such stellar performance is patient hard work, a clearly defined set of goals, and a realistic timeline to accomplish intended objectives. This is a time to figure out if your preparation and foundation stand up under the scrutiny of real-world conditions. As situations change and unexpected circumstances emerge, your predetermined rules of engagement should sustain your efforts and help to maintain your course.

6. SUNDAY. Exciting. A new era has arrived now that Uranus has settled into the Mars domain of Aries for the first time in eighty years. For Gemini people this signals a period of exciting new avenues for improved business profits or a better salary. Career innovations and experimentation during the last several years should now begin to pay off in unexpected ways. This is also a time when stimulating individuals are apt to appear on the social scene, invigorating your circle of friends. If you felt you were getting stale interacting with the same people over and over again, today marks a turning point of greater variety and new dimensions. Prepare to meet somebody totally different who rocks your world as much as you invigorate them.

7. MONDAY. Positive. It could come as a revelation that family members and friends love you for who you are. It's not what you know or say or think that they appreciate and value, it's you just the way you are. That doesn't mean you won't want to change and grow with experience. Just keep in mind the essence which is the core of your being, which will never change through the whole of your life. Birthdays are a time to celebrate this fundamental truth, and people who care for you want to acknowledge you in that special way. Fathers and brothers play a key role now. There is a unique unspoken bond of blood, which gives you confidence and strength because of their undying support.

8. TUESDAY. Subdued. Keeping quietly under the radar might suit for a day or two, just to catch your breath amidst all the action. You have a perfect chance for private conversations with confidantes you trust. Clear the decks of external clutter and commitments so you can totally concentrate. Critical negotiations on a business level may either make or break plans you hope to move forward. Hold out for a little more than you might accept. Gaining the right strong support will mean all the difference, and you can make this happen now. Discreetly arranging financing for a real estate purchase or property renovation might take you into a whole new realm of net worth and personal security.

9. WEDNESDAY. Caring. The plight of other people might take precedence over your own needs. Or you will want to offer kind support and nurturing to loved ones. There may be a relative or an older family friend who is currently hospitalized or in a nursing home and would appreciate a visit. Gemini parents might be concerned with the health and welfare of a child. Discussing various treatment options with a medical specialist can become a priority, but you'll be relieved to know that the condition can be cured.

Don't let the problems and difficulties that others are experiencing burden you. Take some time for yourself to help you relax and calm down. When you're strong you can be strong for others.

10. THURSDAY. Fair. This morning you'll feel like sleeping in or at least enjoying a slow start to the day. Lingering with your lover appeals, and it could be hard to leave. Without your usual bright and early start, you'll take a while to come around. Don't schedule appointments and meetings first thing. Get housework and other chores out of the way before you depart. They'll be simple enough to do, and that way you won't come back to unwashed dishes or a messy room. Take it easy on the job; you won't be sharp and alert until much later in the day. After work, relieve stress or tension through physical exercise rather than getting upset and angry at those you live with.

11. FRIDAY. Dynamic. With the Sun, Moon, and your ruling planet Mercury all in your sign, this is a special day for Geminis. Good health and abundant vitality should be yours, supporting whatever activities you choose to undertake. With renewed self-esteem and a confident trust in your own abilities, you'll feel ready to take on the world. In fact, you might be so enthusiastic that household members find it a bit too much and possibly even annoying. Get out of the house to avoid friction, and plan to be active throughout the day. With your vibrant energy and drive to express ideas so strong, it would be easy to clash and argue with other strong-willed, opinionated individuals.

12. SATURDAY. Bright. The New Moon marks the start of your personal astrological year. Now's the time to put the wheels in motion concerning the brightest ideas for your future. Take the high ground, letting the big picture inform your overall direction. Getting caught up in petty squabbles with family members or friends is a poor use of energy that would only be letting your ego get the better of you. There are more important things for you to do than proving other people either wrong or stupid, or both. Mull over your aspirations for travel and education, then consider options for turning these hopes or expectations into reality. Discriminating decisions will be called for, because you can't have it all.

13. SUNDAY. Helpful. Parents and other older relatives may need support, perhaps both emotional and financial. Be practical about planning their future care. A family business is a good option for a secure income because you'll be able to trust and rely on everyone involved. Any moves or decisions concerning money should be discussed with a professional adviser or accountant. They can help you come up with a well-devised strategy for growing net wealth in the long term. While you have a little time off, it may be worthwhile looking over your records of expenses and income. This will help you clearly know where you stand and ensure that your goals are on track.

14. MONDAY. Innovative. The same old approaches in business and investment won't continue to work as expected. Simply going through the motions in a robotic repetitive routine seems easy enough, but a new era has arrived which requires fresh approaches. An image change could help to maintain interest in your goods and services, so investigate possible options for an enterprise makeover. You may need to take things even further, exploring alternate markets or switching to an entirely different trade or line of work. Certain industries have reached there use-by date, and you won't want to be left behind with diminishing prospects when you could be one of the first to jump on the next big opportunity.

15. TUESDAY. Expressive. Making new acquaintances in the neighborhood will be easy and natural. It could be as simple as striking up a conversation at the bus stop, train station, or checkout line. The next thing you know you'll be on the way to developing a lifelong friendship. Getting to know local shopkeepers means you get good service and choice produce, because personal touches matter. Being recognized in the area where you live promotes a feeling of belonging as well as the security of genuine roots. You're in fine form as a communicator, and any audience will enjoy your style and be persuaded by your message. There's pleasure in sharing information and knowledge, and you'll be acknowledged for your generosity.

16. WEDNESDAY. Fruitful. You should be experiencing growing confidence in your writing and speaking talents. It's not that you need to show off or be the center of attention, but more that you have something valuable and worthwhile to express. Performances of all kinds should be successful. If you need to make presentations or convey a message, schedule this now. Creativity and imagination are peaking. This is a fertile and satisfying period for Gemini performers and artists. Writing, film, drama, visual arts, and graphic design are all possible avenues for successful work which should provide a period of enduring interest. By enrolling in a course to learn more about such activities you'll gain a great deal of useful knowledge.

17. THURSDAY. Active. Repairs and maintenance around the house may occupy a lot of your energy and attention. In fact, there may be so much to do that taking a day off work to handle it all could be justified. Building and renovating are well suited to the planetary action. Make sure that you're on hand to supervise and direct any major work being undertaken. In that way you're guaranteed a thorough job that gives real value for your money. Your physical endurance and stamina are high, making this a day of peak performance for Gemini athletes and sports enthusiasts. Romance can be very intense and even obsessive. Meeting your match in the game of love might lead to a long-lasting relationship.

18. FRIDAY. Cautious. This is the wrong day to skip details and be negligent, careless, or inconsistent. Bosses and other authorities won't accept superficial responses or mediocre efforts. Don't even attempt to sweep mistakes and inadequacies under the rug or fake results. You are being subjected to too much careful scrutiny and attention to detail for sloppiness to escape unnoticed or slip under the radar. Instead of being lazy, take the opportunity to be thorough and professional. It may be tough to get things exactly as they need to be, but there will be the satisfaction of a job well done and likely praise from those in charge. Relating to a parent can be difficult, but maintain respect.

19. SATURDAY. Heartening. A happy contact between Venus and the Moon promises a pleasant day of fun and good times. Relationships with relatives and neighbors are positive and heartwarming. Invite your favorite folk for lunch or an afternoon gathering. There should be plenty of humor, lively conversation, and enjoyable stories to share. With everyone on their best behavior, politeness and diplomacy are the order of the day. One or two friends might prove overly exuberant, but it shouldn't be too difficult to keep them in line. A recent attraction for someone who lives nearby should be pursued. Invite this person on a date, where you can display your intelligence, charm, and wit.

20. SUNDAY. Good. Speaking up for what you want is a good idea. Whether anyone else knows or has guessed your intentions is irrelevant. It's important to give voice to what matters most for you, and to own it clearly. You won't get what you don't ask for. Of course this can be accomplished in the most refined, elegant, and diplomatic of ways, but still maintain an iron fist in a velvet glove. Even if you are initially refused or rejected, it's worth trying again with a different, improved pitch. Perseverance is the key to making things happen. If you find that obstacles and blocks are insurmountable, accept with grace and find a new approach or a new mission.

21. MONDAY. Energetic. You have the ability and motivation to achieve a great deal of work if you harness your energy. Inactivity and laziness will actually feel bad, no matter what excuses you make. Firmly resolve to finish up outstanding tasks and jobs filed away in the too-hard basket, and be done with them once and for all. The timing is perfect for clearing away rubbish and clutter, whether at home or in the workplace. Check every nook and cranny, dumping everything that is broken or irrelevant to your purposes. Your work will then flow much more effectively and with less unnecessary effort. Watch what you say and how you say it when in mixed company.

22. TUESDAY. Productive. Gear up for a hardworking day, following yesterday's groundbreaking efforts. However, there's more flow and less grunt, making for relaxed momentum and steady progress. Pay attention to any aches and pains that develop. You may have pushed a little too hard lately, leading to physical stress and strains which need treatment. It would be wise to schedule a therapeutic massage, acupuncture treatment, or chiropractic session to ease discomfort. Symptoms are early warning signals that can help you forestall a worsening condition. Employees and contractors are worth hiring at top dollar when you can't manage to do it all yourself.

23. WEDNESDAY. Exhilarating. Social appointments and activities gather momentum as the day progresses. Stick to routines early and follow through on commitments and responsibilities. It will be easier to clear the desk and complete outstanding jobs first thing, before interruptions take over the agenda. Expect a roller-coaster ride when eccentric, exciting individuals land on the scene, injecting a vibrant energy with their presence. Younger, wilder, rebellious types feature in the mix, much to your delight. A combination of shock and awe heralds the start of a friendship that changes your life. The doors are flung wide on a network or scene you never knew existed.

24. THURSDAY. Passionate. Your lover or partner should be central today. Make them feel wanted, appreciated, desired, and generally the most important person in your life. With Venus currently traversing Leo, you can lavish as much affection as you want to. People you genuinely care about need to know that now. So be demonstrative and clear about what they really mean to you. You can show this with flashy expensive gifts, but what will really make all the difference is what you say to them and about them. Nothing takes the place of quality time and meaningful attention. If there have been recent disputes, spats, or arguments, they can be quickly resolved and forgiven.

25. FRIDAY. Sensitive. Someone you're close to may be leaving, which is sure to make both of you sad or a bit down. It could be a family member or a partner, but whoever it is there's likely to be a very good reason for their temporary absence or departure. The space that's left in your life could easily and beneficially be filled up by new people you'll now have time to meet and hang out with. When one door closes, another one opens. That's definitely an applicable saying in the present circumstances. An overnight Full Moon will deepen an existing relationship, and may also present business opportunities in a shared venture. Make sure you can afford whatever you promise to become part of.

26. SATURDAY. Purposeful. Further dealings with real estate and housing finances can become a significant priority. It's time to assess the value of your property holdings as an overall component of your net worth. You may require the services of a professional in this regard, who should give you a current valuation that can be relied upon. Perhaps you want to borrow against this or make further investments that require mortgages and loans. A parent could become a part of the process, either as a joint partner or as a guarantor of a finance arrangement. Inheritances, insurance, and taxes can all feature in the mix. Wherever you look, your money seems interconnected and tied up with other people.

27. SUNDAY. Supportive. Paying attention to a parent or other older relative is a duty worth doing today. Try to make a practical difference to the quality of their lives. You could offer to help out with chores and tasks that are difficult for them to handle or accomplish. Better still, remember what they enjoy, and go out of your way to make this a fun day for them. Something as simple as a walk in the park, a picnic, or a trip to their favorite stores will satisfy simple needs for recreation and getting out of the house safely and securely. Attend to property, medical, travel, and life insurance. Get a deal that suits the context as well as your budget. Don't ignore it or just hope for the best.

28. MONDAY. Interesting. Take a break from business as usual and entertain yourself with a cultural event or a social outing.

Maybe you could invite recent acquaintances to your place for dinner. Organize a group of pals to attend the movies, a concert, or a show. Expect a pleasant break. What's important is bringing the spice of variety into life. Then you'll have stamina to keep plodding away at mundane daily routines, which are making slow, steady progress. Legal or official matters involved with membership in an association may need your attention. Whatever the situation happens to be, you'll be required to play by the rules of the game.

29. TUESDAY. Reassuring. Traveling away from people and places you love may prove unavoidable. You could be needed by a family member living faraway. Or property you own in another part of the country may require attention. Keep the trip brief and efficient, then get back home as soon as possible. Meanwhile, call or send a message to say you miss folks left behind. Introducing a love interest to your relatives might arouse disapproval or discussion of the pros and cons if your partner is from a foreign background or of a different faith or race. Perhaps such a relationship won't go too far if this person can't realistically fit into your life. But if you're both determined, then it could work over time.

30. WEDNESDAY. Evocative. If journeys and separation have been part of your experience lately, the truth is you may not mind being away today. The interest and stimulus of different sights, sounds, smells and situations will be uplifting. All this might even provoke thoughts and considerations of moving to another place to live permanently. Gemini individuals are perennial travelers. You appreciate the value and necessity of change. Even if you don't want to move right now, it's always delightful to vacation in a special or exotic location where your spirit can have a free rein. Thought experiments are worth exploring. Imagine yourself in different circumstances and see how that feels.

JULY

1. THURSDAY. Testing. Review your income to see if it covers your expenses. As a Gemini you are not one to put your head in the sand when things get tough. Pressure can be a good motivator to get you to improve yourself. The steady-as-she-goes philosophy might be abandoned now in favor of positive action. Marital differences can become obvious. Instead of getting caught up in the blame game or in deception, own your own contribution to the disharmony. Look at ways to rebalance the relationship together and to reclaim the loving union. When you go to bed tonight, things won't look the same as they did this morning.

2. FRIDAY. Productive. A business venture can get the go-ahead, involving you in all sorts of proceedings and discussions. Don't be disappointed as you watch your original idea get watered down by the powers that be. They are looking for profit and security. You will gain creative license once you get going again. Say no to week-end overtime, and plan to do something fun with your loved ones for a change. Throw a party with friends. Or take a trip to some-where different for inspiration and motivation. Some Geminis seeking affordable real estate will have to convince your family that you need to move away. They'll come around eventually.

3. SATURDAY. Eventful. You can expect to run into familiar faces and enjoy a very social day, with plenty of places to go and people to meet. If you join a volunteer organization and do your bit for those less fortunate, the experience will turn out to be one of the best things you have ever done. Besides helping other people you will make new friends and meet people who will prove to be powerful connections in the future. If you are trying to avoid some-body, you may be unsuccessful now, so don't even bother. Face up to the issues you have with them and try to solve the problem. If you owe money that you can't repay right now, be honest and work out a repayment plan.

4. SUNDAY. Sentimental. A celebration or anniversary can bring you together with family, friends, and people from your past, with fond old memories to reminisce over. You could be easy prey to se-ductive influences and romantic overtures, so try to keep your feet on the ground and your head out of the clouds. A close friend or relative may be leaving, stirring up a feeling of loss and isolation. But they won't be gone forever, and you are sure to have lots of correspondence during the period you are apart. Be careful if you are traveling. Check that all travel arrangements are correct and departure times are up-to-date. There could be some transporta-tion delays that tax your patience and temper.

5. MONDAY. Mystical. An artistic or spiritual influence holds sway over the day, making you wonder whether anybody is truly indepen-dent or whether something much greater pulls the strings. A meet-ing with a remarkable person can open your eyes to new ways of being and spark interest in further study. Just give yourself time to think things over. Don't sign up for anything until you are sure you can afford the price. Someone close may need your support; what-

ever you can do for them will be a great benefit. You have a lot of
energy for beautifying your home and adding value to your assets.
Search for unique and creative ideas to revitalize your environment.

6. TUESDAY. Strenuous. Your tenacity and endurance will prove
invaluable in any ambitious pursuits. Just be sure to have a plan of attack in order to avoid impulsiveness and treading on other people's
toes. Also make sure you don't take on too much or you may burn
out before the day is done. If you can take the day off to work on a
personal project, you will remove a lot of pressure that is currently
on you as well as save some money. If a romantic relationship recently ended, find a good counselor and get some help to work out
your subconscious drives before you start another affair. Emotional
work done now can save you heaps of heartache in the future.

7. WEDNESDAY. Manageable. For the enthusiastic and inquisi-
tive Gemini this is a time to concentrate on the jobs at hand, leaving all new projects for another day. If you can get on top of what
you already have going, you will be happier in the long run. Catch
up with all your correspondence too; there could be someone or
something important that you have forgotten about. An argument
with a loved one can send you packing to lick your wounds. Instead
of feeling sorry for yourself, examine the overall picture for a better
understanding. Writing down your feelings and emotions can provide a more impersonal overview. Retail therapy won't make you
feel better and won't help to conserve your funds.

8. THURSDAY. Beneficial. Lady Luck will be on your side if you
play your cards right. You will have to know what you want and
what is expected. The possibility of becoming overcommitted is
high. You may have stiff competition in the love stakes and might
need to reassess your situation. Decide if you want to have to play
this game forever or if you just love the thrill of the chase. Prepare
well for a meeting in order to show that you know the facts. This
will earn you extra points with your boss, besides the possibility of
a better deal. Appearance and presentation make the difference in
all pursuits, so put some additional thought into both aspects. Be
sure to dress to impress.

9. FRIDAY. Expansive. Mercury, your ruling planet, moves into
the sign of Leo, which is Gemini's natural house of communication.
Over the next three weeks you can expect to have many group discussions and conversations, meet new people, possibly travel quite
a bit, and also have more contact with relatives and immediate
neighbors. Use this time to gather information rather than try to

reach conclusions. There are too many distractions for clear think-ing right now. Take some time out to do something for yourself. Have your hair done, get a massage, or buy an item for your home that makes you feel special. You have been giving a lot of your en-ergy to other people and need to replenish it now.

10. SATURDAY. Powerful. Intense encounters with other people can stir up emotions of guilt, jealousy, or possessiveness in you or someone else. Tact and diplomacy will be vital in order to avoid con-coct and outbursts. Luckily Venus, the planet of love and harmony, moves into Virgo, which is your sector of home and family. You might decide to enjoy quiet hours at home redecorating, cooking, or gar-dening. Venus will stay in Virgo until August 7, so look forward to the closeness and warmth of family living. There is a definite possibility of overindulgence in food and drink with no regard for your diges-tion or your weight, so be mindful of this when preparing meals.

11. SUNDAY. Supportive. The New Moon in Cancer highlights your financial sector and makes this a good time to initiate a budget. Con-coct a financial plan for making and saving more money or start a new job. Your parents could decide to give you financial backing to start your own business, or you may have to help them in their old age to find a retirement home that suits their budget and require-ments. Either way, family support is indicated. Entertaining at home should be fun, and a new neighbor can become a great friend. Try not to make any definite plans for today. Just sit back and let life happen. You might be surprised where you end up at day's end, as a surprise invitation comes your way.

12. MONDAY. Communicative. Intuition and foresight are on your side. When it comes to purchasing large-ticket items such as real estate, trust your good Gemini instincts and you can pick up a bargain. You are in tune with subtle undercurrents that contribute to conversation, which gives you the ability to truly communicate with people. Whether in a mediation situation or other sensitive ne-gotiations, you should come out on top. On the other hand, if you are faced with a long-term contract where the fine print is stacked against you, contact an attorney or a government agency. You will get the support you need for a fair deal instead of being ripped off.

13. TUESDAY. Niggling. Changes are inevitable, and working out how best to adapt to new situations and relationships can cause some anxiety. If you leave things to take their own course, you may have to put up with a situation not of your choosing. Gemini stu-dents could have trouble making ends meet. Try getting involved with other students to start a cooperative for food and textbooks; discover the power of the group. It is time for you to take a stand, whether you are in a problematic relationship, an economic situation that is unsatisfactory, or living conditions that don't suit your needs. When you express your feelings and believe that you deserve something better, it will all fall into place.

14. WEDNESDAY. Helpful. This is a great time for socializing at home. Ask your boss to come for dinner, and show your true worth with good hospitality and organization. A new relationship might introduce different cultural values into your home, which will make life better than it was once you adjust to the alterations. Don't balk at change. You have a lot of energy to put into your residence, and this is a perfect time to start looking for a home to buy or renovate. Your parents or an older relative may need some help to find new living quarters where they can maintain their independence but still have support. Check out senior-care facilities to find the best options.

15. THURSDAY. Disconcerting. This is not a good time to discuss issues that are critical to you. You will find it difficult to maintain your equilibrium and not fly off the handle. However, if someone challenges you unjustifiably, you certainly won't back down without out a fight. The problem is that your sense of perspective may be so distorted that you cannot tell important issues from trivial ones and will defend both with equal vigor. Focus on your desired goals and stick with them. Guard against acting impulsively or hastily without any regard for what you truly want. The need to make a choice between your career and home should be talked over with the folks who matter most in your life and work.

16. FRIDAY. Fruitful. An artistic bent can produce outstanding results right now. This is a very good time to put extra effort into anything you hope to achieve. Loving thoughts and feelings can arise in all sorts of situations, and you need to be discerning about who you shower with your favors. Gemini investors may be surprised with the returns that are starting to come in; a decision may be made to invest even more. Remember, however, that the market is fickle. Only buy what will give you a reasonable return in the short term. Geminis who are bored should look at new hobbies or sports that are inspiring as well as adding plenty of human contact back into your life.

17. SATURDAY. Creative. Gemini writers should find any recent blocks removed. New ideas will lead to a steady stream of accomplishment without too much trouble. The same goes for teachers and students who have been grappling with assorted obstructions. Either getting the point across or just getting the point will lead to a solution that is creative and valuable. Be very careful when if comes to speculation because you are likely to fall prey to false promises or premises. The same goes with the mating game. A very attractive and alluring person might promise a great deal but then expect far more than you can give. You may be caught in a love triangle with an ex. Better end it right now to avoid any more heartache.

18. SUNDAY. Industrious. There is a self-denying nature to the day. No matter how important financial security might be, there is still the personal element and the stress that you should consider. A decision to clean out closets and get rid of items no longer in use could end up with a major family dispute about what should be thrown away and what is worth keeping. If you allow everyone to have their attachments, common ground can be reached and everybody's self-worth will remain intact. When working out a budget, be sure to include some money for fun. Otherwise life will become so gray that the budget will be ignored and will become worthless. Focus on maintaining a happy balance between enjoyment and thrift for well-being.

19. MONDAY. Congenial. You can call on plenty of support for whatever project you are about to embark upon. Don't let nuisance holdups or lack of confidence put you off. You may be your own worst enemy at this time. Get plenty of advice, then trust what you hear rather than focusing on your own doubts and excuses. It is said that fortune favors the brave, and that applies to you. Weight watchers can find a good diet and the resolve to stick to it. A meatless and fat-free regime could be best. If you have health problems, obtain advice about what to eat and what foods to avoid. Start walking in the early morning for exercise and you will be surprised at the people you meet.

20. TUESDAY. Erratic. A momentary lapse of reason can wreck your whole day, so stay on target and keep what is important at the forefront of your mind. People are going to make demands of you that you can't deliver, but don't feel inferior. Instead, realize that they are making unreal requests. If you are working in an environment where there is a lot of backbiting, don't let it get you down. Simply ignore it and it will go away. A legal situation that is looming may be causing much sleeplessness. Instead of stressing out, get some legal advice. You don't have to stick with the lawyer you currently have. You can shop around for someone who suits you better, or even represent yourself.

21. WEDNESDAY. Promising. Your mate or partner may introduce you to someone who can offer much better opportunity than your present job is offering. This will give you the chance to negotiate for the situation you really want, so don't let it slip through your fingers. Saturn, the planet of discipline that is often called the teacher, now moves into Libra, where it is strong and offers its best. This signals a time to put everything in order so that you can have maximum impact. Conserve your energy, treat your body as a tool that has to be well cared for, and be efficient so that your lifestyle matches your intrinsic reality. You can't go wrong when you play fair.

22. THURSDAY. Mixed. Be active in the first part of the day; later on you will not be very effective. You could spend hours on the Internet searching for information that isn't forthcoming, or find that the phone numbers you obtained have been disconnected. Don't get involved in gossip, or you are likely to become a target also. Be extra careful of someone who says they want to get to know you better despite being still married with a family. An agreement or contract in dispute can be discussed, worked on, and some type of arrangement made. Be prepared to make concessions, and some will also be returned in your favor. Conflicts within a relationship can be worked out if you accept your part of the blame.

23. FRIDAY. Encouraging. The Sun is now visiting Leo, your solar third house of communication. Sun in Leo turns your attention to your immediate surroundings and increases your interaction with friends, neighbors, relatives, and work associates. This is a good time to examine how you handle the casual relationships that are so important in your life. There is a certain amount of manipulation going on beneath the surface. Be sure to carefully read all the fine print before signing any long-term contract. A love relationship might simply be an exchange for social security or financial gain. Be cautious about who you pair up with, and be sure that your intentions are what you think they are.

24. SATURDAY. Tricky. Attachments to people and belongings can get in the way of true communication. These can color all discussions, making for a very emotional exchange. If you can maintain an overview of what is going on, you will avoid lots of misunderstandings and conflict. Trouble with the police or other authorities is indicated, so be very careful not to exceed any limits. If you have to travel and are not fit to drive, call a taxi or ask a sober friend to give you a lift. If you get involved in a one-night stand, make sure to take all precautions for your own peace of mind. An investment in renewable energy might be worth looking into despite the initial cost.

25. SUNDAY. Active. Today's Full Moon in Aquarius implies an urge for freedom and the need to break free from any bonds that have been restricting you. As a Gemini you are in a very intuitive and creative frame of mind, which will help you work with anyone who is trying to hold you captive to their desires. An invitation to the theater or to an exhibit can open your eyes to exciting possibilities and ignite a passion for exploration. Don't let initial doubts color your excitement. You can learn some important facts of lasting value. Although you may be thinking of moving for lifestyle reasons, you could find that the opportunities for your line of work are limited. Don't be put out off; by being innovative, you will succeed.

26. MONDAY. Philosophical. Travel arrangements may have to be canceled, but look at it practically and it is probably for the best. Travel to a certain country might have to be avoided due to a political situation. Geminis who go overseas as a volunteer may find the hardship and pain of the citizens too much to bear. However, if you look for spiritual backup you can become an effective and caring helper. Students may have to budget time as well as money. Extra study is designed for making ends meet and putting in revision time will help; that may be necessary to grasp a particular subject. Instead of feeling you need time to yourself, the sacrifice you make now will lead to a lucrative and rewarding profession in the future.

27. TUESDAY. Diverse. All your plans and expectations can go by the wayside as other influences come into play in your life. A new romance might come as a surprise, taking you to unheard-of places. You could find yourself making promises that you thought you would never make. For any Geminis who are suffering from back problems and other health issues, yoga, meditation, or tai chi might be beneficial. The allure of overseas travel can be so strong you find yourself making arrangements for a cruise that promises lots of fun and exotic experiences in foreign ports. You might even begin a new life in another land or start a special long-distance relationship.

28. WEDNESDAY. Demanding. Gemini going on a job interview should try to keep your own ideas to yourself. Make sure you express only those ideas your prospective boss wants to hear. With your emotions coloring your ambitions at the moment, be careful that you don't make a long-term decision on a whim. Turning to drugs or alcohol in an attempt to express your emotions to your mate or partner will only make matters worse. You would be wise to examine your need for false courage. A job proposal might come your way. No matter what you think it entails, you would be wise to investigate the ins and outs of the position before accepting or rejecting it.

29. THURSDAY. Challenging. Professional and business concerns come into focus, but in a way that will test you. Your personal life might be on public display more than usual, making it difficult for you to conceal certain facts about yourself. A public argument with a loved one will be hard to live down, so do your best to stay out of the limelight for now. On the other hand, your emotional sensitivity and empathy toward the people you work with will be a plus, allowing you to gain all the support you need to move into a higher position. You might be asked to take a leadership role that involves some public speaking, and you will be surprised at your popularity.

30. FRIDAY. Energetic. Mars, the planet of action and energy, moves into Libra and your solar house of fun, lovers, and children. This signal can the start of a new relationship, the birth of a child, or a new creative project. A sports interest can put you in the winner's circle. Just make sure you don't overdo your training schedule; keep on doing what has been working for you up to now. A child may need extra attention or discipline. Don't think that love can or will solve all problems. Life is hard, and children need to be able to cope with adverse situations. You may be asked to put in some overtime. No matter how inconvenient this may be, say yes or you might find you don't get any further opportunities.

31. SATURDAY. Social. Invitations are likely to be many and varied, and it is up to you which you are going to accept. Don't be worried about activities you don't want to attend, because it is up to you to choose. You can always come up with a good excuse for those you refuse. You are likely to make some important new contacts. Concentrate on people who can probably give you what you want, because the opportunities won't be there for long. This is an excellent time to start planning for the future. Your hopes and dreams will start to take effect over the next two months. Successful Geminis might receive a bonus from an appreciative boss generously sharing profits.

AUGUST

1. SUNDAY. Invigorating. This is a day for some serious fun in the company of other equally determined pleasure seekers. Gemini sports fans will appreciate an opportunity to test their skills and competitive prowess in a tournament with tough players also out to take the prize. There's no room for letting up in such a win-or-lose, do-or-die situation. After playing hard, it's likely everyone will want to proceed to party hard. Gemini parents, or those involved with a partner who already has kids, can spend the day blending the extended family to make everyone feel included. However, some moments of tough love could be needed to keep all the tribe in line and make them come together.

2. MONDAY. Stressful. Maintaining a secret might bring you to the bursting point. A skeleton in the family closet may be poised to tumble out, but that doesn't mean you need to provide a push. Saying too much might bring shame and embarrassment to someone you never meant to hurt. Discretion will be the better part of valor. If certain information doesn't need to be broadcast for any real purpose, keep quiet. Gossip in a local dining establishment or around the watercooler could be impossible to avoid. If you hear things that are none of your business, put yourself in the shoes of those involved and act fairly. If you feel vulnerable or inadequate when out and about, get home to a safe place with the one you love.

3. TUESDAY. Rebalancing. Take time out to catch up on reading and paperwork that has been piling up. Shut yourself away in a quiet space where you'll be totally undisturbed and get to it. If a pile of e-mail in your inbox has been demanding attention, get to it now. Among all the information overload, you'll turn up a few gems of humor and friendship. Reading for pleasure should be part of your day, but don't neglect the household accounts and family budget. It's okay to have a nap or snooze if you become so comfortable that drifting off happens naturally. Some regular downtime seems part of the cycle of functioning in the most healthy and efficient way.

4. WEDNESDAY. Bright. You'll feel increasingly better as the day rolls on, with more energy and a greater sense of purpose. There's no need to get off to a flying start. Enjoy sleeping a little later than usual, then a leisurely breakfast, before making a relaxed appearance at work. Your keen efficiency in everything you tackle will make up for any earlier absence. You'll be able to fly through tasks, then go looking around for more to do. There should be plenty of time to get some exercise, and you'll be pleased at the obvious progress in your level of fitness. Gemini athletes will be performing at peak performance and be capable of achieving a personal best.

5. THURSDAY. Tricky. Get your head on straight so that conflicting signals and information don't set you at cross-purposes. It will be easy to say one thing while a household member hears something else, making for moments of tension in any shared living space. Any messages and other communication that can get jumbled will do so today. The trick involves listening and reading with extra care and attention to detail. Double-check with the original source to make sure you get it right. Arguments seem pointless when all that's wanted is clarity and understanding. A language barrier can be hard to overcome and might be postponed until a better time. Learning a complex subject may seem appealing but wind up being frustrating.

6. FRIDAY. Restrained. When planning the weekend's recreation, check carefully to determine what your budget can afford. Certain activities may need to be curtailed or cut back due to the cost involved. Gemini parents may be under pressure from kids to pay for extravagant desires and expectations that have been fueled by the media or by well-heeled friends. The need to work and earn a living may mean less fun and socializing over the next few days. This will be disappointing, but it's better to be realistic and to face facts. By applying discipline to your efforts and reining in your expectations, you will survive and prosper in the current climate. Put some cash aside for emergencies and rainy days.

7. SATURDAY. Connecting. Health, fitness, and feel-good factors are all in positive territory, making you upbeat about yourself and life. Relations with family members and among people you live with are currently excellent, encouraging roundtable discussions and meaningful conversations. Geminis looking for a new place to live can find a suitable home, which is also a good value. Finances and real estate blend well, making this an ideal time to buy or sell. Spending money on household items should be a useful and satisfying shopping venture, whether you're in the market for kitchen utensils, decorative items, or garden equipment. An older relative would appreciate a phone call or a thoughtful gift.

8. SUNDAY. Comforting. This is a day when it pays to be grounded in ordinary experience, keeping in touch with your feelings. Rather than taking off on any imaginary flight of fancy, stay tuned to your basic instincts and sensitive intuition. Your heart will steer you to truths greater than heady ideas and pie-in-the-sky concepts. Thinking can sometimes be overrated, and this is one of those times. Make a point of visiting or calling close family members and friends, reminding them how much they mean to you. As the day goes on, you might enjoy a stroll around the neighborhood or a drive out of town. Learning more about a challenging hobby you're committed to makes for a relaxing evening.

9. MONDAY. Good. Welcome a low-key start to the working week. You may be relieved to find that traffic and transport are not busy or cramped. Once you're on the job, check all messages and mail to locate significant information requiring focused attention. Educational and training activities for the period ahead should prove successful and productive. Use available quiet spots in the day to draft important communication. Your brain is switched on, and choice words for eloquent and articulate expression come easily to mind. Take time to get it just right and delay sending it for a few days. Reading and editing will only improve the final result.

10. TUESDAY. Revealing. Last night's New Moon in Leo might have given deeper sleep than usual, or provoked weird and wonderful dreams. It would be wise to write down what went through your head. There may be important clues to the future, ideas that will help you make imminent decisions. If you do not know how to interpret or decode your inner symbolic language, get a book that deals with such matters. Or discuss it with someone who can assist to unravel them. Make it a short day at work so that you can arrive home early to enjoy personal space and a favorite pastime. Serious Geminis should plan the month's budget. Gardeners should prepare new beds and plant seeds for autumn harvest.

11. WEDNESDAY. Constructive. People you live with may think differently than you, yet what they have to offer is smart, insightful, and useful. You may struggle with their suggestions because your style and approach makes it hard to see where they're coming from or what they actually mean. Put yourself in the other person's shoes in order to grasp their perspective and then be able to communicate effectively. You're bound to learn something important from a variety of divergent opinions. A neighbor or relative might propose a business venture of great merit. Unless you give it a fair hearing, you could miss a genuinely worthwhile opportunity. Developing a green thumb and getting your hands dirty will suit this lunar phase.

12. THURSDAY. Easygoing. Look forward to a laid-back day without too much action or energy. This is a timely break, allowing you to even stay home without missing too much. It's the wrong time to start any new venture. Attempts at accomplishing very much are unlikely to succeed. Keep your objectives limited, and be content with achieving small victories. Romance may be planned for this evening with expectant confidence, in contrast to an earlier nonevent. However, the tone is one of serious commitment and genuine love, so you could get in deeper than usual or deeper than you want. Playing the field is not an option. Married couples can renew the vows in a touching private ritual.

13. FRIDAY. Special. Only the superstitious should get spooked by this calendar date. For some folk, thirteen is an auspicious number in a positive sense. Take this day in stride, but pay plenty of attention to what happened overnight. A powerful combination of Saturn, Venus, and Mars has been energized by the Moon, making this an exceptional period of the month. It could herald the birth or conception of a child. Parents may discover a youngster's special talents or abilities that hadn't been recognized or acknowledged before. A new relationship may become a central feature of your life, one you'll cherish for years to come.

14. SATURDAY. Rewarding. Creative pursuits are ideal, and you should have time to pursue them. A quietly brewing passion for an artistic hobby could be giving you the idea of taking it to a more professional level. Gaining further education and training in related techniques and skills will reward you with enhanced performance. Competitive sports may also appeal, whether as a player or a spectator. You'll find greater satisfaction and entertainment from a display of elegant skill and graceful style rather than rough or brutal activity. A high-brow cultural event such as a museum exhibition, classical concert, ballet recital, jazz show, or foreign film festival offers a special treat.

15. SUNDAY. Guarded. Regular exercise and athletic activities are central to a healthy lifestyle. Not only will they keep you fit and in a positive frame of mind, but they'll also provide you with some great fun. Enjoyment is critical in maintaining a steady routine so that you receive the promised benefits. Make a point of encouraging everyone in the household to exercise jointly and spend regular quality time together. Be aware that the dark side of pleasure pursuits could creep up on you if you're inclined to burn the candle at both ends with late nights and poor nutrition. There will be a price to pay for self-destructive behavior, no matter how much you enjoy certain activity at the time.

16. MONDAY. Varied. With the right attitude, this can be an exciting and productive start to the workweek. However, at the outset you may feel you got up on the wrong side of the bed. You may be a bit hung over from the weekend's good times, or thoughtless harsh words may be exchanged during breakfast. Don't let a grumpy beginning create daylong negative vibes. Move on and expect circumstances to improve as you tackle the workload awaiting you. Stubborn resistance to chores and tasks won't help your cause. Once routines are handled and set in motion, you'll have the freedom to follow interesting new career and business leads. Spontaneous social contacts will also spice up the mix.

17. TUESDAY. Vital. Love and sex are in high profile, making other experiences temporarily fade into the background. Geminis who are in a new relationship will find it hard to stop focusing on that special person. You'll be busy calling or messaging in every spare moment, planning an evening together. Your friends and workmates will be pleased for you, supporting this current tilt at happiness. Married couples should arrange a romantic date to rekindle passion for one another and to celebrate being together. If you're single, pleasurable companionship will be easy to find, offering an antidote to any sense of lonely isolation.

18. WEDNESDAY. Harmonious. Relationships flourish in the present planetary climate, making enduring and valuable connections readily available. The focus moves from intimate pairings toward day-to-day friendly contacts. Relatives and neighbors feature in cheerful exchanges laced with goodwill and humor. Make calls, send messages, and schedule personal meetings for maximum positive influence and beneficial outcomes. Salespeople can be particularly convincing and persuasive, landing deals with major customers and earning a hefty commission. Satisfying progress is foreseen for all parties involved with ongoing negotiations, and agreements can be reached. Just don't get hung up on petty details or inconsequential fine print.

19. THURSDAY. Pressured. The tone is heavier today, fulfilling the reputation Saturn and Capricorn maintain among the astrologically savvy. There will be no escape from duties and responsibilities, so don't even contemplate trying. The best approach is to put your shoulder to the wheel, and make a steady effort at getting the job done. If you let someone down or neglect promises you made, the result won't just be disappointment. There is likely to be a negative backlash and severe consequences. Gemini parents need to take special care of children, watching for early warning signs of emerging difficulties or stumbling blocks. Check that insurance is adequate for the unexpected.

20. FRIDAY. Erratic. Mood swings seem to be the order of the day, as people who are usually amicable, easygoing, and cooperative become cantankerous and disagreeable. This Jekyll and Hyde turnaround will let you know the true colors of an individual you thought you could trust and rely upon. Check your own behavior, too; it might be you who is accused of fickle, unreliable responses.

The best course is one of direct honesty, sticking to agreements and promises made. This is clearly a time to treat people the same way as you expect to be treated by them. There is grand opportunity to clear the way for a genuinely committed relationship where love will prevail.

21. SATURDAY. Resourceful. You and your mate or partner need to break out and do something different. Familiarity may not quite be breeding contempt, but it can lead to becoming jaded and disconnected. Taking each other for granted is no way to make the most of a relationship. Changing the scene and taking in a wider world of possibilities will be a breath of fresh air that provides a mutual sense of relief. A potential business venture could be based on a sense of excitement and intuitive instinct. However, somehow knowing this venture could be the next big thing may not be convincing to potential investors. They will require a more substantial business plan, which might be hard to pin down just now.

22. SUNDAY. Favorable. Put entertainment of the highest quality on your agenda. Make sure to get tickets early for chosen events because seats are apt to be in scarce supply for popular activities. Traditional and classical performances are especially impressive. Even if you're a novice in these artistic fields, you'll appreciate the special quality of the experience. Taking classes to learn more about a favorite subject or special interest will reward you with greater knowledge and skill. You'll probably receive far more from your involvement than you expected or paid for. An ongoing romantic scenario with a foreigner can flourish, and even a long-distance relationship shows promise.

23. MONDAY. Ideal. A certain relationship could be experiencing a dream run, making you think you've finally found that special someone and can plan ahead in a serious way. Love is definitely in the air, whatever your current partnership status. As an air sign you are receiving delightful energy from Venus, the planet of love, and from Mars, the planet of sexual desire. This combination makes you attractive and popular. Affection flows freely, and close encounters occur effortlessly. You're at your best to make a lasting impression. Dress for success in high style, and expect to be the center of attention in a most positive way. Couples may decide to start a family in this period.

24. TUESDAY. Encouraging. The Moon has been growing in light and today reaches its peak. Make a point of checking the horizon at sunset for the beautiful sight of a rising Full Moon. This is a time when you are under pressure to get the balance just right between work and your personal life. If there is too much emphasis on one or the other, adjustments will be required. As important as your career may be, your success is now based on having a secure and grounded home base. Forward-looking negotiations and deals are promising. You should be quietly excited by workplace developments as well as by private initiatives you're planning. Prepare to be patient as these work themselves out over time.

25. WEDNESDAY. Useful. Mercury, your ruling planet, has recently gone retrograde in the sign of Virgo. Mercury retrograde happens usually three times a year for about three weeks, signaling a time to review and reconsider plans, activities, and projects. This is especially important in regard to your current career and job, which can be mystifying and perplexing if they had seemed to be progressing well up to this point. Take any delays and obstacles in stride; they give you the opportunity to get things right, preventing any further problems later on. If something needs to be abandoned altogether, that will prove to be the best move in hindsight.

26. THURSDAY. Eventful. Throw yourself headlong into the working environment, and you'll make rapid progress no matter the current circumstances. Like white-water rafting, the pace of events will be exhilarating yet risky. Don't let yourself become intoxicated or spun out. Surf the waves of opportunity where there is least resistance and most to gain. Geminis beginning a new job or applying for a different position can look forward to fresh prospects of greener pastures. However, expect to take a while before everything is fully sorted out. At least you won't be bored with the flurry of activity throughout the day. This evening you could follow up interesting leads and contacts in a social way.

27. FRIDAY. Demanding. The business of earning a living takes priority over recreational distractions, especially this morning. Don't jump ahead of yourself, starting the weekend in your mind before the working week is done. Make a point of completing unpleasant chores and tasks so you won't be anxious over the weekend or have to face them again on Monday morning. Taking part in group activities and team efforts will be a mixed experience. There should be close camaraderie among associates, but tension with outsiders or managers. You could be tempted to bend the rules or take unnecessary risks, but that might backfire. Stay disciplined and stick to the straight and narrow.

28. SATURDAY. Bumpy. Arranging a social outing or gathering could prove difficult. It may be hard to line up everyone so you can be together in the same place at the same time. Agreeing about what you all want to do could also prove almost impossible. What some would enjoy, others may loathe, and vice versa. There may be nothing to do but cancel altogether, postpone until later, or split into two groups for the day. Tension and jealousy may arise among friends due to competition and rivalry. Love, sex, and friendship are currently a challenging mix that may get too hot to handle.

29. SUNDAY. Tricky. You may awake in strange territory and at close quarters. Desire and attraction have been powerful forces lately and can become a heady brew. There is an opportunity to forge close ties and strong bonds. Genuine trust and vulnerability go hand in hand, which could overwhelm or even scare some Geminis. Others may delight in the experience of two people becoming one, reveling in the depths of unknown possibilities. However, if you have gotten out of your comfort zone and don't want to take things further, communicate that clearly and politely. With tact and diplomacy you'll be able to extract yourself from any situation.

30. MONDAY. Calm. Catch up with the month's routine tasks such as household budgeting and office filing. Creating an ordered system for paperwork is a good idea. Also put tools and resources into definite places so that work can proceed efficiently. You'll feel relaxed and productive when you can get your hands on exactly what you want in timely fashion. Clients and customers will also be impressed and confident regarding your services when you appear to have it all together. Head back home early, if you haven't already taken the day off. Make it a quiet evening at home alone or with immediate family members, enjoying a calm, peaceful, and secure environment.

31. TUESDAY. Reflective. It would be easy to sleep in and miss appointments or arrive late at work. Geminis on a tight schedule or with a critical agenda should set a loud alarm or have someone check to be sure you're up. Dreams, visions, and fantasies could be swirling in your head. Try to sort out truly bright thoughts from hopeful projections. At least one current idea has a real prospect of future success, but which one it is may not be obvious among a cloud of possibilities. This could be the time to take the path less traveled, which is risky yet full of promise. However, that doesn't mean rushing headlong into a foolish venture, informed by nothing more than wishful thinking.

SEPTEMBER

1. WEDNESDAY. Confusing. Some days present a cascading information overload, and this is one of them. Trying to make sense of so many ideas and so much communication can seem like a daunting task, even for a Gemini. The key is to take one step at a time, with a clearly organized process. Keep breathing steadily and stay calm, even when the pressure is on to return calls, make decisions, and respond immediately. Travel plans can easily get scrambled, and a previously agreed meeting agenda may be changed on the fly. It may be smart to postpone any new involvement for the day because not much is likely to be accomplished. Back off into your own personal world and don't pay too much attention to external happenings.

2. THURSDAY. Magical. Taking a short break from work would be wise, especially if you've been frazzled and stressed lately. Personal appearance is a major concern. You're naturally attractive and vital, but that doesn't mean you should leave it at that. Take pleasure in enhancing your look with the right mix of cosmetics and accessories. A haircut or hair removal is perfectly timed in this waning section of the lunar cycle. Shop for an eye-catching outfit that will lift your already fine presentation. There's always room for improvement. A romantic date or encounter this evening will be magically uplifting and memorable. Singles should make the most of being seen on the scene.

3. FRIDAY. Problematic. The consequences of financial extravagance may come home to roost. If you've been sensible and disciplined with expenses and budgets, you will only have to worry about a little belt tightening. On the other hand, if you've been reckless or negligent, there could be serious concern over economic survival and paying your bills on time. Whatever the circumstances, you would be wise to eliminate any indulgent spending on luxuries and nonessentials. Figure out where savings can be made. Make a concerted effort to earn as much as possible, and hold onto it for future needs. When times get tough, you need to be prepared. Vacation and education plans may have to be downsized.

4. SATURDAY. Pressured. You'll have little time for daydreaming and recreation. There's business to be done and money to be made. Being resourceful is a priority. Don't let opportunities for improving your circumstances slip through your fingers. Nor should you imagine that chances will keep knocking at your door, because they won't. Research and explore available ways to earn more with a better job. Put in job applications and arrange interviews as soon as possible; otherwise you may find the best positions quickly filled by other eager workers. Sports and hobbies need to be put aside, and entertainment may be unaffordable or postponed. Reschedule a date while you're busy with life's necessities.

5. SUNDAY. Pleasing. This is a perfect day to get out of the house for a drive or a stroll. Meet friends at a local restaurant for a leisurely breakfast or lunch, swapping stories and listening to the latest gossip. Or catching up with close relatives over a Sunday dinner might suit everyone's schedule. Take whatever opportunity for getting together that comes along. Gemini parents will want to spend quality time with youngsters in playful outdoor activities at the park or recreational area. Neighbors offer pleasant conversation, and you may want to invite them to your place so that you can get to know each other better. Exploring your area offers a heightened sense of belonging.

6. MONDAY. Innovative. Don't hesitate to propose creative ideas and presentations. This is the right time to suggest concepts so that they gradually develop and gain acceptance over the coming days and weeks. Futuristic proposals and visionary plans are likely to capture people's imagination, especially if they're packaged in stylish and playful ways. Using a humorous approach and appealing to a sense of fun should work well, whatever you're proposing. Youngsters are sure to be receptive to knowledge when it's in the guise of an entertaining game. Teaching, coaching, and training activities will be well received, particularly when reviewing and reinforcing previous subject matter rather than initiating any fresh new topics.

7. TUESDAY. Motivating. A lot of frustration and complications due to recent delays can reach a climax and a resolution simultaneously. With your ruling planet Mercury still retrograde, many endeavors may be on hold or awaiting decision. Now's the time when solutions begin to present themselves, at least partly because you've finally accepted the existing state of affairs. Move forward with fixes, answers, and strategies that deal specifically with problems. Arrange for needed repairs and maintenance of a car, machinery, or home appliance. While you're at it, you might get a health checkup and physical overhaul yourself. Give special attention to your home and family. Get to bed early for a rejuvenating night's rest.

8. WEDNESDAY. Grounding. Today's New Moon has special importance for Gemini's sense of place and security. This is the time of year to put down roots and enhance the physical condition of your living space. If you have plans to buy or sell real estate, these are likely to be at the bargaining and negotiating phase until next week. A contract can then be signed and a deal concluded with confidence. You may be thinking about moving to a new residence, whether just around the corner or out of state. Renovations and landscaping are ideal activities around your home. Spend time to get the design and planning just right. Think ahead to the next season.

9. THURSDAY. Demanding. Stick to the straight and narrow path, and you won't go wrong. Precisely following rules and regulations works best. Authorities are likely to make an example of rebels and lawbreakers, no matter that person's age or experience. There may be legal matters to deal with concerning children, possibly about custody and maintenance or regarding their education. You'll be expected to honor your part of each and every agreement or bargain you've made. If you delay paying the mortgage, child support, or other regular bills, you could jeopardize your credit rating. Unfortunately this is a day when you won't get much credit for what you do well, but you are apt to be hammered for any errors, mistakes, or misbehavior.

10. FRIDAY. Creative. Artistic efforts will be well received, making this a good time to display, publish, or exhibit your work. A project you've been focusing on for weeks may have reached the point where you're finally ready to launch it. Prepare the way with appropriate advertising and promotion so your intended audience or market knows what to expect. Gemini parents may be required to attend a school event where kids are putting on a show. If you feel in need of a decent dose of fun, plan to leave work earlier than usual or even make it a long weekend. This evening enjoy a hot date, a new affair, or romancing your loved one in a passionate way.

11. SATURDAY. Comforting. After an impassioned or entertaining evening, now's the time for talking. Enjoy a lively family meal where everyone shares recent adventures. Comparing notes on shows and movies is a great way to find out what's worth going to see. Gemini singles who have made a deep impression on each other may start discussing the prospect of living together. Relationships are on solid ground physically and emotionally, making this an ideal time for meaningful communication about practical issues. Put last-minute touches to a project or plan of action. Most importantly, be sure that it feels right and makes good sense. The opinion of someone you trust will give you added confidence.

12. SUNDAY. Satisfying. Cleaning up around the house makes sense if you're too busy during the week to take care of all the chores and home maintenance that pile up. You'll have ample energy for tackling jobs requiring strength and stamina, so plan to deal with the tougher ones. Everyone who lives with you should be urged to pitch in. Many hands make light work of less than pleasant tasks, and there will be a real sense of satisfaction once the work is done. Clear out unnecessary stuff in closets, attic, and garage. Make a genuine attempt to dispose of it all, decreasing the load of material goods around the place. Streamline your life so you can be mobile when the mood strikes.

13. MONDAY. Volatile. It's easy to find yourself at cross-purposes with your mate or partner, especially concerning living arrangements and lifestyle. One of you may have had a change of heart about a prior mutual decision, resulting in the current standoff about what's going to happen. It could be something as basic as purchasing new furniture, or as important as where you will live. Singles who had planned to move in with that special someone might now have a different view. Keep the lines of communication open and the dialogue ongoing. You can come up with inventive solutions to any problems if you think laterally and remain open-minded. Practice tolerance toward opinions that are different from your own.

14. TUESDAY. Interactive. It may seem difficult to cooperate with other people, but that doesn't mean you should give up trying. Interactions and encounters are currently a major part of your busy life, so make the most of them. Certainly it will help to maintain a sense of humor; a dash of wisdom and compassion wouldn't hurt either. If you want to make a real attempt to understand other people, put yourself in their shoes and try your best to see things from their perspective and through their eyes. If you're able to do so in even the most difficult situations, the insight you gain can bridge the gap and make all the difference.

15. WEDNESDAY. Diverse. It's days like this that can send you over the edge, making you think perhaps you've gone a little bit crazy. Expect to encounter wild antics and inexplicable behavior, which even you may be prone to as well. There can be surprising breakthroughs as well as unexpected breakdowns. Either way, able support will be on hand to help come up with a fix to solve problems. Sometimes it takes reaching a point of total stress or an extreme experience before it's possible to truly understand someone or something, even yourself. Be prepared to try new behavior if you want to change and transform outcomes constructively. A deep conversation or professional guidance will produce a lasting impression.

16. THURSDAY. Supportive. Welcome the outstanding rapport between you and those closest to you. A whole network of interpersonal relationships is ready for affirmation and reinforcement from you. Aim for straight talking and direct communication. This might even include a dose of honest but fair criticism, so that everyone knows exactly where they stand with you. Gemini parents will have special influence on youngsters. Kids will benefit from consistent discipline and from the boundaries you set, even if they're not happy at first. Employees need to be given clear instructions about what's expected and about the consequences of breaking rules or not delivering. Fair but firm is the best approach in all dealings.

17. FRIDAY. Constructive. Carefully studying what your business competitors are doing right and wrong will help you succeed better. There may also be mutual benefit in getting together with others in your line of work to share resources and know-how. Creative approaches along with sensible financial management is sure to be a winning combination. Risks and innovative strategies are fine as long as the budget can handle it. Quality family time is a wise plan for this evening. If the household gets together for a shared meal, the easygoing atmosphere is likely to lead to deep, meaningful exchanges. Entertain at home in style, or throw a spontaneous party if there's a reason to celebrate.

18. SATURDAY. Strategic. Organization is a strong feature of today's efforts and activities. Well-laid plans and detailed strategies should pay off in every way. Travel, whether short or long journeys, will proceed on schedule like clockwork, delivering all of your expectations. A visit to family or the old hometown will prove very satisfying, especially if you spend some time with older relatives who may not be as mobile as they once were. Enjoy getting back in touch with your roots and origins. You are apt to be inclined to avoid routine weekend chores, preferring to be out and about instead. If you decide to attend an art exhibit or a cultural event, delegate some of the housework to the kids, your mate or partner, or someone you hire.

19. SUNDAY. Starred. A serious spiritual tone encourages attending devotional services. Put high-brow entertainment on the agenda as well. Appreciation of traditional arts is growing, reflecting a greater maturity or increasing sophistication in your taste.

Gemini parents might want to expose children to a refined performance that cultivates and expands their awareness. Such experiences are best in small doses of the very best quality, so be discriminating in your choice. A thorough, densely packed educational course would be challenging and gratifying. You're ready to take your understanding of a special interest or hobby to a deeper, more professional level.

20. MONDAY. Challenging. Start off on the right foot at work this week. Arriving early and hitting the ground running will impress higher-ups, who will appreciate such a show of eagerness and enthusiasm. Problems or obstacles that emerge on the job may not respond to usual remedies and brute force intelligence. Instead you'll be challenged to think laterally, to use your good Gemini intuition to move forward and to succeed. Amid all this busy activity and productive effort may be a compelling workplace attraction. This could be a stunning new coworker or a customer; whoever it is, they're sure to have your total attention. A romantic love story might become an event of social notoriety.

21. TUESDAY. Advantageous. With Venus and Mars both in Scorpio, the dance of the sexes becomes irresistible. Passion, power, and positioning can be used advantageously by both men and women. Males appealing to females in power may be chosen for jobs or promotion. Women who want to prevail in competitive arenas might use their desirability to men in charge. While such tactics seem shameless, gender plays and preferences are a reality and could be used to get ahead where decently possible. It may be especially hard to keep your mind on the job if there are other compelling interests grabbing your attention.

22. WEDNESDAY. Opportune. Many Geminis have been in line for career advancement and promotion this year. If such success has eluded you so far, be aware that further opportunities are on the horizon. You'll need to be sharp to grab them. Stay on the lookout, as they may appear suddenly out of the blue in the least expected place or from a surprise source. Those of you in the market for a new job could land an exciting position that's even better than you'd hoped for. Changing your profession, industry, or role at work is a tempting proposition, especially if you're bored or have outgrown your current situation. However, lay the groundwork with family members for change.

23. THURSDAY. Balanced. The Full Moon in Aries early this morning shines a light on your social life, leading you to consider how much fun and joy you've been having. If you've been busy at work and preoccupied with paying the bills and getting ahead, now is a favorable time to bring more balance to the equation. Spending time with coworkers at lunch or after quitting time, just relaxing together could be one way to achieve this balance, especially if other contacts are limited. There's sure to be at least one or two associates you like and would enjoy knowing better. Join a club or team that offers sports activities or a hobby interest. Create a strict schedule for personal recreational time and stick to it.

24. FRIDAY. Active. Pulling together in a cooperative effort can achieve a great deal. In contrast, trying to go it alone and do everything yourself will be tough and will only accomplish a limited amount. Become a team player; appreciate that the whole is greater than the sum of its parts. If you're leading or coordinating a group of people, delegate to competent subordinates and trust in their ability to get things done. This is the right time to expand an enterprise by adding new people, allowing you to take on more work. Choose from several candidates who look promising and should do a good job for you. Although there may be personal matters on your mind, there won't be much time for them today.

25. SATURDAY. Slowing. An extended family outing is sure to be enjoyable. Make the kids the center of attention; give them a special experience they've been waiting for. Today is a perfect opportunity to bring stepchildren and stepparents together, creating a positively functioning blend based on trust and respect. Later on you might want to take a break from all that is going on. Shut down your computer, cell phone, television, and any other distracting device so that you can chill out in a place of personal peace and calm. Trying to have fun in usual ways won't prove as satisfying as you expect. Sometimes you need to come to a complete stop, which can be hard for a Gemini's persistently active mind.

26. SUNDAY. Solitary. Devote yourself to personal affairs and interests. Make this a private day where you can indulge yourself however you want. Make it clear to everyone that you're not interested in an outing or in chores, that you need a block of time where you're totally undisturbed. Even your mate or children should understand that this is essential for your well-being, although it may not particularly suit them. Being a bit selfish on occasion is healthy. After all, you know best what you need. A secret passion might be simmering quietly inside you, tempting you to initiate a clandestine romance. However, think over the consequences before you act. Keep a diary or journal to process your feelings.

27. MONDAY. Mixed. Set an alarm if you need to be at work or at an appointment early; it could be all too easy to sleep in longer than usual. You might wake up in a groggy cloud of confusion, maybe exhausted from an overactive night of dreams or possibly hung over for other reasons. You'll become progressively more effective and alert as the day progresses, but it could be a slow start. Take time off this morning if possible, gathering your wits and clearing your head. Ask a fellow worker or employee to fill in for a while to provide help and support. You may be vulnerable to infection, so dose up on vitamins and health supplements to ward off potential sickness. Conserve your energy for tomorrow.

28. TUESDAY. Vibrant. In contrast to yesterday, you should now be on top of everything and fighting fit. Your positive attitude will help ensure that everything you attempt is achieved with efficiency and provides satisfaction. Organizational skills are at a peak, allowing you to tackle the biggest and most complex projects with confidence. Any sense of getting sick has likely been shrugged off with a renewed sense of vitality. You'll accomplish more working independently and without distraction. Leave complicated interpersonal issues for another day, and strike out to make your mark solo. Because you're so competent now, you'll probably have sufficient spare time for a hobby, sports, and exercise.

29. WEDNESDAY. Strenuous. Use this day to make sure that whatever you're responsible for is together and accurate. Upcoming unexpected happenings can create instability. But if you've prepared as best you can, then everything should be fine. Being too caught up in your own thoughts and activities may lead to neglecting your appearance. Pay extra attention to your style and how you look. A sloppy presentation could give people the wrong idea about your character, ability, and intentions. Mental overload can lead to anxiety and burnout. Make sure you're getting enough healthy exercise, fresh air, and quality nutrition. With competing demands from career and family, your own needs might have to come last.

30. THURSDAY. Uneasy. Money is apt to be tight, causing problems if you haven't been sticking to a budget. Even large plans and projects with carefully planned expenditures may experience cost overruns and need extra funding. If you're not earning enough to meet monthly bills, it might be time to negotiate a new payment arrangement. Gemini parents know how much it really costs to raise kids these days. The whole family will need to tighten their belts, which likely means less cash for entertainment or other luxuries. Use this pressure as an incentive to improve earnings and income through committed effort and strict penny-pinching.

OCTOBER

1. FRIDAY. Opportune. An excellent job opportunity looks set to come your way, promising to improve your social status as well as your bank balance. Be mindful of what you will wear to the interview or audition. Whatever else you do, do not try to use your influence or make an impression by name-dropping, charm, or sexual allure. A relationship might be on the rocks and leave you feeling insecure and lonely. Get out and meet new people, join clubs, apply for interesting positions, and volunteer for community service. That way you can turn your misfortune into fortune fairly quickly. Go shopping and deck yourself out in new glad rags. Put your very best foot forward, then you can't go wrong.

2. SATURDAY. Fortunate. Gemini salespeople can make the sale of the century and really give yourselves a kick ahead. So get out there and start talking. A family member or close friend might come to you for counseling. If you are prepared to give them the time, you can make a big difference to their prospects right now. Your intuition is spot on at the moment, and your suspicions regarding a work mate could be justified. Make sure you cover all your bases because someone might angle to take you down with them. A hot date could be canceled this evening. Don't worry. You'll get another chance. Catch up with old contacts over the phone, which will be to your advantage in the future.

3. SUNDAY. Lively. Your ruler Mercury, the planet of communication and short-distance travel, moves into Libra, which is your solar sector of fun, lovers, and children, and instigates plenty of social events, parties, and the like. You will have a chance to make new friends and, if single, to form a new romance. Gemini parents who want to help a child with studies will start to take the role of a teacher at home. Make sure kids have some outlet for fun to create a balance. Perhaps taking up a sport they're interested in would suit. Planning a vacation can turn out to be a pain in the neck if choice places are all booked out, leaving you with no other option but to reschedule everything or look elsewhere.

4. MONDAY. Variable. The morning is likely to be quiet and thoughtful. Many ideas and feelings can go and come, but you would be better off getting into an artistic outlet and allowing your internal processes to take care of themselves. Otherwise, your mind might concoct all sorts of wrong ideas about people and situations. Tread carefully when talking about personal issues, as everyone is likely to be a touch oversensitive right now. Spend some of your savings on making your home more comfortable. For Geminis who are looking for new living quarters, today might present the perfect place, especially if you are moving in with a lover. It will be the love nest of your dreams.

5. TUESDAY. Scintillating. Romance and innuendo are in the air. Someone you have never considered eligible might arouse passion. Various conversations about banalities or business can seem seductive and volatile, promising all sorts of zany dating and flash-crush scenarios. An inheritance of some sort can open doors and turn problems into solutions, doing wonders for your self-confidence. A new job or position might test your mental powers and your ability to walk the talk. However, if you stop trying too hard and just wing it, you'll probably do just fine. Trust your ability to communicate, which as a Gemini you have in spades, and you will probably start new walks and talks.

6. WEDNESDAY. Suspenseful. An aura of change can affect your mood and create feelings of insecurity. Yet this will pass as the day grows old. By nightfall you will feel confident and ready to party late into the night. Relationships could be testing your level of commitment. Your natural Gemini mutability may make you think of moving on and considering other possibilities. But maybe it is yourself you need to get to know and learn to live with. So don't project your anxiety onto your current companion. Proper exercise and diet can overcome many health issues you may be experiencing now, and also can enhance your enjoyment of life. Try to work with a personal trainer and dietician.

7. THURSDAY. Influential. Today's New Moon in Libra impacts your solar house of speculation, fun, and children. It might inspire you to plan a grand vacation and start paying for it, or to invest in real estate that will give you the lifestyle you've always craved. Whatever you decide, be sure to research interest rates and the seller's credentials before giving information about your financial assets. Students might have to take on a large debt to gain entry to a preferred school. However, this won't matter if you can earn big bucks after graduation. An interest in art or music could be the start of a lucrative public career. Just guard against pushing your child to live your own dreams.

8. FRIDAY. Positive. Your good relationship with a coworker will pay off when they recommend you for a promotion. Be aware, however, that they may have a hidden agenda you know nothing about. Make sure you stay informed and in the loop so that you won't be duped. A person who seems very nice can suddenly turn into someone who is not so nice. This is a good time to clean up around the house. Sort out all your bills and other paperwork. Start a new diet or exercise regime, or research lifestyle changes. By putting your own backyard in order, external situations will be resolved as well. Unemployed Geminis might apply to the armed forces where you can learn a trade.

9. SATURDAY. Rebalancing. Venus, the planet of love and attraction, is now retrograde in Scorpio until November 8, then retrograde in Libra until November 18. This will alter conditions involving love impulses, partnership considerations, and finances in relation to your work, service, and physical well-being. Relationships with coworkers, health professionals and service providers can change and contracts be renegotiated. Loving relationships may come under the sway of practical considerations. Financial mismanagement from the past can be brought to your attention. This is a great time to finish artistic or creative works previously left unfinished before venturing into new projects.

10. SUNDAY. Restful. Get any work you have planned for today done early, because there is not a lot of hope of getting anything done in the afternoon. Friends may call and disrupt your plans. But if you relax and enjoy their company, a good day will be had by all. A local farmer's market could be a lot of fun. You can pick up fresh and organic local produce to put quality nourishment on your plate and probably save a few dollars as well. If you are trying to save money, why not visit your local library and choose free materials to entertain you. Take a break from today's consumerism and ask the neighbors over for a game of cards and good conversation.

11. MONDAY. Cooperative. Problems can be solved through cooperation focused on a common goal, which can be nurtured through an open and honest information exchange. A loving relationship may enter the next stage of commitment with a proposal of marriage and be the beginning of lifelong plans. A former rival in love can turn out to be a best friend if you are willing to let go of old resentments and expectations. A new relationship could come with a ready-made family and put you in the role of stepparent. Don't become a competitor for attention and affection. A legal matter might be resolved and surprise you with how cheaply and successfully you have managed to come through it.

12. TUESDAY. Impulsive. Extravagance and generosity are rife and good feelings can mark this as a very enjoyable day. But if you overstep the mark, there may be strife between you and your partner. Make sure you talk things over before you spend any substantial amount of money. Social interests can interfere with your work performance and put you on the wrong side of the boss. At this point in time, any tardiness or sloppy performance will not go unnoticed. The costs of a social function could escalate and demand a total rethink on what you are doing and why. Go back to the drawing board to start all over again. Legal matters should be postponed today.

13. WEDNESDAY. Limiting. Expansion and contraction are part of the same cycle now. You might have to take a step backward to consolidate before you can move forward again. A minor theft or accident could bring home the benefits of insurance. It would be worth your while to do some research on all the different types of coverage available before you fork over your money. A major rethink on the use of your resources can be timely. It will ensure that you are making use of everything available to you. The busy Gemini might overlook some very valuable assets, friends and associates included, so don't hesitate to ask for assistance if needed.

14. THURSDAY. Revealing. Pressure to make an important decision could bring up many other issues besides the matter at hand. If you are completely honest with yourself, you might be able to gain a little insight into the workings of your psyche. Counseling would be timely now. Even such things as art therapy, where you can access deep-seated emotions through creativity, will help. Self-destructive tendencies can also become noticeable. You might be overworking to a point where you have lost your joy in life. See if you can moderate your behavior patterns. Let friends and loved ones look after themselves while you take some time out to relax and nurture your inner child.

15. FRIDAY. Easygoing. After the last couple of days, today will be a pleasant change. Take advantage of the relief from stress and tension and do something nice for yourself. Plan your next trip. Visit the travel agent to get the ball rolling, or go on the Internet to find the cheapest fares now while time is on your side. A legal matter that has been haunting you could be dropped surprisingly, and end up costing you little compared to your expectations. Maybe the lesson for the day is to have no expectations. Simply enjoy whatever life dishes up, then you won't be disappointed. You may be interested in exploring different spiritual lifestyles that will benefit your health.

16. SATURDAY. Entertaining. Chores and domestic duties won't be a problem for you today. It is quite possible that your idea of fun will involve a cleaning spree, taking the meaning of spring-cleaning to the max. Ask friends or family over for a meal. Enjoy creative culinary delights with lashings of fun and interesting conversation. Serendipity, the faculty of making desirable but unsought-for discoveries, will touch you often. Sudden surprise guests or the return of a long-lost suitor can beneficially alter your life. Listen to the weird tips or inside information you receive. The door to enlightenment might open a crack, giving you insight into what is possible.

17. SUNDAY. Expansive. Sensitivity to your surroundings is greatly increased, as is your empathy with those around you. Be willing to listen to a friend's problems, or discuss your own problems. You will pick up on the moods of other people as if you were a social sponge. Just be careful about associating with negative people who are not able or willing to discuss their emotional problems in a rational manner. Poetry and art, especially escapist art or literature, can take you away from whatever is bringing you down. Your creative mood might lead to new skills and a positive outcome. There is a distinct possibility of discovering a talent you never knew you had.

18. MONDAY. Restrictive. The temptation to spend time daydreaming will be stifled by the necessity to work and to fit in with what those around you expect. Lighthearted conversations might occasionally include interesting mentions of fantasies, dreams, and ideals. A new romance might make it very hard to keep your mind on practical everyday issues. Whispered phone calls or furtive e-mails could earn you a black mark with your employer. An afternoon meeting will give you a chance to prove your worth and show your ability to find solutions through genius strategies. Be sure to take notes of what's discussed so that you have a record of ideas being proposed and who suggested them.

19. TUESDAY. Idealistic. This is a lucky day. You are able to act with a complete picture in mind of what you are doing now, planning with greater foresight while avoiding the pitfalls others may call bad luck. You can advance your interests and are not about to accept any offers unless they fit in with what you really want. Some Geminis may turn down a lucrative job offer because it involves work in an environmentally dangerous field or in conditions that are exploitive and possibly illegal. Romantic idealism can hold sway in a relationship. Be careful not to put someone up on a pedestal, as the inevitable fall can really be a shock.

20. WEDNESDAY. Lazy. A late night or sleeplessness can affect your mood and incline you toward escapism, such as shutting the door, turning on television, and not answering the phone. It is good to have a day of rest occasionally. But be sure you are not avoiding a problem that will only gain in momentum through neglect. If the latter is the case, consider seeing a counselor to learn more effective coping methods and to take the pain out of living. Excessive physical strain should be avoided, as you are now more subject to minor infections, chills, and fevers. If you suffer from allergies, be mindful of what you eat and drink so that you do not suffer the consequences.

21. THURSDAY. Spirited. Your ruler Mercury, the planet of communication, has moved into Scorpio, which is your solar sector of health and work. Mercury visits Scorpio until November 8. You will be more attentive to detail than usual and especially concerned about using the best techniques available. Be careful not to be too critical, though, as your striving for perfection could irk others and your criticisms seem too personal. Nervousness and anxiety might dog you as you strive for perfection. Pursue relaxing pastimes. Just stay away from substance stimulants such as alcohol, coffee, even caffeinated tea. Improving your diet and hygiene will lead to heightened physical condition and buoyant mental attitude.

22. FRIDAY. Rewarding. Problem solving as an intellectual tool suits Gemini's mental nature. Give your mind something to do if you have time on your hands. A business proposition may come your way, giving you plenty of things to investigate such as your rights and responsibilities within the business deal, the tax arrangements, and the market viability. Don't make any decisions until you have covered all aspects. Then you will be sure you know what you are getting yourself into. Tonight's Full Moon in Aries highlights your social life. Consider heading out for an evening of fun with friends. Gemini singles are likely to meet someone who will play an important role in your life.

23. SATURDAY. Rejuvenating. The Sun moves into Scorpio today and joins Mercury, Venus, and Mars there, signaling experiences with health and work that add emphasis to this already highlighted area of life. A new diet and exercise regime can truly inspire you. Pick and stick with a healthy regime, not a faddish diet that does more harm than good. A trip into the great outdoors will inspire, too. If you hang out in your local area, you are likely to run into people whom you haven't seen for a while. They might suggest new activities and new encounters that generate both excitement and personal growth, helping you to replace old habits with fresh and healthful ones.

24. SUNDAY. Tiring. Stay home this morning and relax with the newspaper and your favorite breakfast. You shouldn't bother about anything now, as you need to rest and recuperate from a busy week. Some Geminis may feel a bit lonely, but only ask someone over or get involved with people who don't need anything from you. Otherwise, they might take more energy than they give and will make you feel worse. Stay positive. A good comedy film would pick you up better than negative company. Or maybe you will spend some time getting to know yourself better. Start a journal, or go through your photo collection and catalogue these stills of your life and history. You might learn something new.

25. MONDAY. Sensitive. The Moon moves into your own sign of Gemini this morning. So for the next two days personal and subjective considerations will override everything else. You are very sensitive to the moods and feelings of the people around you. This puts you right there whenever someone needs your sympathy, warmth, and understanding. But you can become touchy, and objectivity may be difficult. If somebody disagrees with you, you might take it more personally than it was intended. This is a perfect time to initiate new projects that you have on your drawing board. Focus on your appearance and presentation. Beautifying your environment will also give you a lift.

26. TUESDAY. Supportive. Powerful associations can be a great help in the area of work and recognition for service. Don't hesitate to contact them if you are having trouble in the workplace, especially with such problems as sexual harassment or bullying. Subjects such as psychology, the occult, yoga, or other techniques of personal transformation will attract you, and they would be very good for you now. A separation from a long-standing friend could be difficult, and you may feel guilty for your part if not totally responsible. Don't let consideration for other people's feelings inhibit your own personal growth. Remember, you are the most important person in your life.

27. WEDNESDAY. Volatile. The willfully independent and rebellious spirit in the air will make it difficult to find agreement when it comes to group activities. You have a strong need to be free and to do something different, maybe even a little wild. Someone new in your workplace could threaten your feelings of security and make you feel you have to work harder or faster. However, don't jump to conclusions or make hasty decisions. This feeling will pass, and you will then be in a stronger and more secure position. Concentrate on setting up a budget you can afford and live with, one that will help you work your way out of debt. Home repair problems can be costly to fix, especially plumbing.

28. THURSDAY. Harmonious. The central issue today is self-expression through creativity and relationships. You will be assertive, but only to gain the attention of those you love or would like to love. Once you get out and socialize, you will make new contacts and friends who are warm and generous. Guard against overindulging; too much of anything can have unpleasant consequences in the months to come. This is a favorable day for all kinds of financial activities as long as they are not extravagant or self-indulgent. Advice from a financial professional will be beneficial, especially if you are planning to set up your own business and become self-employed doing what you do best.

29. FRIDAY. Stimulating. Mars, the planet that rules energy and action, has moved into Sagittarius, your solar sector of intimate and business partnerships. This influence will make you more self-assertive than usual. If you have been stifling parts of yourself for the sake of a relationship, you are likely to air your grievances now and hopefully clear the air between you. Sometimes this Mars transit can signify legal conflicts. You will need to be aware of the level to which you allow your self-assertiveness to be expressed, as conflicts and controversy can follow. Communication should flow well. Contracts and agreements can be finalized satisfactorily without undue compromise.

30. SATURDAY. Challenging. Minor crises can arise that present some sort of challenge to the structure of your daily life. While not necessarily serious, they may force you to pay more attention to what is happening. Singles could start a relationship over the Internet and find yourself organizing a face-to-face meeting for the first time. Students and writers will find a burst of emotional and physical energy that spurs creativity and concentration. If you are feeling nervous or worried, practice deep breathing. You'll find the extra hit of oxygen very helpful in grounding you and calming the nerves. Short-distance travel is indicated. You could be stuck inside the car for a while.

31. SUNDAY. Erratic. Your mental processes may be scattered, making it very easy for you to lose something of value or forget an important event. Write everything down and remember to look at your list. Then you will avoid disappointment. Gemini parents could be roped into helping at a sporting event or social fundraiser, and end up feeling that you have been used and abused by the organizers. When accepting volunteer positions, be mindful to point out exactly how much valuable time and energy you are happy to donate, and how much you are not. A theater performance or art exhibit will transport you to a creative space, thoroughly entertaining all aspects of your psyche.

NOVEMBER

1. MONDAY. Difficult. Being cranky or angry with people at home or at work is no way to start the new week. Make sure you think long and hard before unfairly criticizing those you're closest to and depend on most. Forget the saying that familiarity may breed contempt; it doesn't justify any harshness. Forgive the mistakes of others, and they'll forgive your ill temper. Then the day should improve immensely with much that can be accomplished in enjoyable fashion. Gemini with a new romance on the boil may discover that your family doesn't approve of your choice of partner. Your lover may not like your relatives either. That leaves you in the middle of a sticky situation.

2. TUESDAY. Testing. By keeping your head, you'll manage tricky and demanding circumstances that arise. Geminis who are familiar with the job easily handle sudden emergencies or pressure. However, if you're new and inexperienced in a particular trade or profession, you'll have to learn fast and think on your feet to keep it all together. Whatever the challenges there are to meet, tackle them headlong and you'll learn valuable lessons for the future. Juggling work demands and personal needs can be done by staying calm and focused while taking things steadily, one at a time. That way you can show just how smart you are, which should make an impression on the right people.

3. WEDNESDAY. Steady. This should be a calm day in a stormy, crazy period. You can rely on the continuing energetic support of coworkers and employees, who will help you get the job done through thick and thin. Give some serious consideration to the quality of your current work. It may not be as enjoyable or fulfilling as it once was, but this is not the right time to rock the boat or abandon ship. It's more than likely that you really like and care about the other people at work. Gemini parents may want to hire a tutor for a child who needs extra learning support. Improvement in sports may come from a qualified coach or extra practice time.

4. THURSDAY. Imaginative. During this dreamy period you're likely to engage in fantasy and escapism. You won't have much enthusiasm or interest in applying yourself to anything that requires effort or seems dull and routine. If there are creative outlets for your talents at work, pursue them productively rather than wasting time avoiding boring tasks. You'll be very pleased to get away from work as soon as possible. Look forward to focusing on a hobby and artistic interests, where you can excel. Sports and games should also be fun, whether you're a spectator or a player. Romance is on the agenda, although it may be different from what's usual and expected.

5. FRIDAY. Intense. A certain relationship could take on an obsessive quality. Serious love is in the air, but to do what you do best you need to lighten up. Someone you have been trying to avoid may have you in their sights, making you feel caught in a fatal attraction. A person who initially seemed pleasant might reveal a difficult side of their nature, which is unappealing. If you're not really interested, don't string that person along. Otherwise it will become more and more difficult to extract yourself from the involvement. However, if you want to impress a hot date, cook a special meal. Your partner will be most surprised and grateful if you offer to do the housework.

6. SATURDAY. Deceptive. Overnight the New Moon in Scorpio brings sensitivity and wariness. It will be unusually easy for you to upset people carelessly. Be vigilantly aware of what you say and do that might be taken the wrong way. This is no time for fooling around with anyone's feelings or heart. Consequences of doing so may be devastating, because everyone is not able to take things in stride like you do. Practical jokes might be taken seriously, and tall stories could be accepted as factual truth. Mistakes and errors in the workplace may result from having the wrong people in the wrong job. Don't trust everything you hear. Use your good Gemini intuition to sort out what's really going on.

7. SUNDAY. Lively. Expect a day filled with feisty encounters and spirited competition. Plan a round of golf or a game of tennis with an arch rival, determining once and for all who's got the right stuff. If called upon to adjudicate a contest, it will be difficult not to take sides and be biased. What starts as an argument, dispute, or conflict could surprise you by turning into a fortunate encounter. A collision, physically or emotionally, might be your lucky break. Gemini parents need to maintain harmony for the sake of children, which will be easy once you're all sharing an enjoyable day together. Singles who have a new love interest may find that this person becomes a permanent feature on the scene.

8. MONDAY. Sociable. Many varied personal exchanges make this a busy day. You'd be wise to leave some time available for a full schedule of meetings, appointments, and encounters. Even if there are no formal plans, spontaneous events will pepper the day in random ways. An interview for employment or some other role or position should be easygoing and positive, with a favorable outcome. Business negotiations should result in a mutually satisfying agreement. Sales and deals can be concluded profitably, with the likelihood of future transactions. Now that retrograde Venus has slipped back into Libra, a special person could return to the scene after being away. Expect to revisit happy days and good times.

9. TUESDAY. Influential. After yesterday's informal meetings, you might find yourself getting in deeper with serious individuals. This may involve a second round of interviews with top managers who want to assess your background and potential in depth. Anticipate thought-provoking, searching questions, and be sure to have documents and references in order. Professional advice might be required, which can be difficult to accept yet essential to heed. Contacts and networks you've recently acquired may lead to associating with movers and shakers who will support your ambitions to make it to the top. A potential partner with significant investment resources can help a big venture become reality.

10. WEDNESDAY. Reassuring. Being busy might mean you don't have as much time for your family as you'd like. This can be a major problem, especially with very young children. Reassure them that you'll all go on a special outing or vacation as soon as possible. Arrange quality care in your absence, whether from a professional or a relative who can be trusted. An expensive hobby could be affecting your credit, increasing monthly payments each time around. Bring personal discipline to bear on the situation and set things in order before it's too late or too hard. Success and progress depend on your people skills and your financial responsibility.

11. THURSDAY. Focused. Because of your experience and persistent efforts, work matters will come together surprisingly well. You're in line to make rapid advancement in your career, with higher-ups sure to notice your competence and commitment. Keep up the good work, and you'll go far quickly. If you're self-employed or own a business, borrowing to expand your enterprise can prove a wise investment, improving your market share and enhancing your reputation. However, personal experiences may be less pleasing. Differences with a lover could put romance on hold, at least for today. Pleasurable entertainment you have been looking forward to could be canceled or postponed. Be pragmatic, taking the good with the bad.

12. FRIDAY. Positive. Long-distance relationships need consistent and patient effort. Positive connections can be established and consolidated with people out of state and overseas. However, it's important that you be the one to initiate contact, giving the impression that you're enthusiastic and committed. Gemini students will receive much benefit from direct one-on-one tutoring, where there's a lively exchange and immediate feedback. A friend who is taking the same course might be helpful, supporting you with understanding and by reinforcing key knowledge and core information. Learning another language comes easily for Gemini people, but you need someone to converse with so that you can test your skill.

13. SATURDAY. Uplifting. Your intentions to renovate or develop a property may run into a logjam of bureaucracy involving regulations and endless paperwork. Get the design and planning stage resolved before taking further action. A planned journey or vacation may have to be postponed or delayed because you're not feeling well enough to leave. This will only be a minor hiccup in what proves to be an enjoyable trip. Romance is in the air, making this a perfect day for an inspiring date. Arrange an outing that is stylish and inspiring. Whatever entertainment you decide upon, make it elegant and top quality, clearly demonstrating high esteem for your mate or date. Indulge whimsy and imagination rather than being overly practical or down to earth.

14. SUNDAY. Stressful. Geminis who work closely with customers and clients might receive annoying calls demanding service and attention. For the sake of the company's reputation, and because you want to do your job as well as possible, you'll need to deal with them calmly and politely. If you find yourself caught up in career and business concerns over the weekend, your mate or partner is sure to be upset. Listen to this disapproval without buying into an argument. The work that you need to do isn't going to take care of itself, so it will be up to family members to take on extra roles. It may be all too easy to stumble into disagreements, which adds to stress.

15. MONDAY. Improving. The workweek starts out with an air of tension and lingering resentment, but don't hold on to negative feelings or anger. Life will settle down, and you will find solutions as the day goes on. It is doing your health no good to bear grudges or replay past animosity. Business deals that have been in a dynamic process of negotiation, with plenty of push and shove, can now move toward a final mutually acceptable agreement. Despite concerted competition and challenging obstacles in the workplace, you will succeed due to your worthy efforts plus a dose of luck. People who are for you outweigh the influence of those opposed to you.

16. TUESDAY. Fortunate. Today brings the sort of relief that comes after heavy rain breaks a drought. Important goals have either been accomplished or they are within reach and assured. In the midst of a busy and active period at work, there will be no time for joking around and having fun. Put social and personal demands aside until you complete the mission. An enterprise may be growing faster and larger than you anticipated. If you need to employ help to keep up with the demand, do it now rather than cutting corners or delaying. Events move speedily, bringing exceptional career opportunities that must be grasped immediately. Stalling or procrastinating could be disastrous.

17. WEDNESDAY. Upbeat. People are at their lively best, so don't miss out on the social action. Amidst all the cheerful conversation and good-humored banter, certain genuine attractions can develop. There's apt to be an unmistakable spark and passion in an encounter that could cause you to look twice at someone you thought you already knew. If you've been having second thoughts about getting more deeply involved and going further with a certain relationship, what happens between both of you now could seal the deal. Current energy favors bold and courageous action, with no looking back once you've made your move.

18. THURSDAY. Volatile. There may be some difficult choices to make. You can't have it both ways, so don't try to walk the middle ground. Whatever you opt to do, there will be happiness and disappointment simultaneously. Accept the home truth that everyone can't always be a winner. The best solution or strategy is to do what you really want, without attempting to compromise or to please anyone else. Your mate or steady date might need to accept your desire to be with friends who are significant people in your life. Gemini parents may genuinely need a break from the kids or a night out together alone. Get up and go, no matter how other family members respond.

19. FRIDAY. Empowering. The Moon in Taurus indicates that time of the month when you need to draw back and consider your affairs from a calm perspective. Venus in Libra, a position of strength, has gone direct again. Love and all its associated affairs take a turn for the better. All you have to know is your inner truth about what and who you desire. Geminis who have already made a move need to observe the effects and consequences. And if you are still poised before making a decision, give yourself another few days before revealing your hand and casting your lot. Advice and counsel from a wise, experienced elder will help you reach an understanding.

20. SATURDAY. Tricky. This is the wrong time to listen to the off-hand reactions and rash opinions of others. They probably don't appreciate your circumstances, and they may not even really care. Certain people seem intent on stirring you up or even attacking you verbally. You've always got something to say for yourself, but a better tactic for now is to remain silent. Refuse to be drawn into any sort of combat or competition. Instead, play your cards close to your chest and keep your powder dry. A better moment to respond will present itself. If you're out and about tonight, stay away from dark or dangerous places and don't stop to help strangers.

21. SUNDAY. Spirited. Today's Full moon focuses on what you really want. This is a time of year when personal relationships are of major importance, becoming a priority. However, at this point you're in a position to consider them from an individual perspective, taking your own needs and welfare into account. An ultimatum may be presented by a partner or steady date who wants to know where your relationship is going. You need to hear them out before responding. Neighbors and relatives could feature in the scenario that unfolds, clearly expressing their opinions. A visitor or guest might travel to meet with you in order to stage a face-to-face encounter.

22. MONDAY. Forceful. There can be a face-off with a strong-minded individual. You're probably used to such encounters lately. In fact, they should be starting to make you think about what you're doing that is contributing to these situations. You are only responsible for your own behavior, and other people need to take care of their actions or inaction. With common sense, respectful patience, and genuine goodwill, any differences can be bridged. Mutual agreements that are acceptable to both sides can be achieved now. Be open to a successful negotiation rather than arguing, reacting, or trying to prove a point. Competitive sports are a great way to release built-up stress.

23. TUESDAY. Excellent. Peace and calm should prevail today, offering a well-deserved break from recent volatile conditions. Gemini creative types who can find a tranquil, undisturbed space will produce exceptionally fine work that will be appreciated and broadly distributed. Extraordinary sensitivity in your communication skills allows a big audience or market to hear your message loud and clear, with positive responses. Advertising campaigns and presentations are destined for success. Teaching and transmitting quality knowledge can be accomplished with flowing style. Romance blooms and seeks to express itself in the wider world. Celebrate love and beauty in all its forms.

24. WEDNESDAY. Bumpy. With the Sun in Sagittarius, your opposite sign, you need to work harder to stay on the front foot. Making a buck today can seem an uphill struggle. There's plenty of competitors who are challenging your share of the market. Instead of being discouraged, do what you do best and stick to your core business. If earnings are down temporarily, use it as an incentive to cut costs and expenses that don't contribute directly to your profitable bottom line. Commercial success requires emotional stamina as well as smarts. If you let fear or greed rule you, there will be a problem sooner or later. As an individual entrepreneur, it can be tough to compete with large corporations.

25. THURSDAY. Fortunate. What a difference a day makes! Now a lucky break can happen for you when least expected. Maybe you land a big account or make a bumper sale, something that really adds to the bottom line in a major way. Small enterprises are sure to prosper, especially if they're involved with appealing cutting-edge technology. Geminis climbing the corporate ladder may receive an extra boost, perhaps getting a promotion into the upper echelons of management. You'll be tempted to spoil loved ones with extravagant gifts to celebrate this financial turn for the better.

Fortune is smiling on you, so you can risk a modest wager at the track or at a casino.

26. FRIDAY. Heartening. Relations with near neighbors are at an all-time high, making this the right night for a block party or get-together at your place. Getting to know all the folks nearby is fun and also makes for good business. You'll be surprised when you discover that characters living in the local area are potential customers, or that they have influence in your company or industry. Building a network from grass-roots contacts makes good sense. A brother or sister could propose some type of investment or joint venture. They may already be successful and want to include you. Gemini singles venturing out this evening will find a pleasant companion close by.

27. SATURDAY. Pleasurable. Last night's partying could continue today as well, offering everyone an opportunity to let their hair down and have a good time. There should be chances of taking fun video footage, then even uploading the results onto the Net for public viewing. Relationships can flourish in the current positive planetary conditions, whether they're long term or one-nighters. Make a play for that especially attractive person you've had in your sights, sweeping them off their feet with gestures of grand romance. Old-school manners will be appreciated. Dress to impress, including the best jewelry you own.

28. SUNDAY. Meaningful. All fun and games eventually come to an end, and so it is today. What was previously light and carefree now becomes serious. If a relationship has become deep and meaningful, you will have to decide if you want to take it any further. Everyone wants understanding from those who are close, and that need surfaces clearly at this point. Be prepared to enter a vulnerable, intimate period with the person you love, where each of you can express your truth. Practical considerations of domestic and family needs may interrupt more profound moments. Couples should honestly consider the suitability of living together at close quarters. Separate living spaces may still allow for a happy ongoing relationship.

29. MONDAY. Confrontational. Frustration mounts with people who won't listen to instructions. Your irritation may turn to rage if you discover certain individuals are being purposefully obstructive. Heated family arguments could occur in a climate where everyone seems ready to take offense and go on the attack. You may not see eye-to-eye with a parent. If you live together, that won't be able to continue under such conditions. Or you may not be inclined to visit frequently, if at all. Be careful what you say in an angry moment, because your outburst can't be taken back no matter how much you apologize later. A troublemaking friend could bring mischief and mayhem to your household.

30. TUESDAY. Demanding. It's time to make peace with everyone you've been at loggerheads with recently. Bearing grudges is not happy or productive. Make a genuine effort to meet people at least halfway in order to mend the situation with as much goodwill as possible. But certain people may have gone too far, making reconciliation neither possible nor desirable. If so, no amount of forgiveness can change that. Mull over the real meaning of good and evil in your world, and make a clear-cut choice between them. If you've been involved with a crowd that has been leading you astray, now's the time to make a clean break.

DECEMBER

1. WEDNESDAY. Cautious. Many plans for business deals and investments could be on the drawing board, but you need to look at all the fine print and research the legality of them before committing to any of them. There is an aspect of corruption influencing this day, so make sure you are not the victim of someone else's greed. On the other hand, if you have a plan to make easy money, don't think you can get away with ripping anybody off, or your actions will come back to haunt you in the future. Partnered Geminis might find that your mate is better equipped to handle joint funds. Be ready to listen to advice.

2. THURSDAY. Calm. Interesting conversations are the hallmark of the day, but be careful of gossip. A story making the rounds could veer far from the facts. A new work colleague can introduce you to some influential people. Look your best when leaving the house and you will be sure to impress. Romance is high on the day's agenda, and a blind date might be more than a little impressive. If you want the relationship to continue, use this introduction to get to know each other but don't go too far. The allure of the mysterious can be far more interesting. Business demands may involve long-distance travel. You may be able to take your partner on this journey.

3. FRIDAY. Variable. Think twice before bounding off on some wild-goose chase. Your fascination for all that is eccentric might leave you with lingering embarrassment. Accidents are also a possibility. Check all power outlets before using electrical appliances. Stick to the speed limit if driving, and don't take the wheel if sleepy or under the influence. Conversations can be a source of interesting and useful information. If you run into people you haven't seen in ages, stop and chat for a while; you will be glad that you did. Employment opportunities can open up in an alternative field to the one you are presently in. Don't be closed-minded; change might be worth your while.

4. SATURDAY. Placid. Spend the morning cleaning and getting all of your chores out of the way. Nothing will happen before lunch; if you have early plans, be prepared for them to be canceled. Conflicts with other people are apt to be surprisingly emotional, and you might find it difficult to maintain much detachment and objectivity. A desire for change and excitement can inspire you to start renovations around the house. Or plan an afternoon doing something different with your loved one to help rekindle romance. Because you are particularly sensitive to environmental influences, be mindful of where you go and with whom. Allergies are possible, so watch what you eat.

5. SUNDAY. Harmonious. Today's New Moon in Sagittarius, your relationship sector, heralds new beginnings and possibly the start of a serious relationship for Gemini singles. You will want to be close with the person you love most. This is a good time for sharing feelings and emotions, ultimately strengthening the bonds of intimacy and deepening the understanding you have of each other. Your competitive urge is strong, but be careful in group activities that you don't make enemies by being pushy or too personal. Dealings with the public are indicated. You could make a lasting impression on an important person thanks to your diplomacy and leadership qualities.

6. MONDAY. Active. Your energy level is high and you are likely to act with extra vim and vigor. However, be sure to put aside some time for planning before you act, which will guarantee that you are productive. Arguments are possible because you won't take kindly to anybody getting in your way or demanding a block of your valuable time. People are more likely than usual to get on your nerves, and someone might try to push you around at work. Bite your tongue and be civil for your own good. If you receive a hot tip regarding an investment, follow it up. A romantic introduction can get your heart racing, but don't rush in too fast.

7. TUESDAY. Profitable. Shared resources are difficult to manage at the best of times, but today you need to sort out finances so that everybody knows and agrees with what is going on. On a business level, make sure correct contracts are in place and insurance is paid up. Within a personal relationship you can turn shared resources into a tidy nest egg if you pay strict attention to where your money goes, what you have to invest, and then where to maximize potential profit. Consulting a financial planner would be a wise move. A job offer may seem well above your current expertise, but you have plenty of support and that spells success.

8. WEDNESDAY. Transforming. Mars, the planet that rules action and energy, moves into Capricorn, your solar sector of sex, death, and rebirth. This will arouse issues that make you think and cause you to change some aspect of yourself. Business deals and negotiations can get bogged down due to ego conflicts. It is also not a good time to apply for a loan. An intimate relationship can force you to do some soul-searching. You and your partner might decide to see a marriage counselor for objective and constructive help. An attraction to the occult is indicated, and you may start studying one of its many aspects in an attempt to know more about what makes people tick.

9. THURSDAY. Trying. Travel arrangements may have to be rearranged due to illness or the need to get vaccinated prior to departure. Be aware that health problems could occur due to travel. Older relatives may be a source of irritation with their many different opinions about how to manage your daily affairs. If you can keep opinions to yourself, you will leave with your relationship intact. A spiritual frame of mind may rule as you become increasingly aware of the bigger picture apart from all the mundane details that seem to consume your days. This will put you in touch with your basic ideals and help you see if you have deviated from your desired path. It's not too late to get back on the right track.

10. FRIDAY. Upbeat. Your creative flair is on fire, and what you express will influence or inspire other people. Don't let a lack of confidence stymie you. If you want to paint, sing, act, or write, get some lessons to start you off; your natural talent may surprise you. A new relationship might be based on physical attraction alone; enjoy it while it lasts and you won't come to any grief. Collaboration and cooperation are highlighted, making this a good time for group or community effort. Someone needs to be in control, however, to orchestrate the event without too many different opinions holding up the work. A spiritual meeting will be uplifting tonight.

11. SATURDAY. Easygoing. This morning use your time to tie up any loose ends that have been bothering you. Eating light and right for the day will give your body a rest and also boost your energy reserves. Gemini gamblers may enjoy playing games on the Internet with play money, a good way to bet without actually using your own money. If you have trouble resisting real money games, you might need to get some counseling. Later today you could be in the limelight, finding yourself so high in the popularity stakes that you have trouble choosing which invitation to accept. Whatever your decision, you will have a good time.

12. SUNDAY. Fine. This is one of those days that start out well and just keep getting better. If you have a backlog of work you can get a lot finished, which will put you ahead of your associates. Your pride in the job will also give you a boost. A cultural display or exhibit might be worth your time. Besides being stimulating personally, you could make an important contact for your work. You may even receive a job offer or a new assignment that is too good to refuse. However, if somebody suggests anything illegal or underhanded, say no immediately and walk away. With today's aspects you are likely to get caught and suffer the consequences.

13. MONDAY. Uneven. You won't want to do anything by halves. The difficulty is that you may be spurred on to do more than you can comfortably handle. Guard against involving yourself in projects that require more energy than you have or that overextend your resources unnecessarily. Similarly, don't be overly generous or extravagant or you'll be sorry later on. If people close to you seem to act erratically or impulsively, cut them a bit of slack and be willing to lend some support. They might be going through emotional turmoil and just be calling out for a helping hand. Work that requires concentration could be impossible. You might be better taking a sick day and pleasing yourself.

14. TUESDAY. Unsettling. An undercurrent of emotional tension creates all sorts of innuendos and miscommunication. Sometimes you might find that you are reading things into a conversation that really aren't there, but it's difficult to know the difference. Play it safe by taking everything at face value and keeping life simple. Problems in your primary relationship might overshadow the whole day as the need to make a decision about staying or leaving plays with your emotions. If you decide to abide by your commitment and look at ways to hold your relationship together, counseling would be a good start. If a child is causing problems, seek some outside help for the child's sake as well as your own.

15. WEDNESDAY. Bright. Gemini singles might meet a future partner through a chance introduction by a friend, giving you reason to feel on top of the world. Joining a social or hobby group can be the best thing you have ever done, broadening your circle of friends and putting zest back into life. If you are thinking about starting a family, the next few months disclose a fertile time period. If you don't want to start a family, make sure you take precautions. Your political views are developing. This is a good time to become active in local area government, and for exercising your democratic right to bring change and improve the community.

16. THURSDAY. Mixed. Shortcuts and quick fixes could be the order of the day, although you will probably have to come back and redo work at a later date. If you have been on a waiting list for a medical procedure, you might finally receive a date and can start to prepare for this event. Frequent visits to a neighbor, relative, or friend who is in the hospital will cheer them up no end. Your bright chatter and smiling face are sure to speed up the convalescence. Lock securely if you are leaving town for a short trip, as the possibility of a theft is on the cards. You could be very lucky now, so buy a lottery ticket or a chance on a charitable raffle.

17. FRIDAY. Fair. Too much interference will set you back today. You would be better off finding a secluded spot to do your work, a place where you are likely to achieve a lot. Someone may be working against you. However, you have allies behind the scenes who can negate such opposition, so don't hesitate to ask for help. If you can get away from regular duties, go for a break. Fresh air will do wonders for your thoughts, and the extra oxygen will energize you. A trip out of town with your partner is an occasion to share a bit of serenity together. Enjoy a change away from home. Be spontaneous, exploring the area and refreshing your senses.

18. SATURDAY. Reflective. Your ruler Mercury, the planet of communication, retrogrades back into Sagittarius today and gives partnered Geminis a chance to reflect on how well you communicate with your partner. Talk it over together and see what comes up. Contracts and agreements are likely to be stalled again and probably won't be settled until year's end when Mercury goes direct. Check on your holiday list to make sure you haven't left anybody out, which is possible. You tend to be more self-critical than ever now. So be kind to yourself. Give yourself the understanding and compassion that you allow others. Meditation techniques can shut down internal chatter.

19. SUNDAY. Good. At this busy time of the year you might want to limit your social activities to friends and family, enjoying the intimacy that it affords. If you have to go shopping, be very wary of spending too much and running up debt. You are in danger of blowing your budget right now. Sometimes simple gifts are just as nice as expensive ones. So think outside the box, and buy unusual or practical items that are affordable and will remind the recipient of you every time they use them. You are likely to suffer from mood swings today. Rest and wholesome food will do you a world of good. Take a break from coffee, and drink plenty of water.

20. MONDAY. Varied. Nervous exhaustion is on the cards through overwork today. Pay attention to your energy level, and get some relief before you burn out. Plan a break away from home this holiday period, even if you just go to stay with a friend who lives in an out-of-the-way spot. The change will be as good as a rest. Practice your photography skills by taking still lifes or action shots from different angles. Foreign contacts can be useful now, enabling you to expand your business dealings into more lucrative markets. Start the ball rolling and it will gain impetus. For a fresh look to your appearance, try a new hairstyle or color. Sometimes image is everything.

21. TUESDAY. Diverse. Get up early and enjoy the Full Moon in your own sign of Gemini. Bathe in the Moon's cool reflection of the solar fire and hopefully get an insight into your own inner workings. The day looks to be full of contradictions and conflicting interests. So be prepared to talk fast and give compliments, or you might step on some VIP's toes and live to regret it. An investment could look shaky, but don't react hastily. Chances are it will recover in the next day or so. Your arrangements for the festive season may also have to be changed due to unforeseen circumstances. If you take care of your close family and friends, the day will be a success.

22. WEDNESDAY. Intriguing. The Sun has moved into Capricorn, which represents your eighth solar sector of joint or collective enterprises and anything to do with other people's money. This can herald an inheritance of some sort, or you may receive a grant for research or community work. Get your submissions to the government or private sector before the month is over. Your Capricorn eighth solar sector also represents sex as a tool for transcendance, urging you to explore your relationships. They can become a minefield. It will be easy to unwittingly push the wrong buttons and start a conflict. Understanding the buttons instead of blocking them will prove very interesting.

23. THURSDAY. Interesting. Messages can arrive from people you haven't heard from in ages, giving you a rundown on their doings and starting you thinking about contacting other old friends. An important meeting or interview could test your nerves. If you trust your instincts, you will be successful. The roads are likely to be a nightmare of traffic jams, so avoid driving as much as possible. Public transport probably won't be much better either. Merriment after work could continue into the wee small hours. Be smart, go home early, and be bright for tomorrow without having to worry about any embarrassing moments that often happen at office parties. Instead, you can enjoy gossip about others.

24. FRIDAY. Supportive. If you are very careful and thorough in your approach to any kind of work, you probably need not repeat any task or have anyone tidy up after you. You may have to take care of someone today, perhaps an elderly parent or a young niece or nephew. Shopping should be very productive, with your ability to sniff out a bargain in top form. If you have any problems, you might benefit from talking to your parents because they have lived longer and experienced much. They might surprise you with their wisdom. Carols by candlelight will be a moving performance, making you feel a part of something memorable from humanity's past.

25. SATURDAY. Merry Christmas! The focus is on your home and family this holiday. An intimate gathering of close family and friends should be everything you have planned. You will enjoy all the domestic duties that go along with hosting and nurturing the ones you love. For those members of the family who couldn't make it, hook up over the Internet and have the next best thing. Someone may drink too much and become a problem, so monitor the alcohol consumption for everybody's sake. A child could be disruptive, with a few tempers frayed by the end of the day. But a good time should be had by all. Impromptu visitors will top the day off very nicely.

26. SUNDAY. Constructive. This is a perfect time to start a new project, especially an exercise regime. You do need to be aware of overdoing, so take it easy. Some Geminis heading off on a trip will find tidying up, packing, and getting going a breeze. Others may be setting up a business from home and are making the most of your break to work on it. The more you beautify your surroundings, the more successful and happy you will feel, which is bound to rub off on the profitability of your enterprise. Those of you in the market for some land in the country may be looking at various properties that fit your bill. Stop and talk to the locals to learn more about each area you visit.

27. MONDAY. Reassuring. You may be holding on to loved ones or possessions too tightly due to your need for security. Yet if you learn to let go a little, you will be less likely to lose it. The same holds true with children. In your desire to protect them, you can deprive them of learning individual responsibility. Learn to trust in the universe a bit more. You or your partner may be in the process of changing careers, which could arouse all sorts of insecurities. Go out to the theater for a thought-provoking evening of live entertainment. Enjoy conversation about the plots and subplots of the show. It might give you some insights. Keep the drama on stage rather than in your life.

28. TUESDAY. Quiet. An introspective mood can make any social engagements more of a chore than fun. Business negotiations could fall into disarray because of haggling over minor details and dragging in irrelevancies. If you feel up to it, take control and keep everyone focused on the agenda as much as possible. A child may be having trouble with another child, but let the kids sort it out themselves. By getting involved, you might end up alienated from the other parents long after the youngsters are friends again. If you think you need to do more for your fitness, consider taking up a sport. Enjoy competing, learning a skill, and mixing with others while you are having fun.

29. WEDNESDAY. Heartening. The urge for fun and excitement will make for a spirited day. Plans to enjoy a favorite pastime or creative project will go smoothly. Pleasure seeking could be too wild, though, and extreme sports could pose risks not worth the adrenaline lift that you crave at the moment. An old friend may visit unexpectedly and ask to stay with you. Be very careful what you say because it might be hard to evict them once they get a foot in the door. Focus on your health now. It would be wise to make an appointment with a practitioner to see that you are in good shape. Geminis need lots of rest to balance your active life.

30. THURSDAY. Focused. Your daily routine will be very enjoyable. Doing routine tasks will soothe and restore your energy while you are organizing yourself efficiently. Use your time to follow up all your paperwork and to put your filing cabinet in order. If your wardrobe needs rejuvenating, go have fun shopping or at least window-shopping. Bargains abound. So buy loved ones a gift to let them know you care. Enjoy getting outside for fresh air. Stop at a local café and chat with a few neighbors, catching up on the local gossip. Some interesting information might be very profitable for you.

31. FRIDAY. Stimulating. This is a great time for socializing. Single Geminis might meet an interesting and passionate newcomer. The mood for the whole day is one of indulgence. It will be easy to overdo anything right now, so you need to have your wits about you if you want to keep your reputation intact. It is a favorable time to start a home beautification project and for entertaining at home. The possibility of breaking a diet is really high. It might be better to call a truce and just enjoy yourself. You can have fun discussing all the New Year's resolutions that your friends are making. Give some thought to what you would most like to change in your own life.

GEMINI
NOVEMBER–DECEMBER 2009

November 2009

1. SUNDAY. Variable. Fun-loving Venus is in Libra, your house of pleasure and recreational pursuits, as the new month begins. So time spent enjoying yourself is well worth it now. However, you may need to curb the tendency to splurge on high-priced or luxury items if the bank account is leaning toward the low side. Your Gemini ability to articulate in a clear and concise manner is enhanced. Still, avoid acting as if you know everything and do not use sarcasm as a form of wit. Arguing with neighbors and siblings would be a no-no. Try to limit contact with people of a volatile nature. Retire early to bed this evening in order to recharge run-down batteries.

2. MONDAY. Sensitive. An emotional beginning to the day is foreseen. It would be best to tackle each problem as it arises. Logic and common sense are also required so that issues are kept to a minimum. The Full Moon culminates in the sign of Taurus, and this lunar cycle can bring an end to an old desire. Old wounds could be reopened and must be addressed before closure can come. Learning to let go of the past also means that you are willing to release things you have outgrown. Single Gemini should be prepared for an instant attraction. Although a love affair might be extremely pleasant, any chance of it lasting a long time is unlikely.

3. TUESDAY. Dreamy. Your head might be in the clouds today. If you have plenty of leisure time, exploring spiritual connections and New-Age topics can be a pleasant way to while away the hours. Your keen intuition should be used to ensure that you are on the right pathway. An individual or a situation from the past could return. Take care that you don't revert to old patterns. Instead, try to resolve the issue and move forward. An unusual invitation might be presented. Saying yes would provide an opportunity for you to move in different social circles. After a heavy day at work or at play, be wise and relax at home.

4. WEDNESDAY. Diverse. Wednesday is your ruler Mercury's day, and also the Moon is whizzing through your sign now. So you probably will be talkative and busy. Be careful about disclosing personal information. Make sure you trust people before revealing confidential matters. Inspirational Neptune begins going direct in Aquarius, your house of travel and education, which will help to remove delays in these areas. Any holiday plan or legal action that has been on hold could now move forward. You can expect to make a good first impression with your brilliant ideas and friendly manner. A creative streak should be utilized as a form of relaxation.

5. THURSDAY. Sparkling. The Gemini Moon guarantees a good day for you. But stop talking long enough to listen to what others say. Grasp opportunities as they appear, and they should lead to fine results. The Sun is merging with your ruler Mercury, making it a very busy time with lots of things to do and people to see. This is a favorable day to assess your employment choices and lifestyle routines. You will want to update your resume and obtain a clear picture of what lies ahead. Research all sources if you are looking for work or hoping to move up the corporate ladder. Employment interviews, staff meetings, and auditions should proceed smoothly.

6. FRIDAY. Nurturing. The Moon now glides through family-oriented Cancer, conveying a need to nurture yourself and loved ones. Make sure you don't spend money just to gain emotional comfort. Buying trinkets and treats could be a temptation, and later you might regret the cost. Mechanical breakdowns could loom on the horizon, and repairs might be an unexpected expense. Have an electronic diary close by, as an appointment could be overlooked in the course of a busy day. Joint finances are likely to bring tension to a committed partnership. Geminis who share expenses with roommates may run into a number of irritating obstacles.

7. SATURDAY. Productive. Under the Cancer Moon you have a strong desire for financial independence. You can assist this goal by regularly checking that passwords and bank pin numbers are safe. Go over your credit card statements and look for errors. See that essential bills are paid on time. Venus, the lover of the good life stops, now visits Scorpio, your house of employment conditions, physical well-being, and the daily grind. Those of you actively trying to reform current working conditions are bound to attract supporters. Those of you unemployed should find it easier to settle into a new job of choice. Household duties could seem less of a chore now.

8. SUNDAY. Good. Rise and shine early on this foreseeably busy day. The Moon is sliding through dramatic Leo. So running errands, visiting, shopping at the markets, and playing or watching games are all satifying activities. This is an excellent period to help people who are experiencing a few problems. Your Gemini counseling and communicative skills are to the fore, but be assertive and not aggressive. If you don't agree with anyone's opinions, say so because you don't have to support everything. But say it gently and without arrogance. Promising more than you can deliver is a failing that needs to be guarded against.

9. MONDAY. Promising. Career and business possibilities indicate a financial boost. This is an excellent period to approach an authority figure for a pay increase, a promotion, or your own car park. The Moon in Leo is showering Gemini with amorous influences. Seductive Venus and passionate Pluto are happily entwined. Romantic desires move upward. If you are feeling a need for emotional comfort, arrange a special date with your significant other. Curb any jealous tendencies and make this a night of love and affection. A secluded setting under the stars, music for lovers, and a few delicious treats will help create an intimate ambience.

10. TUESDAY. Eventful. This morning the Moon moves into practical Virgo, accentuating your place of residence, family members, routine chores, and daily activities. Property matters are highlighted. Those of you who have been considering relocating can begin looking around for a new abode. Home improvement projects should proceed without snags as long as you are patient. Expanding or changing your living space can be an exhilarating experience. Meeting former coworkers for lunch or a shopping spree can also add a dash of excitement to your day. Tonight take your mate or favorite pet for a leisurely walk and forget about the cares of the world.

11. WEDNESDAY. Varied. Mixed trends prevail today as your ruler Mercury harmonizes with unique Uranus and challenges dreamy Neptune. Attempting honest and open communication could be fraught with difficulties and may be better left for another day. Distinguishing the forest from the trees may be impossible when confusion clouds the issues and the situations that are confronted.

Restless tendencies might encourage reckless action because standing still isn't an option for the on-the-go Gemini. Implement relaxation techniques to help calm down anxiety and to reduce the chance of overload and meltdown. A few minutes of deep breathing can restore a sense of tranquillity.

12. THURSDAY. Constructive. Your home front takes priority this morning. An older family member may be required to make a major decision, so you should be on hand to provide support. It is a good day for those of you on the job. Put innovative ideas into a structured form so that colleagues will be impressed by your high level of expertise and productivity. Gemini sales representatives and commission agents can expect to receive a number of top leads that will yield financial gains. Someone eligible could appear on the employment scene, taking you by surprise when your heart strings begin to flutter.

13. FRIDAY. Active. If you are superstitious, don't fret about today's date. The stars are mainly swayed in your favor. As a Gemini, sitting still can be extremely difficult. Moving around is more to your liking. Being helpful is also very important, and for some of you there is nothing that irritates you more than people wasting time or doing nothing. Offer assistance to people who need help or who are struggling to keep abreast of their workload. Dinner for two and lots of good conversation could be the preference of committed couples. Singles may be in the mood for mingling and flirting. A letter from a lover stationed overseas will bring tears of joy and hope.

14. SATURDAY. Spirited. Resilience and determination will pave the way to successful outcomes now. Leisure, lovers, and children may take precedence today. Infants and the newborn could be the center of attention of Gemini parents. Dropping youngsters off at football, ballet, or the movies will keep you moving on foot and in the car. Impulsive behavior might lead you into a tight spot, so watch it. Have plenty of variety planned over the weekend to keep boredom at bay. Secure the enclosure of your favorite pets tonight and the next morning, or they may no longer be where they are supposed to be.

15. SUNDAY. Helpful. Implementing a responsible health and hygiene strategy will prove very successful. Be vigilant monitoring your diet and fitness programs. Your ruler Mercury slips into Sagittarius, your house of personal and business relationships. Sagittarius here boosts the flow of discussions between partners. Specialized counseling received now should be helpful. If you are unclear about what direction to take in life, you would greatly benefit from the guidance of a career or life-skills professional. Seek legal advice before signing a binding employment agreement. Thoroughly read everything contained in any important document.

16. MONDAY. Important. A major celestial influence is in play as serious Saturn disputes with powerful Pluto, creating stressful situations with love and shared finances. This is not the best time to take on extra responsibilities or any duties that would jeopardize a personal relationship or a business commitment. Borrowing money for a child or lover should be avoided. Refuse to guarantee a loan for anyone, or you might be left with a large debt to pay. A fresh cycle begins today with the Scorpio New Moon emphasizing health and employment. Now is an excellent period to consider the overall state of your physical fitness and to maintain the conditions that will help you live a long and healthy life.

17. TUESDAY. Supportive. The spotlight remains on relationships, including both intimate partners and professional partners. Getting everyone working as a team shouldn't pose too many problems. People will be more than happy to follow your lead. Close associates depend on your cooperation to get things moving. A significant other might need extra attention lavished on him or her, so turn on the charm and make up for past neglect. Keeping in top condition is often easier for the active Gemini than some sedentary individuals. If you intend to lose a few pounds, hire a personal trainer, purchase home fitness equipment, or schedule gym workouts to achieve a trim, taut, and terrific physique.

18. WEDNESDAY. Cooperative. Make cooperation the keyword for today. As you start, you might feel like it is one step forward and two steps back. Dealing with a cranky boss or authority figure can be challenging at times. But by day's end you will realize how much has been accomplished. Avoid hesitation, be prepared to take a leap of faith. If there is an important issue to be discussed with a partner, now is a favorable period to initiate open and honest communication. Ask another couple to join you and your lover for a night out. Unattached Gemini will have fun socializing with close companions.

19. THURSDAY. Manageable. Today you need to be scrupulous and discerning, particularly when it comes to matters involving your love life. Possessiveness and aggression should be avoided. Be realistic, Gemini. An overly indulgent lifestyle could jeopardize your financial status, causing economic problems and ever-increasing debt. Care is required with important financial and legal documents. Remember to check all facts and figures. An issue with a coworker that has been simmering on the back burner might come to the fore, ready for action to be taken. This is not a favorable day to purchase a new car.

20. FRIDAY. Challenging. Intensity mounts as the Moon zooms through the sign of Capricorn, your house of jointly owned assets and resources. Close associates could become envious without provocation, and there might not be much you can do to change the situation. Rather than arguing with those around you, set about organizing a new strategy to boost your financial status. A creative project will hit the right mark with people who have the clout to promote your work. This may mean the beginning of a successful career in public view. Studying the financial markets and how to invest can open up a new field of interest.

21. SATURDAY. Disconcerting. Past extravagant spending could catch up with you now, resulting in an argument with a partner. Self-employed Gemini should consider implementing a stock count or hiring an independent bookkeeper if you are not sure of the correct accounting figures. Seductive planet Venus is in dispute with jovial Jupiter, so don't expect much activity and passion to occur with a lover or in the bedroom. Over the next few weeks a significant new alliance could begin. Coupled Gemini might find yourself in the midst of the delightful task of preparing wedding arrangements. Changes in domestic plans may need to be made to suit the requests of relatives.

22. SUNDAY. Empowering. Overnight the Sun enters your opposite sign of independent Sagittarius, further accentuating your house of the other people in your life and just in time to begin celebrating the festive season. Happy news is likely to arrive for your partner, and you can expect to be sharing the good times with others. Energy applied to study can be of huge benefit. Gemini students need high marks to follow your dream. Foreign lands are in the frame. Travelers can expect most things to go to plan, except around lunchtime when risky action should be avoided. If you want to broaden your horizons, check out various travel options and begin plotting your journey.

23. MONDAY. Demanding. Your willpower might be very limited now. If so, moderation should be the day's guiding principle. Steer clear of department and specialty stores. The temptation to spend could be so strong that you buy impulsively without due consideration of how much you actually can afford. Expect travel to be exciting and adventurous. Still, tourists should beware pickpockets, street vendors, and sellers of pirated goods. Business operators importing or exporting products could run into problems with paperwork not filled out correctly or shipping containers stuck at the piers. Review plans for hosting a special function to ensure that costs have not surpassed the budget.

24. TUESDAY. Lively. Today is great for just about anything, Gemini. If you have plans set in motion or you want to get away from the everyday routine, consider acting now. The Sun and Saturn are making positive aspects to each other. So partnership affairs, legal issues, and professional consultations should progress favorably. A rough patch at work in late afternoon might mean that some of you are required to stay on the job rather than head home or take off to socialize. However, your departure is likely to be delayed only for a short time. It shouldn't take the organized among you long to resolve a problem and then finish off a task.

25. WEDNESDAY. Satisfactory. Make use of your artistic and innovative flair on the job. Thinking outside the square comes easily now. Once again, you should have problems solved in half the time it takes teammates to find an answer. Creative self-expression will win the day at work. This is your chance to finish off various tasks waiting for attention. When it comes to love, a few obstacles strew the roadway for singles seeking a commitment. Finding romance might not be difficult. But keeping the blinkers off will be the challenge because an enduring relationship is unlikely under current cosmic influences. Social events are highlighted, so accept invitations and have fun.

26. THURSDAY. Favorable. There can be a great deal of conviction behind your words today. Both speech and memory are apt to be sharper, and you may recall a lot of things that can assist your progress. Beware using sarcasm or appearing too forceful, as this behavior could work against you now. Geminis in a long-distance relationship should avoid too much socializing and mixing with singles if you value your current love affair. An assortment of tasks should be added to your list of things to do in order of urgency. Start with tasks that require mental application and concentration to detail because your focus is very strong.

27. FRIDAY. Fulfilling. Strong humanitarian impulses are likely to come to the fore now. Many of you may consider joining a group that aims to protect the environment in general and wildlife in particular. Gemini folk could also be the recipient of the generous spirit of others. Accept gracefully, then vow to help others in the same plight when you are back on your feet. An attraction to a like-minded group of people dealing with issues that stimulate the mind could see you becoming a member and an activist. If you are on the job today, put your head down and get moving to meet deadlines so that you are free from work this weekend.

28. SATURDAY. Happy. A pleasant day dawns when you should have a free schedule to relax and to focus on long-term personal goals. Typical Gemini folk have the wonderful ability to mix with various and diverse people. Attend a meeting of a local organization that deals with community issues and learn interesting things. Emotional comfort comes from good companionship. Socialize with friends who can introduce you to an assortment of lively individuals who will stimulate your mind. Don't be surprised if someone with creative ability suggests that you collaborate with them on a special project. It could lead to a lucrative partnership.

29. SUNDAY. Fortunate. This is a great day for anything but work, so it is just as well it is the weekend. Gemini confidence is high, and luck is on your side. Explore your daydreams and fantasies. These can be the source of creative inspiration. You could be asked to speak at a local place of worship or at a religious gathering. If public speaking is something you are not proficient in, don't stress. The words needed to convey a message will come as if by magic. Beware secrets, intrigue, and promises that have little hope of being kept. Travelers should choose sightseeing trips that feature notable monasteries and cathedrals.

30. MONDAY. Mixed. Proceed slowly. The cosmos is in favor of a quieter period today. It would be wise to rest and to review your thoughts. Talking business is unlikely to be productive. This is no time to take on competitors. Negotiations and transactions should be kept to a minimum, and impulsive action avoided. Gut feelings can guide you to opportunities for new projects, but be wary of whom you trust. Changeable influences are likely to create upheaval. The mix between your ruler Mercury and excitable Uranus impels you to be busy, chatty, sociable, and mentally stimulated, all of which will increase any restless tendencies.

December 2009

1. TUESDAY. Sparkling. If life has been very stressful for you lately, you can now look forward to a happier period arriving. Creative inspiration and artistic expression are high. First-time authors could finally see your name in print, while talented artists may be thrilled to have your work hung in a well-known gallery. Fun-loving Venus slips into your opposite sign of independent Sagittarius, encouraging you to put more effort and attention into a one-on-one relationship. A smart appearance and a change of style may be essential now. The outside facade can bolster inner feelings of confidence and self-assurance, so arrange an appointment for a new hairstyle and visit a favored boutique.

2. WEDNESDAY. Significant. Important cosmic patterns are to the fore today. For many Twins, various changes could occur that will be life changing. Both professional and personal goals remain at the forefront of your thoughts. Uranus, planet of chaos, is now moving forward in Pisces, your house of business and career. Uranus going direct can remove obstacles that may have been limiting your commercial success. Your enthusiasm and originality return to peak strength, aiding progress in making decisions about occupational interests. This morning's Full Moon in your own sign of Gemini places the accent on connections with other people. This lunar influence can either destabilize a romantic relationship or make it stronger.

3. THURSDAY. Tricky. Bringing stability to this day will be challenging. Heightened emotions could make you and other people quickly become rattled and agitated. If you are prepared for conflict at the onset, there is less chance of getting irritated and upset yourself. Patience will need to be exhibited when passions and desires run deep. But this might not apply to a partner who is too preoccupied to react to an immediate problem. Shop smart, preferably before lunch, and save your money. Later on, you may be tempted by sales signs and bargain prices. Although these may represent good buys, spending on them would strain the budget.

4. FRIDAY. Promising. It is a better day to head to the shops. You will be in a grounded and levelheaded mood. With an eye for quality at bargain prices, you will instantly know if you need something or not. The attitude of an associate or business partner could be subject to change, so hold off making final decisions until issues are clarified. Romantic trends are more subdued now. Your interests are focused on the practical side of a relationship rather than passion and desire. This is a favorable period for coupled Geminis to move in together, plan a wedding, or become engaged. Singles might meet an eligible newcomer who is older and more mature than you are.

5. SATURDAY. Reassuring. Endurance is the key to success today. Your empathy and compassion for the plight of others, as well as your ability to tune in to what is happening around you, are on the rise. Your ruler Mercury now takes up residence in the solid sign of Capricorn. A realistic approach toward love and romance continues. You can get right down to the nuts and bolts of relationship issues and goals. Curb your tongue, think before speaking. Words better left unsaid could tumble out, provoking discord. Unless you have a major social function to attend this evening, it might be a good choice to curl up with a good book or a lover and relax.

6. SUNDAY. Steady. A trip to the weekend markets to browse goodies on offer could be a delightful diversion and an occasion to buy gifts for the holidays. Geminis experiencing relationship problems should find discord beginning to disappear this morning. If you have pressing issues to discuss with a partner, do this now while the cosmos is supportive. Assuming the worst would be a mistake. Be patient, even forgiving, and maintain a tolerant attitude. Twins who need a break from weekend responsibilities could visit the local library, attend an interesting lecture, or participate in a community activity.

7. MONDAY. Uplifting. Seize the day and secure your future. An optimistic perspective and a positive attitude will enable you to assess any opportunities being presented now. Decisions affecting long-term investments can be made with a good chance of beneficial outcomes. Helpful advice and valuable information can also pave the way for a lucky break that will expand the bank balance. In-depth research carried out at this time should reveal everything you are looking for, and possibly more. Disputes relating to property, inheritance, or divorce should be settled in your favor. Geminis entering counseling will find comfort from the words of wisdom imparted.

8. TUESDAY. Varied. Gemini loves to gather knowledge whether it is trivial or probing. You can continue to broaden your horizons by listening to the news, watching and reading documentaries, and joining blog sites. Keep busy. If possible, steer clear of people who have a tendency to push your buttons. Your tolerance for close companions may be low, especially if their behavior rubs you the wrong way. Choose your words carefully. Try to work away from the hustle and bustle and noise of teammates. Take it easy while driving. Walk, don't run. Be more aware of potential injuries that could occur when traveling by bus or train.

9. WEDNESDAY. Fair. It should be a fairly quiet day on the work front. The festive season is coming closer. If you are hosting celebrations, set aside time now to make decisions regarding catering requirements. Cooking, cleaning, restocking the pantry, and preparing for guests are all chores that most of you will relish now. An awkward family situation might need to be resolved. But unless you are directly involved, remain neutral rather than becoming entangled in endless disputes that only drain your time and energy. An early night can help you maintain your physical reserves, also remove you from potential conflict.

10. THURSDAY. Vital. Energy is on the rise. This is the time to put special plans into action. Get an early start, and you can stay on track with allocated tasks and also reach a benchmark. People are likely to follow whatever direction you take, so lead by example. The Moon is gliding through Libra, enhancing your creative urges and your desire for love and romance. Social life should be on the rise as the weekend approaches. Expect to receive invitations to plenty of lively parties and celebrations. Attending children's concerts and plays should give delight. Participating in favorite pastimes will be both enjoyable and relaxing. A first date should prove successful.

11. FRIDAY. Bright. The pace continues to pick up, as does your creative streak and artistic flair. Instead of searching for special gifts for loved ones, consider making a few hand-crafted pieces with your own stamp of individuality. Besides, if you shop, you may be drawn to luxury items that will not suit the recipient. Conversation and discussion with a romantic partner should be kept lighthearted. Watch out for minor deception. Rely on your intuitive powers, your gut reaction. If you perceive that someone is telling you little white lies, they probably are. Tonight your guests should be impressed by your gracious hospitality and genuine friendliness.

12. SATURDAY. Accomplished. It is an ideal day to make handicrafts for the festive celebrations, volunteer for the school working bee, or rearrange the domestic environment. Get loved ones involved in preparing greeting cards and decorations. The kitchen of Gemini cooks could become a hive of activity. Goodies that tantalize the taste buds are churned out for all those lucky enough to sample your fare. If any health issues affecting someone in the household should emerge, you will take time from a busy schedule to focus on everyone's well-being. Plan to visit convalescent friends and relatives who need cheering up.

13. SUNDAY. Comforting. It is another day when preparing food could be on the agenda for Gemini folk. A new recipe book may be the inspiration needed to get you started. Healthwise, it may be time to cut back on rich and fattening food. If you have been overindulging recently, your stomach could be a little less tolerant now. Animals can be a source of comfort and love. Right now give extra back in the way of care and attention to your favorite pet. Dental problems can make life a little miserable for those of you who have been lax in keeping your teeth in good repair. If you experience even minor twinges, get an appointment sooner rather than later.

14. MONDAY. Lucky. Good fortune arrives today as well as a large dose of restless energy. Use a load of tact and diplomacy when dealing with the complaints and issues of clients and members of the general public. Success in a legal matter is more than likely. Gemini travelers should have a great day wherever you are in the world. Students can make progress, as distractions should be minor, and exams should be a breeze if you prepared. There will be lots of variety in your day to keep boredom away. A surprise incident with a partner could lead you to make a decision that has been long in coming.

15. TUESDAY. Liberating. Ambition on the job takes a backseat to your free-spirited creativity. If you haven't organized for the holidays, today you could be inspired to deck the halls with holly. Gemini folk are not known to be shy and retiring. But if you are one who is, abandon this approach now so that you can enter into party mode. Someone from overseas could spice things up no end, injecting excitement into home and hearth. A creative writing course explaining the basics of publishing your own novel would be an interesting experience. This is also a good time to send a manuscript to an editor or agent.

16. WEDNESDAY. Charming. Another great day dawns for Gemini to move special projects ahead. Those of you in retail sales, advertising, and public relations should experience better than expected profits. A New Moon in lucky Sagittarius this morning illuminates your horoscope zone of business partnerships, intimate relationships, and all contacts with others. Some lucky Twins are likely to receive a wedding proposal. Some of you may be in the throes of making preparations to walk down the aisle. Soft-pedal around any tricky situations to ensure that a happy atmosphere prevails around the home and working environment.

17. THURSDAY. Positive. Any Twins now experiencing a rocky patch in your relationship can utilize today's positive vibes to initiate honest and open discussion with a partner. Ongoing issues can be more easily resolved without tension or discord. As your creativity rises, those of you who write poetry or romantic stories should find that productivity increases. Gemini fashion and interior designers can also benefit, as inspiration flows and your ability to mix and match color schemes is high. Love and passion rule the nighttime, especially for young lovers and the reunited.

18. FRIDAY. Variable. Morning trends are not conducive for harmony and accord. Don't rock the boat or insist on having the last word, and you should make it through to more tranquil vibes around midday. Love remains a priority. The mood to make romantic plans with a significant other can be acted upon. A candlelit dinner for two and sweet anything's whispered will set an amorous scene. Geminis who haven't yet finished the festive shopping should make a start now. If a special gift for a lover needs to be purchased, you should find exactly what you are seeking. Lovely surprises can be expected, so be prepared to be pleasantly surprised.

19. SATURDAY. Disconcerting. Expect the unexpected. It is another day of surprises, but these may lean more toward shock and revelation than anything else. Upheavals are foreseen, especially in a romantic relationship or business partnership. The temptation for you or a partner to slip into old patterns of behavior can be overpowering. This could prompt you to end a permanent alliance or to seek some form of counseling. Solo Gemini seeking romance shouldn't have to look too far. Just enjoy the moment without expectations, as your lover is unlikely to stick around for very long.

20. SUNDAY. Mixed. Weight watchers and those of you who have to stick to a diet for health reasons will need to exert extra willpower today. Communications with family or friends living abroad will be challenging when technology lets you down. It may be time to use your land-line phone to confirm holiday arrangements if cellular and Internet connections are lost. Your imagination is working to capacity, urging you to put talents on display for all to see. Your interest turns to all things foreign, so plan to dine at a restaurant serving food with an exotic flavor. Then take in an art-house movie to round out an enjoyable cultural experience.

21. MONDAY. Easygoing. Energetic Mars has gone retrograde in Leo, which could help slow things down a bit. Even the most active Gemini should take a break and pace yourself as the countdown to the busy festive season begins. If the call of distant lands becomes stronger and louder, talk with a travel agent. Even if you can't go away right now, getting ideas for the future will be motivating. This is still a good period to hit the books and to join a discussion group that combines learning with socializing. At midday the Sun arrives in the practical sign of Capricorn, just in time to bring a thrifty approach to gift giving and spending.

22. TUESDAY. Gratifying. Business and career matters rise to the fore today, so thoughts about the upcoming festivities should fade into the background. Commercial and professional opportunities open up now. Some of you could land a new and better job or a promotion at your current place of work. Mixing business with pleasure may provide a few laughs but might not be immediately profitable for the small or independent entrepreneur. Think long term, though. Establish new contacts. Build relationships with customers and clients. Such connections will be useful at a later time. Be vigilant guarding personal possessions when out and about this evening.

23. WEDNESDAY. Manageable. It is natural to feel a bit stressed at this time of year. Most Gemini people thrive on being busy and on the go. But you will need to keep emotions in check if you become a little frazzled. Satisfaction will come from working hard now to complete outstanding chores, to fill orders, and to make record sales. You could soon be taking a step up the career ladder occurs and receiving a bigger than expected bonus. Keep alcohol consumption to a minimum, especially if you have trouble curbing your tongue after taking a few drinks. A romantic dinner could be a perfect end to the evening.

24. THURSDAY. Spirited. With the Sun merging with intense Pluto, this is a great day to make solid plans for future happiness and financial security. The Moon dances to the tune of Aries this day before Christmas, so relax with family members, neighbors, and friends. A kind gesture extended now could make this a happy time for another who may be in need, lonely, or far from home. Consider offering hospitality to an associate or colleague who is unable to make it home for the holidays. You will feel the joy that comes from sharing. Join community carol and worship services this Christmas Eve.

25. FRIDAY. Season's Greetings! Today is likely to be what you make it. Those of you celebrating this special holiday will be happy if you remain cool and calm even when confronted by the usual array of mix-ups, delays, late arrivals, and badly prepared food. It can be an intense time, although peace will reign as people reach out to each other. Lovely Venus entering the sign of Capricorn today spreads an aura of harmony. Close and extended family mingling together will create new memories while talking about bygone days. Your energy may be at a lower peak than normal, so make sure you ask guests to help you with cooking, serving, and cleaning up.

26. SATURDAY. Quiet. This can be a day when enjoyment comes by relaxing alone or with friends and family. Group conversations should be spirited. You might decide to hit the post-festive sales. Or you could clean up the domestic environment, eat leftovers, and watch TV. If you have active plans, try to complete them before early afternoon. By then, your energy will become depleted. Listening to music might be the most appealing choice of amusement for tonight. Venus now visiting Capricorn, your sector of shared assets and resources, puts your focus on future financial security.

27. SUNDAY. Uncertain. Your ruler Mercury has now gone retrograde in Capricorn, which can pose delays to matters involving shared business and financial assets. Partnership funds are tricky. You could be a little battle weary and out of sync with people around you. If your plans are flexible, spend some time at home relaxing and recharging your energy. Be warned that minor quarrels could erupt with siblings, children, neighbors, or a lover due to crankiness or indiscretion when it comes to words spoken. Take care when sending e-mails that you say nothing to give offense.

28. MONDAY. Loving. The cosmos has swung your way when it comes to love and romance. Passion is intense. This is a perfect time to take off for a first or second honeymoon or to propose to a long-time lover. Gemini singles eager to meet someone should go slowly. Your burning desire might cloud your judgment. If possible, defer signing anything of importance for the next three weeks while your ruler Mercury is retrograde. But don't stop looking around for opportunities that could raise your financial status. A favorable period exists to catch up on paperwork, clean out your files, and remove clutter. Throw, sell, or give away to a charity things no longer in use.

29. TUESDAY. Productive. Relationships with intimate and professional partners remain in the spotlight. However, there is a more subdued atmosphere. This morning could be a case of whatever you do, be prepared for something to go awry. The Moon slips into your sign, which can be empowering as long as you focus and follow through. The good thing is that as a Gemini you usually learn by experience and are not prone to making the same mistake twice. You would do well to return to procedures that worked well for you in the past. Pay attention to share financial responsibilities, especially debts.

30. WEDNESDAY. Diverse. Gemini personal appeal is heightened, enabling you to persuade people that your way of thinking has merit. Take charge of shared funds if your partner is not thrifty. Be wary if shopping on line. So-called bargains could be misleading, and you might find the exact same product cheaper in a department store. If you are planning to travel with a group tour, make sure you take the required amount of spending money. Otherwise, getting cash through a foreign exchange could cost you in fees. Pack sparingly and keep your luggage weight under the limit to avoid extra costs.

31. THURSDAY. Good. An eclipsed Full Moon in the sign of Cancer can provide the encouragement you need to go through the attic, garage, and closets to remove old and useless items of clothing, furniture, and even out-of-date food stuff. Clear away the tired and useless things that are cluttering up your life. Make way for the new and the fresh. Geminis driving anywhere today should take care on the roads. Travel at a safe speed to avoid fines or minor traffic accidents. Mechanical breakdowns could also occur, so check tires and gas before going too far. New Year's Eve parties will be memorable for years to come.

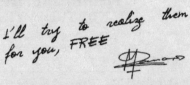

❑ **22.** Have a country house

❑ **23.** Get promoted at work

❑ **24.** Find a job which is enjoyable and pays well

❑ **25.** Find true love at last

❑ **26.** Be madly loved by someone

❑ **27.** Marry the person I love

❑ **28.** Attract men

❑ **29.** Attract women

❑ **30.** Be on TV

❑ **31.** Make new friends

❑ **32.** Have more time to do things that I like

❑ **33.** That my children have a substantial monthly income

So that's it! Have you chosen your 7 wishes? Then quickly complete the original of the Form below and return it without delay to Maria Duval.

Nothing to pay, everything is FREE!

Yes, Maria Duval wants to help you free of charge, and that's why she doesn't want any money in return for the help she's going to give you. All you need to do to benefit from Maria Duval's free help and to see your Secret Wishes coming true in your life is to simply indicate on your "Special Wish Fulfillment Form" the 7 Secret Wishes that you'd like Maria Duval to realize for you, and then return it as soon as possible to the following address:

Maria Duval c/o Destiny Research Center, 1285 Baring Blvd. #409, Sparks, NV 89434-8673.

Please, don't hesitate. Remember, you have nothing to lose, and EVERYTHING TO GAIN!

SPECIAL FORM FOR FULFILLING YOUR WISHES

Complete and return as soon as possible (by this evening, if possible) to:
Maria Duval c/o Destiny Research Center
1285 Baring Blvd. #409, Sparks, NV 89434-8673

YES, my dear Maria Duval, I accept your offer with pleasure. I would like you to try and realize the 7 Secret Wishes which I have indicated below FOR ME, FREE OF CHARGE.

I understand that I'll never be asked for any money in return for the realization of my 7 Secret Wishes, neither now nor later.

Subject to this condition, please see below the 7 Wishes I'd most like to see coming true in my life:

Indicate here the number corresponding to the 7 Wishes you'd most like to see coming true in your life (no more than 7):

I have chosen wish No. 4, so the amount I'd like to win is: $ _____

In a few days' time, you are going to receive a large white envelope containing your secret instructions. Read them carefully, and I expect to see some big changes taking place in my life after a few days.

IMPORTANT NOTICE – Answer the following *confidential* **questionnaire:**

1. Do you have any financial problems? ❑ yes ❑ no
How much money do you urgently need?
$ _____

2. Are you unlucky (do you feel like you're born under a bad star)? ❑ yes ❑ no

3. Are you working? ❑ yes ❑ no
Are you retired? ❑ yes ❑ no

4. Are you married or do you have a spouse? ❑ yes ❑ no

5. Are there major problems in your love or family life? ❑ yes ❑ no

6. Do you feel lonely or misunderstood?
❑ yes ❑ no

7. Do you feel as if a spell has been cast on you, like someone has sent bad luck your way? ❑ yes ❑ no

IMPORTANT – Please write below, in a few words, the question that disturbs you the most (IN CAPITALS):
_____
_____
_____

Age: I am ___ years old Date of birth: _____
Hour of birth: _____/_____ ❑ AM
(if you know it): Hour Minute ❑ PM

Place of Birth: City/ Town: _____

State/Province: _____ Country: _____

I confirm my astrological sign is: _____

(IN CAPITALS) ❑ Ms. ❑ Miss ❑ Mrs. ❑ Mr.

FIRST NAME _____

LAST NAME _____

ADDRESS _____
_____

TOWN/CITY _____ STATE _____

ZIP _____ 3D003

Email address: _____

FREE
PARTY LINE

Make new friends, have fun, share idea's never be bored this party never stops! And best of all it's FREE!

Never Any Charges!
Call Now!

712-338-7722